THROUGH
NEW EYES

THROUGH NEW EYES

Developing a Biblical View of the World

James B. Jordan

Wipf and Stock Publishers
EUGENE, OREGON

Wipf and Stock Publishers
199 West 8th Avenue, Suite 3
Eugene, Oregon 97401

Through New Eyes
Developing a Biblical View of the World
By Jordan, James B.
Copyright©1988by Jordan, James B.
ISBN: 1-57910-259-X
Publication date: July, 1999
Previously published by Wolgemuth & Hyatt Publishers, 1988

To our friends at Westminster
and Good Shepherd

CONTENTS

DIAGRAMS

ACKNOWLEDGMENTS

From 1980 to 1988, we lived in Tyler, Texas, and were members of Westminster Presbyterian Church, which became Good Shepherd Episcopal Church in 1987. This book is dedicated to our friends of those years, a group of godly people who have borne with grace the "slings and arrows of outrageous fortune." You have our love.

Part of this book was written while I was employed by Westminster Presbyterian Church as administrator of Geneva Ministries, then a ministry of the Church. After I left that position, Dr. Gary North of the Institute for Christian Economics provided me with a living by commissioning me to do some background studies in Leviticus. Because of his generosity and support of my labors, I was able in my spare time to complete the present book. Many thanks, Gary.

Parts of this book have seen more informal circulation elsewhere in the past. I have noted where this is the case. In 1987, Geneva Ministries put out two sets of tapes, each with a workbook, that gave in lecture form the gist of much of this book. The series "Rocks, Stars, and Dinosaurs" concerns basic worldview symbolism; the series "The Garden of God" concerns the transformations of the world in history, focusing on the Garden of Eden, Tabernacle, Temple, etc. The material in the present book supersedes what is found in those tape sets.

I must also thank the following people who read the manuscript and provided encouragement and sound advice: Messrs. Michael Hyatt and George Grant of Wolgemuth & Hyatt, Publishers.

INTRODUCTION

There are a number of books available on *Christian* world-view, but precious little on the *Biblical* worldview. By drawing this distinction, I am not belittling the former. There is certainly a place for books that set out the Christian view of philosophy, history, art, science, man, etc., using the vocabulary of our modern age. There is also, however, a real need for books that dig into the Bible and set out the Bible's own worldview, explaining the Bible's own language. The Biblical worldview is not given to us in the discursive and analytical language of philosophy and science, but in the rich and compact language of symbolism and art. It is pictured in ritual and architecture, in numerical structures and geographical directions, in symbols and types, in trees and stars. In short, it is given to us in a premodern package that seems at places very strange.

For instance, when we come to the Bible with questions about animals, we think in terms of biology, the nature of genuses and species, and the like. The Bible, however, discusses animals in terms of "kinds," distinguishes between "clean and unclean" beasts, and tells us to observe the "ways" of animals as they live. The Biblical worldview of animals, while it does not necessarily *contradict* the findings of modern biology, is certainly different. Similarly, if we approach the Bible with questions about botany, we find that the Bible discusses plants and trees in terms of how they symbolize various kinds of men, or in terms of their usefulness for food and medicine.

When we look at the stars, we imagine millions of suns very far away from us. There are cepheid variables, double stars, neutron stars, galaxies, and quasars. In the Bible, however, stars are given as "signs and seasons, and for days and years" (Genesis

1:14), because "the heavens declare the glory of God, and the firmament shows His handiwork" (Psalm 19). While the Biblical perspective does not invalidate telescopic investigation of the starry heaven, could it be that we are not seeing all we should see when we look at the stars? Do we need new eyes?

A philosophy of history is extremely important for man, especially today after Hegel and Marx, Toynbee and Spengler. When we go to the Bible for a philosophy of history, however, we encounter covenant renewals, sabbaths, festivals, Jubilee years, and the Day of the Lord. If we intend to apply the Bible to this modern problem, we shall first have to acquire the Biblical perspective.

Geography for us is a study of maps, some marked with contour lines; others with natural resources; others with political divisions. While the Bible is obviously not ignorant of these things, the Biblical worldview speaks of such things as the "four corners" of the earth, and of "holy ground."

Modern science assumes that the world is governed by impersonal natural forces, such as gravity, coriolis, and electromagnetism. Such forces explain the actions of winds and waves. In the Bible, however, trust in such natural forces is called "Baalism." The Bible encourages us to see God and His angels at work in the winds and waves. Is this mere poetry, or does it give us a perspective badly needed in our modern world?

We wrestle with the problems of church and state, but the Bible gives us priests and kings. It gives us the relationship between seers and judges, and between prophets and monarchs. It gives us blood avengers and kinsman redeemers. It gives us kingly palaces and priestly sanctuaries. Are we familiar enough with the Biblical worldview to apply these categories to modern concerns?

We are concerned about law, and we distinguish between state law and church law. We speak of "moral" law, of "criminal" law, of "civil" law, of "canon" law. And when we turn to the Mosaic Law, we expect to find these categories, but we don't. We find what look like "moral, civil, and ceremonial laws" all mixed up together. In fact, we find that the Mosaic Law is not law at all, in the modern sense, but *Torah*, something radically different and more profound. And what should we do with this Mosaic Torah? Should we try to apply it to modern circumstances, or should we ignore it?

Finally and in summary, twentieth-century Christians are used to discussing worldview questions in the language of philosophy, while the Bible sets forth its worldview very often in the language of visual imagery (symbolism) and repeated patterns (typology).

We should not be surprised if men do not view God's world rightly. Romans 1:20 tells us that "since the creation of the world [God's] invisible attributes, His eternal power and divine nature, have been clearly seen, being understood through what has been made." This means that all men are confronted constantly with God's true worldview, because they "clearly see" the true nature of things, including the nature of God Himself. Yet, as Romans 1:18 says, men "suppress the truth in unrighteousness." That is, they refuse to see the world rightly.

It is possible to suppress the truth by means of a direct contradiction, but that is hard to do. If we contradict the whole world, we shall have to commit suicide, which indeed is the way out for some people. It is more common, however, for men to take part of the truth and abuse it in order to negate the rest of the truth. Men take a small part of the truth, and then pretend that this fragment is the whole truth. That way they can "suppress" the true world picture, the true basic interpretation of reality.

For instance, modern man takes part of the truth about the arrangement of the universe—that it is peppered with various kinds of suns called stars, arranged into galaxies, etc.—and uses this truth to suppress the more important truth that the heavens declare God's glory, and that the heavenly bodies were made for "signs and seasons." To take one more example, modern man notices that animals resemble each other and human beings. The Bible says that these resemblances are by creation design, so that men can learn about themselves by studying animals. Modern man takes this truth and perverts it into the error of evolution, the belief that men are genetically related to animals.

The relationship between modern science and the Bible has been well described by Vincent Rossi. He writes,

> Living symbolism [by which he means a Biblical *view* of the world] does not deny science as a mode of knowing about our world, but serves to place scientific fact and methods of proof in a

large, multi-dimensional context that includes spirit, revelation, prophecy, and the Sacred as modes of meaning and knowing. For example, events of the past can be seen to have symbolic meaning that may instruct, warn, or nurture the present life. In the teaching of the Fathers this is called *typology*: past events serving as types or models of present or future reality. Symbolism, not science, is the true universal language.

The God-centered principles contained in the Bible give us the vision to correct the one-dimensional, earth-bound, man-centered meaning that the secular world-view puts on the facts. . . .[1]

Correcting the secular worldview brings us to the purpose of this book. Our purpose is not to deal with modern social problems, important as they are. Nor is our purpose to try and set out a Christian philosophical worldview, as much as we need to keep working in that area. Rather, *our purpose is to get into the Bible and become as familiar as possible with the Bible's own worldview, language, and thought forms.* Our purpose is to learn to think the way people thought in Bible times, so that we see the world through new eyes — through Bible eyes.

Thus, my job in this book is to try to familiarize you with this archaic worldview as much as I can, and then show you the benefits of learning to think God's thoughts after Him — because there are real benefits to looking at the world through Bible eyes.

There are two ways we can proceed. One is to take each Biblical symbol or pattern and discuss all the possible interpretations of it, debating various points among ourselves, and inching toward a consensus. If this book had been written that way, it would be thirty thousand pages long, with five million reference notes. The other way to proceed is for me simply to lay it all out, as I see it, without arguing *in depth* for *every* single point along the way. In this way, the overall system I am setting out will speak for itself, even if some of the individual points are debatable.

That, obviously, is what I have chosen to do. After the first three chapters, which are introductory, we shall look in Chapters 4 through 9 at the fundamental furniture of the world: rocks, stars, plants, animals, men, angels. In order for us to get familiar with these things, I'll be giving lots of illustrations from the

Bible. Some of the illustrations may be debatable; that is, some scholars may think I should use this verse and not that one to make my point. That is all well and good, but I have elected not to debate the point extensively in this book.

In the third and fourth parts of this book we shall look at the succession of worlds as the Bible sets them out: the worlds of the Garden, of the Flood, of Abraham, of Moses, and so forth. Each of these worlds has its own symbolic structure, its own mode of existence, its own peculiar laws, and so forth. Moreover, each world takes up the preceding world and transforms it, so that each new world builds on the one that comes before it. Again, in order to make this point, I shall be giving lots of illustrations, particularly from the symbolic world-models that were in use in each age (the Garden, Noah's Ark, Tabernacle, Temple, Jerusalem, etc.). Scholars may (yea, doubtless will) take issue with some of my particular interpretations. The point, though, is the overall Biblical worldview framework that I am setting out. Specifics can be debated.

Of course, if I have not done my homework, then this book is nothing but a lot of speculation and hot air. So, there are reference notes at the back of the book. Students and critics can put a bookmark in the End Note section, and follow along. The end notes accomplish three things. Some of them refer to other books and essays that substantiate what I have written in the text, or that at least give further arguments. Other end notes provide the arguments themselves. My third kind of end note gives additional information that may be of interest to the Bible student. Those who consult the end notes will find references to some specific background studies that I have written, that support the findings presented in this book, and that are available from Biblical Horizons, P.O. Box 132011, Tyler, TX 75713. I invite the interested reader to write for more information on these.

Additionally, I have supplied a somewhat annotated bibliography. I have listed here a number of books that have been of help to me. Some are written from liberal perspectives, and must be used with care by evangelical Christians. I have tried to give guidance, so that those who want to pursue the themes of this book can do so.

The last chapter of this book consists of my thoughts on what I think the "cash value" of all this is. Can studying Biblical symbolism really help us understand modern problems? Obviously yes—as a Christian, I believe all the Bible is relevant to modern problems. There are some particular benefits that I believe can accrue to the student of Biblical worldview, and I have set these out in Chapter 19.

PART ONE

THE NATURE
OF THE WORLD

It is the glory of God to conceal a matter, but the glory of kings is to search out a matter.

—Proverbs 25:2

ONE

INTERPRETING THE WORLD DESIGN

What do we see when we go outside and look at the world? Has it become so familiar to us that we pay no attention to it at all? Or perhaps when we look at the blue sky do we think of the refraction of light? When we notice the sun, do we think of a nuclear furnace? When we see a fox in a zoo, do we think of what we learned in biology class about its bones and organs? And beyond this, when we step back and view the world, how do we see it? Blue sky, green fields, brown earth, blue water—does this set of images mean anything at all, or is it "just the way things are"? How do we *view* the world?

The Bible is concerned to give us a basic worldview model and begins with it right away. The first chapter of Genesis tells us about the design of the world, as it came from the hand of the Designer. There is a separation of light and darkness. There is a blue sky as a ceiling over the earth, a sky that becomes black and filled with stars at night. There is a separation between land and sea. Moreover, there are creatures apportioned to each of these environments: lights and birds for the sky, beasts and creeping things for the earth, fish and great "monsters" for seas. And over them all, yet under God, is man himself, the captain of creation. In this chapter we want to start becoming familiar with the nature of this worldview grid.

The Six Days of Genesis 1

From time to time in the history of the Church, the interpretation of Genesis 1 has been obscured by a tendency to read it in terms of current science. Bringing a scientific worldview to Genesis 1 has resulted in two errors. One is to take the chapter liter-

ally but try to interpret what it says in terms of scientific categories. This tendency appears in the *Hexameron* of St. Basil the Great
(330-79). Basil takes Genesis 1 as it stands, but constantly tries to
integrate it with the "earth, air, fire, water" science of his day.
The opposite tendency appears in St. Augustine's *Literal Meaning
of Genesis*. Since Genesis 1 does not always seem to square with
the scientific (and philosophical) understanding of the world,
Augustine tends to take it allegorically.[1] Both approaches have
modern advocates, though the science has changed. While it is
not the purpose of this book to discuss the chronology of the
Bible or the ins and outs of creation in six days, it will be helpful
if I declare my own position. I am personally persuaded of recent creation, and in six twenty-four-hour days, as the Scriptures set it out.[2] God did not have to build the world in six days;
He could have spoken it into fully developed existence instantly.
The Bible states that God developed the creation over a six-day
span of time, and it is very difficult to figure out a way to evade
the force of this. Scripture elsewhere affirms the simple fact of
six-day creation (Exodus 20:11), and nowhere provides any evidence to support a purely symbolic view of the text.

The motive for escaping Biblical chronology and six-day creationism is the honorable desire to make the faith relevant and
credible to its intellectual despisers. Some good men feel that
there is no way to reconcile a "literal" interpretation of Genesis
with the "certainties of modern science." Those who know the
history of science, however, will not be so sure of these "certainties."[3] We gain no intellectual credibility by using dodges that
don't work.

Moses, educated in all the learning of the Egyptians (Acts
7:22) — which was thoroughly "evolutionary" in its commitment
to a "scale-of-being" philosophy — was doubtless as surprised at
Genesis 1 as any modern philosopher would be. No impersonal
forces here! No gradual shades of "being" from animals to man
with all sorts of things (satyrs, sphinxes, etc.) in between.[4] No
huge cycles of time. Just a series of immediate personal acts, in a
brief span of time, initiating linear time. This was not what
Moses had been taught by his Egyptian tutors.

Six days meant then what it means now. The text even tells
us that God defined the meaning of the term: "And God called

the light *day*, and the darkness He called *night*" (Genesis 1:5, emphasis added). Day is "lighttime." That is its fundamental meaning. The use of the word "day" for the whole twenty-four-hour period (see the second half of verse 5) is an extended meaning, and shows that day (light) is the more basic component of the period. The (twenty-four-hour) day begins in dark, and moves (eschatologically) to light (day). Moreover, the use of "day" for an age or eon of time is also an extended meaning.

Some have argued that the first three days might have been longer than twenty-four hours, since the sun was not made to measure days until the fourth day. This, however, puts the cart before the horse. The day as a period of time already existed, and the sun was made to fit it. The book of Revelation shows us that even after the sun is gone, the daylight of God's glory will continue to shine (Revelation 22:5).

Another alternative is the "framework hypothesis." Some have called attention to the structure of the six days, as six panels in a larger picture. They argue that the days are not spans of time, but *only* a literary convention for presenting a six-fold creation. The fundamental problem with this view is that it needlessly opposes a theological interpretation to a literal one. The observations about the interrelationships among the six panels or days are valid, but that does not change the fact that the Bible presents the events as taking place over the course of a normal week. If we allow this kind of interpretive procedure, we can get into real trouble: Shall we deny the physical resurrection of Christ just because we have come to understand its theological meaning? We dare not pit the historical aspect against the theological aspect.

Moreover, and to me this is the important point, the theological dimension of creation in six days lies precisely in its being a temporal sequence, as we shall see in Chapter 10 of this book. God had no reason to make the world in six days, except as a pattern for His image, man, to follow. Where the Bible later uses a three-day, or six-day, or seven-day pattern theologically, it is always in terms of the flow of time from a beginning to an end. The "framework hypothesis" Platonizes the time sequence into a mere set of ideas. In its attempt to be theological, the "framework hypothesis" misses the whole theological point.[5]

The Language of Visual Appearance

Genesis 1 is written in terms of visual appearances, not in terms of scientific analysis. Genesis 1 speaks of "lights" in the sky, not of "sun and moon." It says that these lights function as symbols and as clocks (1:14). Ancient science was concerned with the proportions of earth, air, fire, and water in these heavenly bodies; modern science is interested in them as nuclear furnaces, sources of heat energy, and the like. Modern science is surely closer to the mark, and nothing in Genesis 1 contradicts its observations on this point, but this chapter in the Bible is concerned with a different aspect of these heavenly bodies. Similarly, while modern science separates lizards, insects, and rodents into three different groups, Genesis 1 lumps them together as "creeping things" (Genesis 1:24) — again the language of appearance.

The language of appearance accomplishes two things in Genesis 1. First, it gives a true description of the world as it is. It is not merely poetic to call the sun a "great light," for the sun *is* a great light. Nor is it merely poetic to refer to "creeping things," because the animals thus designated do, in fact, creep on the ground. Thus, provided we do not try to press the language of Genesis 1 into some scientific mold, ancient or modern, there is no reason not to take it literally.

At the same time, however, the language of visual appearance in Genesis 1 serves to establish a visual grid, a worldview. By writing in terms of visual appearance, the Bible sets up categories of visual imagery. Unfortunately, modern readers often have trouble with this. We who live in the post-Gutenberg information age are unfamiliar with visual imagery. We are *word*-oriented, not *picture*-oriented. The Bible, however, is a pre-Gutenberg information source; while it does not contain drawings, it is full of important visual descriptions and imagery. This *visual* imagery is one of the primary ways the Bible presents its worldview. There is nothing to indicate that Genesis 1 is *merely* symbolic. At the same time, however, by using the language of visual appearances, Genesis 1 sets up a worldview grid that is used later on in Scripture for symbolic purposes.

For instance, Genesis 1 sets up certain categories of animals. They are as follows: monsters, sea creatures, winged birds, cattle, beasts of the field, and creeping things. These six categories recur in Scripture. For instance, in Leviticus 11, where we find a discussion of clean and unclean animals, there are five categories: domestic animals (cattle), fish, birds, wild animals (beasts of the field), and creeping things. The distinction between clean and unclean is symbolic, and is set out in terms of Genesis one's categories. The great monsters are also used symbolically in Scripture, often to represent the nations in revolt against God. The best-known instances of this usage are the beasts of the books of Daniel and Revelation.[6]

There is no reason to be surprised at the notion that the world and its creatures have a symbolic dimension. Romans 1:20 tells us that God's invisible attributes are "clearly seen, being understood through what has been made." In other words, the creation reflects the character of its Creator, and points us to Him. An example from common life will help to clarify this.

You get into your automobile, and turn on the radio. One station is playing music by the Rolling Stones. You twist the dial and come to another station playing music of Bach. You can tell the difference immediately. Why? Because Bach's music reflects his person and style, and the music of Mick Jagger reflects his. If you have a trained ear, when you hear a piece by Bach you've never heard before, you might say, "I'm pretty sure that's by Bach; it sounds like Bach."

Just so, the universe and everything in it reveals the character of its Creator. God *designed* the universe to reveal Himself and to instruct us. The problem we have is that sin has made us deaf and blind. We need new eyes and ears, and the Scriptures can help us get them.

Reading Biblically

Modern literature is not written the same way as ancient literature, and this presents a problem for Bible students. George Mendenhall has written,

Ancient thought is associational, not "scientific," and therefore tends to create the maximum of relationships between experience, language, and art, not the minimum which is so characteristic of modern over-specialization.[7]

Before the modern era, and before Gutenberg, there were few books. The few men who wrote books wrote them very carefully. As a result, ancient writings, including the Bible, are very tightly and precisely written. Every word has its place.

This fact is generally ignored by "liberal" scholarship, which usually assumes that any part of the Bible is a sloppy conflation of several sources. This viewpoint grew up to explain apparent contradictions and paradoxes in the text.[8] A proper reading of any ancient text, including the Bible, would take the apparent contradictions as stimuli for deeper reflection. For example, in 1 Samuel 14:18, the High Priest's ephod is called the Ark of the Covenant. According to 1 Samuel 7:2, however, the Ark could not have been present on this occasion. Liberal commentators assume that we have here two sources, and whoever put 1 Samuel together was so stupid that he did not even bother to make his book internally consistent. Other commentators (conservatives) explain the "error" in 14:18 by saying that there has been a textual corruption in transmission, and "Ark" should be changed to "ephod." Deeper reflection, however, shows that the Ark and ephod correspond one to another, and there are important theological reasons why the ephod is here called the Ark. The Ark was present with the people in the form of the ephod.[9]

Ancient and medieval literature abounds in numerical symbolism, large parallel structures, intricate chiastic devices, astral allusions, sweeping metaphors, typological parallels, and symbolism in general. Modern literature, whether fiction or non-fiction, is almost always written in a straight line. You don't have to go back and forth in such books to unpack allusions or get "hidden" messages. In other words, you don't have to *study* such books in a literary fashion. You just read them and get the message. Ancient and medieval literature, however, must be studied.

Modern American Christians have trouble understanding the Bible for other reasons as well. Not only are we unaccustomed to reading ancient literature, we are also unfamiliar with visual symbolism. The symbols of the Scripture are foreign to us in a way that they were not foreign to previous generations. When the Psalms were at the center of the Church's worship, Biblical symbolism was much better understood because the Psalter abounds in it. As Campbell has written, "The key to the figurative and symbolic language of Holy Writ is the Book of Psalms."[10] Also, the traditional liturgies of the Church, being thoroughly grounded in Scripture, communicated Biblical symbolism. God's people were also familiar with such imagery from the architecture and decor of their churches. All this has disappeared from the modern American church, and the result is that it is much harder for us to read the Bible accurately.

Happily, this situation is rapidly changing. We are seeing a rebirth of careful exegesis, a new appreciation for the Biblical philosophy of metaphor and typology, a new recognition of Biblical symbolism, a new desire to take the literary structures of the Bible seriously.

It is, of course, possible to jump enthusiastically into the Bible and find all kinds of symbols and allusions that sober study would discount. We moderns lack the kinds of instincts needed to be able to pick up on such things without effort. We have to read and study the Bible, immersing ourselves in its worldview, and then we will be able to discern valid symbols and allusions. Even so, it is doubtful if any twentieth-century expositor can do a perfect job of this; there will always be room for debate and discussion over particular passages. We can, though, set out some canons, or rules, for proper Biblical interpretation.

Rules for Interpretation

First of all, *Biblical symbolism and imagery is not a code.* The Bible does not use a symbol when a literal statement will do.

> Biblical symbolism, like poetry, is evocative language, used when discursive, specific language is insufficient. The Bible uses evocative imagery to call up to our minds various associations which have been established by the Bible's own literary art.[11]

In other words, if John in Revelation 13 had wanted to say Nero, he would have said Nero. Instead, he said "beast." By using the symbol "beast," he was not just giving a code for Nero, he was bringing to mind a whole series of Biblical associations: the beast in the Garden, Adam clothed in skins of beasts, Nebuchadnezzar turned into a beast (Daniel 4), the beasts in Daniel's visions, the human beasts who rioted against

Paul at Ephesus (1 Corinthians 15:32; Acts 19), etc. By associat-
ing the beast with the number 666, he alluded to the dimensions
of Nebuchadnezzar's idol (Daniel 3:1), to Solomon's fall into sin
(1 Kings 10:14), and more.[12]

Second, *Biblical symbols do not exist in isolation.* Symbols

> have meaning within a set of symbolic relations, or within a
> symbol system. This means that symbols have to be interpreted
> within the "symbolic design" in which they are located. Within
> such a symbolic design symbols function as part of a "network
> of relationships."[13]

In the Bible, the entire symbolic world is one organized and
unified worldview, a worldview that actually takes its rise in the
first chapters of Genesis. The symbolic meanings and associations of earth, sea, rocks, stars, plants, animals, serpents, trees,
fruit, and all else are set out in these chapters. The rest of the
Bible simply unpacks their meanings.

Third, in coming to understand Biblical symbolism, we may
receive some clues from other ancient literature, but *we must
always have clear-cut Biblical indication for any symbol or image we think
we have found.* We don't want to read the modern secular worldview into the Bible, but we don't want to read the corrupt worldview of ancient Near-Eastern paganism into it either. In recent
years, failure to keep this rule in mind has marred many potentially useful studies of Biblical symbolism and typology.[14]

Fourth, *the heritage of the Church in systematic theology and in the
history of exegesis is always a check on wild speculation.* According to
Ephesians 4:8, the ascended Christ has given gifts to men, and
these gifts are explained in verses 11-12:

> And He gave some as apostles, and some as prophets, and
> some as evangelists, and some as pastors and teachers, for the
> equipping of the saints for the work of service, to the building
> up of the body of Christ.

The godly wisdom of these gifts, these men, is part of the
treasure of the Church, and to ignore it is to despise the gifts of
the Spirit.

Fifth, *Biblical symbolism must be interpreted in terms of Biblical presuppositions and philosophy.* In the early Church, the school of Alexandria became notorious for allegorical and symbolic exegesis; but their problem did not lie in the fact that they studied Biblical imagery. The problem was that they were trying to squeeze Biblical teachings into the categories of Platonic philosophy, and to do so they had to interpret the Bible allegorically. The Bible has its own presuppositions and its own philosophy of type and allegory; we do not need to borrow anything from Plato.[15]

Finally, since so little work has been done in this area until recently, *the student of Biblical imagery must be alert to the work of other scholars.* Exegesis must never be done in a vacuum.

Conclusion

The Bible is not written in terms of modern science or philosophy. To a great extent, the Bible is written in the pregnant language of imagery. Genesis 1 describes the creation of the world in the language of appearance, and this sets up for us a visual, worldview grid. The world and its contents are not a bunch of random facts but were created with a design and purpose. The world and all that it contains were made, in part, as pointers to God. Thus, in some sense they "symbolize" God's attributes to us. Because of sin, we tend not to see this, and our worldview is askew. The Bible, however, will help us see God's world through new eyes.

All creation is the most beautiful book of the Bible; in it God has described and portrayed Himself.

— Martin Luther[1]

THE PURPOSE
OF THE WORLD

To help us understand the nature and purpose of the world as God created it, let us imagine an alternative world. Let us imagine an infinite, or at least nearly infinite, flat plain. This flat plain is inhabited by people. These people exist to glorify God. They do this by praising Him, and by developing in their social relationships with one another. These people never need to sleep, and so there is no alternating of night and day. These people get their energy directly from the Holy Spirit, so there is no need for food. There are no animals, plants, or gemstones in this world. There are only people, interacting with God and with other people, on a nearly infinite flat plain.

God could have made such a world, but He didn't. And this raises the question of why God chose to fill up the world with all kinds of things. Why create geographical diversity: mountains, rivers, seas, wildernesses? Why create animals, plants, bushes, trees, fish, and birds? Why create alternating days and nights, weeks and years, with sun, moon, and stars measuring them? In other words, why *this* world?

We cannot give a direct answer to this question. Ultimately, God made the world the way it is because it was His pleasure to do so. We can say, however, that this world was made for man, and that all its furniture and features were made for man's good.

David sets out man's position in the world in Psalm 8:

When I consider Thy heavens, the work of Thy fingers,
    The moon and the stars, which Thou hast ordained;
What is man, that Thou does take thought of him?
    And the son of man, that Thou dost care for him?

And Thou hast made him a little lower than God,
   And dost crown him with glory and majesty.
Thou dost make him to rule over the works of Thy hands;
   Thou hast put all things under his feet,
All sheep and oxen,
   And also the beasts of the field,
The birds of the heavens, and the fish of the sea,
   Whatever passes through the paths of the seas. (vv. 3-8)

Notice how David's statement differs from what we often hear today. "Man is just a speck in the vast cosmic universe" is a common modern viewpoint; it is not David's. David begins by considering the heavens, which he knew symbolized God's people, according to God's word to Abraham (Genesis 15:5). The stars are splendid, yet God does not take thought for them, but for man. How much greater is man!

Man was originally created, says David, only a little lower than God Himself. Of course as a creature, man was infinitely "lower" than God; yet as God's viceroy over creation, man was just under Him in the chain of command. This is not the end of the story, though, says David. It is only the beginning, because man is to grow and develop and eventually be crowned with glory and majesty.

Man's dominion over the world as God's viceroy and man's growth in glory and honor are connected with the world, says David. All things were put under man's feet. The highest forms of the natural world, made on the fifth and sixth days of creation, are the animals, and these are listed as under man's dominion. This implies that the animal world, and the rest of creation, was made to assist man in his growth in glory.

This is because all these things reveal God. It is our interaction with God that causes us to grow. It is because everything in the world reveals God to us that we can grow by interacting with the world. We need to explore this in some detail, because it is fundamental to the Biblical view of the world.

The World Reveals God

Romans 1:20 tells us that the world reveals God: "For since the creation of the world His invisible attributes, His eternal power and divine nature, have been clearly seen." Psalm 19:1-2 tells us that the heavens reveal God: "The heavens are telling the glory of God; and the firmament is declaring the work of His hands. Day to day pours forth speech, and night to night reveals knowledge." Job 12:7-9 tells us that the animal kingdom reveals God:

> But now ask the beasts, and let them teach you; and the birds of the heavens, and let them tell you. Or speak to the earth, and let it teach you; and let the fish of the sea declare to you. Who among all these does not know that the hand of the LORD has done this?

We mentioned earlier that any work of art bears the impress of the artist who made it. The music of Beethoven does not sound like the music of Josquin. The Apostle Paul's writing style is not the same as the Apostle John's. We can hear and detect these differences, even if we lack the particular expertise to explain what accounts for them.

But suppose that the only composer who ever lived was Johann Sebastian Bach. There is no music in this world except that of Bach. Whenever we hear music in this world, it sounds like Bach's music. It may be played well or badly but the fundamental raw material is always Bach, only Bach, nothing but Bach. Now, since there is no other music to compare this music to, would we be able to "hear" Bach's personality in the music? Or would it be easy for us to forget about Bach, and assume that "music simply *is*"?

The problem with hearing or detecting God's authorship of the world is just like this. There is no other world to compare God's world to. There is no "music" except God's. It can be "played" well or perversely, but there are no other raw materials at hand. God's personality is fully displayed in the world, but it is easy for us to become deaf to this fact.

The Bible tells us that this deafness and blindness is sin: "For though they knew God, they did not glorify Him as God, or give thanks; but they became futile in their speculations, and their foolish heart was darkened" (Romans 1:21). This verse describes the origin of secular philosophy. The sinner does not want to see God's personality displayed in His works, and so he comes up with alternative explanations of the universe. The "universe simply *is*." In philosophy, this "*is*-ness" is called "Being." Ultimately, all non-Christian philosophy assumes that the universe is un-created and made of neutral "Being." Such a universe is silent. For the Christian, however, the universe is created by God, and constantly speaks of Him.[2]

We have seen that God's personality is revealed in every-thing in creation. Let us return, for a moment, to the question we raised at the beginning of this chapter: Why this world with all this diversity? Why not just man and God, interfacing together, with man growing and developing from this inter-action? I believe the answer to this, in part, lies in the fact that God is infinite and man is finite. We simply cannot grasp God's infinite tri-personality all at once. For this reason, God chose to reveal the infinity of His personality in the diversity of this world. Various things in the world reveal various things about God. As we interface with these different things in the world, we are indirectly interfacing with God, who is revealed in them.

The great conservative nineteenth-century theologian, Herman Bavinck, put it this way:

> We do not see God as he is in himself. We behold him in his works. We name him according to the manner in which he has revealed himself in his works. To see God face to face is for us impossible, at least here on earth. If, nevertheless, God wills that we should know him, he must needs descend to the level of the creature. He must needs accommodate himself to our lim-ited, finite, human consciousness.[3]

Accordingly, "Scripture calls upon the entire creation, i.e., upon nature in its several spheres, and especially upon man, to contribute to the description of the knowledge of God."[4]

St. Augustine provides an illustration:

> On earth a fountain is one thing, a light is another. When thou art athirst, thou seekest a fountain, and to get to the fountain thou seekest light; and if it is not day, thou lightest a lamp to get to the fountain. God himself is both a fountain and a light: to the thirsting a fountain; to the blind a light.[5]

Theologians call God's self-revelation in the world "natural revelation."[6] As Professor John Frame explains,

Everything in creation bears some analogy to God. All the world has been made with God's stamp on it, revealing Him. Creation is His temple, heaven His throne, earth His footstool. Thus Scripture finds analogies to God in every area of creation: inanimate objects (God the "rock of Israel," Christ the "door of the sheep," the Spirit as "wind," "breath," "fire"), plant life (God's strength like the "cedars of Lebanon," Christ the "bread of life"), animals (Christ the "Lion of Judah," the "lamb of God"), human beings (God as king, landowner, lover; Christ as prophet, priest, king, servant, son, friend), abstract ideas (God as spirit, love, light; Christ as way, word, truth, life, wisdom, righteousness, sanctification, redemption). Even wicked people reveal their likeness to God, with, of course, much irony — see Luke 18:1-8.[7]

Similarly, Bavinck wrote that God

is compared to a lion, Isaiah 31:4; an eagle, Deuteronomy 32:11; a lamb, Isaiah 53:7; a hen, Matthew 23:37; the sun, Psalm 84:11; the morning star, Revelation 22:16; a light, Psalm 27:1; a torch, Revelation 21:23; a fire, Hebrews 12:29; a fountain, Psalm 36:9; the fountain of living waters, Jeremiah 2:13; food, bread, water, drink, ointment, Isaiah 55:1; John 4:10; 6:35, 55; a rock, Deuteronomy 32:4; a hiding place, Psalm 119:114; a tower, Proverbs 18:10; a refuge, Psalm 9:9; a shadow, Psalm 91:1; 121:5; a shield, Psalm 84:11; a way, John 14:6; a temple, Revelation 21:22, etc.[8]

All this can be boiled down to a simple fact: The universe and everything in it symbolizes God. That is, the universe and everything in it points to God. This means that the Christian view of the world is and can only be *fundamentally symbolic*. The world does not exist for its own sake, but as a revelation of God.

Man Reveals God

Genesis 1:26 tells us that man was made as the preeminent and particular image of God: "Let Us make man in Our image, after Our likeness." Man, then, is the special symbol of God. As Bavinck put it,

Something of God is manifest in each creature, but of all creatures man is endowed with the highest degree of excellence.

The exalted title: image, son, child of God, is borne by him alone. The name: God's offspring (Acts 17:28), is peculiar to man.[9]

Van Til writes, "Man was created an analogue of God; his thinking, his willing, and his doing is therefore properly conceived as at every point analogical to the thinking, willing, and doing of God."[10]

Thus, says Bavinck, whatever pertains to man can be applied to God,

> especially "human organs, members, sensations, affections," etc. God has a soul, Leviticus 26:11; Matthew 12:28; and a Spirit, Genesis 1:2; etc. Mention is never made of God's body, although in Christ God assumed a real human body, John 1:14; Colossians 2:17; and the church is called the body of Christ, Ephesians 1:22; but all the terms expressive of bodily organs are applied to God: mention is made of his countenance, Exodus 33:20, 23; Isaiah 63:9; Psalm 16:11; Matthew 18:10; Revelation 22:4; his eyes, Psalm 11:4; Hebrews 4:13; his eyelids, Psalm 11:4; the apple of his eye, Deuteronomy 32:10; Psalm 17:8; Zechariah 2:3 [sic, 8]; his ears, Psalm 55:1; nose, Deuteronomy 33:10; mouth, Deuteronomy 8:3; lips, Job 11:5; tongue, Isaiah 30:27; neck [sic, back], Jeremiah 18:17; arms, Exodus 15:16; hand, Numbers 11:23; right hand, Exodus 15:12; finger, Exodus 8:19; heart, Genesis 6:6; the "yearning of his heart" (A.V.: "sounding of his bowels"), Isaiah 63:15; cf. Jeremiah 31:20; Luke 1:78; his bosom, Psalm 74:11; foot, Isaiah 66:1. Further, every human emotion is also present in God; e.g., joy, Isaiah 62:5; rejoicing, Isaiah 65:19; grief, Psalm 78:40; Isaiah 63:10; anger, Jeremiah 7:18, 19; fear, Deuteronomy 32:27; love, in all its variations; e.g., compassion, mercy, grace, longsuffering, etc.; furthermore, zeal and jealousy, Deuteronomy 32:21; grief, Genesis 6:6; hatred, Deuteronomy 16:22; wrath, Psalm 2:5; vengeance, Deuteronomy 32:35.[11]

Thus, it is clear that each human being is a symbol of God. The faculties of the human person reveal aspects of God and portray Him in the world.

But not only is each individual an image or symbol of God. The same is true of groups of men, of societies. God, after all, is both a Person and a Society, both One and Three. Notice how

Genesis 1:27 gives us both perspectives: "And God created man in His own image, in the image of God He created him [individual], male and female He created them [society]." For this reason, there is a symbolic relationship between the parts of the individual human person and the parts of the corporate "body" politic.

> For even as the body is one, and has many members, and all the members of the body, though they are many, are one body, so also is Christ. For by one Spirit we were all baptized into one body, whether Jews or Greeks, whether slaves or free, and we were all made to drink of one Spirit. For the body is not one member, but many. If the foot should say, "Because I am not a hand, I am not of the body," it is not for this reason any less of the body. And if the ear should say, "Because I am not an eye, I am not of the body," it is not for this reason any less of the body. If the whole body were an eye, where would the hearing be? If the whole were hearing, where would the sense of smell be? But now God has placed the members, each one of them, in the body, just as He desired. . . . Now you are Christ's body, and individually members of it. And God has appointed in the church, first apostles, second prophets, third teachers, then miracles, then gifts of healing, helps, administrations, various kinds of tongues . . . (1 Corinthians 12:12-28).

This social diversity also symbolizes various aspects of God's infinite person. Since Bavinck has done the homework for us, let us quote him once more:

> Furthermore, God is often called by names which indicate a certain office, profession, or relation among men. Hence, he is called bridegroom, Isaiah 61:10; husband, Isaiah 54:5; father, Deuteronomy 32:6; judge, king, lawgiver, Isaiah 33:22; man of war, Exodus 15:3; hero, Psalm 78:65; Zephaniah 3:17; builder (architect) and maker, Hebrews 11:10; husbandman, John 15:1; shepherd, Psalm 23:1; physician, Exodus 15:26; etc.[12]

The World Reveals Man

Bavinck states,

Whereas the universe is God's creation, it follows that it also reveals and manifests him. There is "not one atom of the universe" in which his divinity does not shine forth. Secondly, Scripture teaches us that man has an altogether peculiar position among creatures. Whereas creatures in general exhibit "vestiges" of God's virtues, man on the contrary, is the very image and likeness of God.[13]

When we put these two truths together, we see that it inescapably follows that just as the world symbolizes God, so also the world must symbolize man, the image of God. And it is at this point that we can see the "cash value" of this symbolic world design. Man is supposed to image God; and to assist us, God has filled the world with pictures of Himself that show us what we also are supposed to be like as His images. By portraying God for us, the world also portrays the human ideal.

God is like a rock (Deuteronomy 32:4), and so should we be (Matthew 16:18).

God is like a lion (Isaiah 31:4), and so should we be (Genesis 49:9).

God is like the sun (Psalm 84:11), and so should we be (Judges 5:31).

God is a Tree of Life (Proverbs 3:18), and so should we be (Proverbs 11:30).

In this way the world models for us what it means to be a "symbol of God." At the same time, because of sin we often do not look at the world the right way. The Bible, however, will provide us with new eyes.

Conclusion

What emerges from this discussion is that if we want to acquire a Biblical view of the world, we shall have to make a study of Biblical symbolism. The way the Bible uses symbols shows us how to interpret God's natural revelation. When we see how the Bible speaks of stars, gemstones, lions, lambs, fish, trees, and thorns, we will be able to walk outside and appreciate God's world. We will also be able to see in the world pictures of human life and society.

Since a study of symbolism is so important, it behooves us to take a closer look at the nature of it, and how it functions in human life. To that consideration we now turn.

Unto this catholick visible church Christ hath given the ministry, oracles, and ordinances of God, for the gathering and perfecting of the saints in this life, to the end of the world; and doth by his presence and Spirit, according to his promise, make them effectual thereunto.

The Westminster Confession of Faith (1643),
Chapter 25:2

SYMBOLISM
AND WORLDVIEW

The study of symbolism is seen by some as a curiosity, rather far removed from the central matters of life. According to them, anyone who spends time studying Biblical imagery and symbolism may well be getting into a "dangerous" area. Persons who engage in an "overly symbolic" interpretation of Scripture are to be regarded with suspicion. What matters is the study of *reality*; symbolism is secondary.

This attitude betrays the influence of the Greek view of the world. According to the Greeks — and actually all pagans — the world was not made by God. Rather, the world, or the raw material of the world, has always existed. This always-existing stuff just *is*, and so it is called "Being." This "Being" stuff is like a blank slate. It is silent and meaningless "raw material." It does not bear the impress of any Creator, and it does not joyfully shout His name (Psalm 98:4-9).

How did our present world come about, then? Well, the ancients believed that a designer or maker came along, often called a "demiurge." This demiurge imposed order on the primeval raw material. He *imposed* meaning, structure, and symbol on the neutral, always-existing world. Human beings, according to the pagan view, are like little demiurges: We go through life imposing meaning and structure and order on the world. Modern philosophy, especially after Immanuel Kant, has taken an even more radical view. The modern view is that there is no demiurge, and that the universe is really ultimately chaotic. Whatever order and meaning there is in the world has been imposed by human beings, and by no one else. We create our own worlds by generating our own worldviews. All meaning, all symbols, are man-made.[1]

Very often this approach to symbolism is brought over, unintentionally, into our view of the Bible. It is assumed that the symbolism in the Bible is ultimately arbitrary, not grounded in creation design. More liberal commentators assume that the men who wrote the Bible used the man-generated symbolism of their day to express their ideas. More conservative commentators assume that God just decided arbitrarily to use this or that item to symbolize this or that truth. Such an approach, however, implicitly denies the doctrine of creation, as we have seen it in Chapter 2 of our study. Symbolism is never arbitrary or secondary.

In the Western world for several centuries, men have assumed that the proper way to express truth is by means of abstract, philosophical language. Wherever we find imagery, parable, symbolism, or typology, we ought to translate such language into proper abstractions. This, however, is not how God chose to reveal Himself to us. To be sure, some parts of the Bible are written in abstract language, especially the epistles of St. Paul. Most of the Bible, however, is written in stories, histories, poems, symbols, parables, and the like. As far as God is concerned, this way of revealing truth is equally as important as abstract philosophizing.[2]

Notice, for instance, the way in which our confessions of faith and catechisms are written. They are virtually devoid of imagery. Solomon wrote Proverbs to instruct youth, but for centuries Christians have used catechisms that consist basically of definitions of terms: What is justification; what is prayer; what is meant by the fourth petition; etc. The contrast of approaches is quite startling. It illustrates for us the problem we have in recovering the Biblical worldview.

The Primacy of Symbolism

Symbolism, then, is not some secondary concern, some mere curiosity. In a very real sense, symbolism is more important than anything else for the life of man. As we have seen, the doctrine of creation means that every created item, and also the created order as a whole, reflects the character of the God who created it. In other words, everything in the creation, and the creation as a whole, points to God. Everything is a sign or symbol of God.

And not only so. Just as everything in creation is a general symbol of God, so also man is the special symbol, for man and man alone is created as the very image of God (Genesis 1:26). Each individual human being, and the race as a whole (Genesis 1:27), symbolizes God in a special way. What is this special way? Theologians have debated the issue, and no one will ever fully understand it (since to do so we should have to understand fully the nature of the God whose symbol we are). All the same, this much can be said: *Man is the only symbol that is also a symbol-maker.* The first part of Genesis 1 is the context in which it is then said that man is the image of God. God has been presented as one who determines, creates, evaluates, names, takes counsel among Himself, etc. These things are what man uniquely images.

Symbols vary. This is ultimately because, as theologians would say, in the *opera ad extra* of God, one or the other of the Persons and/or attributes of God is always highlighted. What does this mean, in simpler language? Well, the *opera ad extra* are the works that God does outside of Himself. Some of these works are more particularly the work of the Father, some of the Son, and some of the Holy Spirit; though in every case all three Persons are active, because "all of God does all that God does." Also, some of these works more particularly show God's wrath, others His grace, others His forbearance, others His jealousy, and so forth; yet in a general way, all of God's attributes are present in each of His actions.[3]

In a general way, everything in creation points to all three Persons of God, and to all of God's attributes, if we could but see it. But in a special way, each item particularly discloses one or another of His attributes and/or one or another of the Persons.

How are we going to read these symbols? By guesswork? Happily, we have the Bible to teach us how to read the world. The Bible lays out for us the primary symbol of God (man), and four classes of secondary symbols: animals, plants, stones (non-living things), and stars (heavenly bodies). The Bible also discusses angels, though whether angels should be regarded as, like man, special symbols (images) of God, is a matter of theological debate. Since each of these signifies God, it also signifies man, as well. The Bible teaches us how to interpret these symbols, as we shall see in later chapters in this book. Some symbols are verbal and some are non-verbal. Or better, some are relatively more verbal, and some are relatively more non-verbal. Without words we can never understand anything, so that there must be at least some words to go along with non-verbal symbols. On the other hand, verbal symbols (such as what you are reading) still have shape and sound, and thus are not wholly verbal. We are used to thinking only of non-verbal signs as symbols; but we should realize that all language is symbolic, for words are signs that point to things or relations.

The power of symbols is the power of worldview presuppositions. It is the greatest power in the world. All of language is symbolic, of course, but symbolism is not limited to words. Symbolism "creates" reality, not vice versa. This is another way of saying that essence precedes existence. God determined how things should be, and then they were. God determined to make man as His special symbol, and then the reality came into being. Bavinck puts it this way: "As the temple was made 'according to the pattern shown to Moses in the mount,' Hebrews 8:5, even so every creature was first conceived and afterward (in time) created."[4]

Similarly, man is a symbol-generating creature. He is inevitably so. He cannot help being so. He generates good symbols or bad ones, but he is never symbol-free. Man's calling is to imitate God, on the creaturely level, by naming the animals as God named the world (Genesis 1:5ff.; 2:19), and by extending dominion throughout the world. Notice that naming comes first. Man first symbolizes his intention, conceptually, and then puts it into effect. Symbols create reality, not vice versa. Or, more accurately, for God, symbols *create* reality; for man, symbols *structure* reality. Man does not create out of nothing; the image of God's creativity in man involves restructuring pre-existent reality.

God's actions are *creatively constructive.* He speaks, and it comes to pass. Thus, His symbols are copies only of His character and intentions. Man's actions, however, can only be *receptively reconstructive.* He is to learn God's symbols, and generate his own in terms of God's. Thus, for man, reality reflects God's original symbols, so that man learns symbols in part from reality; but then, man restructures reality in terms of his own symbols (either righteously or sinfully). Always, God's symbols are primary; man's, secondary.

The heart of the Biblical doctrine of salvation lies here. Justification, sanctification, and glorification are inseparable, but which has primacy? Justification. First God redefines us, resymbolizing us as righteous, and then He remakes us. Similarly, Paul in Romans 6 says that we are to reckon ourselves dead to sin and alive to righteousness, and then we will live that way. Symbols bring about reality, not vice versa.

The primacy of the symbolic is not the same thing as the Greek philosophical notion of the primacy of the intellect, for symbolism often does not operate at the conscious or rational level of the human psyche. Symbolism points us to the equal ultimacy of the rational and non-rational in man, and resists rationalistic attempts to shave away the mysterious. To put it another way, the error of intellectualism focuses on the verbal aspect of symbolism to the detriment of the non-verbal.[5]

Three Special Symbols

As a copy of God, man is a symbol-making creature. It is always possible for man to seek to elevate his own symbols to the level of God's, or even replace God's with his own. This sinful tendency has cropped up over and over in the Church herself. To be clear on this, we have to isolate what God's own specially appointed symbols are. All things generally symbolize God, but He also has given three special symbols.

We are told in Scripture that everything is confirmed by the testimony of two or three witnesses (Deuteronomy 19:15). There are, accordingly, three special symbols that God has given which reveal Him to His people. They are as follows: man himself (the image of God), the Word, and the Sacraments.

Satan has sought to pervert these symbols, and thus redirect the history of the world. He perverted the Word in his conversation with Eve. He perverted the sacramental symbols of the two trees, saying that there was no harm in eating from the wrong tree. He perverted the revelation of God in man by bringing man into sin.

Grace restores these three special symbols. Grace gives us the Word of God. The Bible itself can be taken as a testimony of two witnesses, Old and New Testaments. Indeed, historically the Church has appointed two or three readings (Old Testament, Epistle, Gospel), which are read from two sides of the altar/table, to form the testimony of double witness. The Bible itself is one of the three special symbols.

Grace gives us the sacraments. There are two of them, forming a non-verbal testimony of two witnesses: Holy Baptism and Holy Communion. Indeed, the Lord's Supper itself has two witnessing elements.

Grace gives us redeemed and restored men. The saved are re-symbolized as righteous and whole before God. Here again, we have two witnesses, the royal priesthood (believers) and the servant priesthood (elders).

Books have been written on the interrelationship of the three special symbols: Word, Sacrament, Person.[6] Here my point is simply this: These are the three special symbols God has set up. The restoration of the whole fabric of life takes place when these symbols are restored to power.

Secondary Symbols

We have spoken of God's primary symbols as special and general. Here, speaking of secondary symbols, we refer to those made by man. Man generates special and general symbols, just as God does. Because of sin, however, man's symbols are often perverse.

God's Primary Symbols:
- Special (Word, Sacrament, Humanity)
- General (the world)

Man's Secondary Symbols:
- Special (special words, special memorials, and special roles for men)
- General (all of life)

Let's look at the three areas or zones of symbolism we have already described. *First of all, language.* Men generate special language symbols when they take oaths, which bind them to certain words. Examples of special man-made symbols are contracts, the U.S. Constitution, and Church confessions. (The subdivision of systematic theology that studies ecclesiastical confessions is called Symbolics or Symbolic Theology.) Men also generate general language symbols all the time, as in conversation and writing.

Second, non-verbal arrangements, or memorials. Examples of special non-verbal symbols set up by men (analogous to God's sacraments) are liturgies (rites), church architecture, the national flag, national anthem (music), and particular works of art by artists designed to express some particular point or viewpoint. At the same time, men are always making non-verbal arrangements that shape and define their lives, such as their daily routines of life (dance), the homes in which they live, their evening meals, and the like.

Third, men themselves. Here we are speaking of clothing. At the general level, men and women dress themselves to look attractive. At the special level is the uniform, designed to identify a man with a special office or calling (physician, policeman, clergyman). These are ways in which men generate symbols around themselves, to give definition and direction to their lives.

We don't often think about these general symbols, such as conversation, dress, and the arrangement of our furniture. Men do, however, take very seriously the special symbols they create. In modern rationalistic Western society, men do not understand the power of non-verbal symbols and of dress, with the result that they are enslaved by them.[7] They do, however, generally understand the power of words. Thus, they place great store by their confessions, constitutions, manifestoes, and the like. It's all right to do that, so long as these man-generated symbols do not become more important than the symbols authored by God. Sadly, that is what usually happens, however.

The Reformation of Symbols

At this point it is clear that symbolism is intimately related to worldview. Our symbols create and reinforce our worldview. They pattern our thoughts and lives, often in ways we are not consciously aware. In order to be delivered from enslavement to our modern worldview grid, we must become familiar with the Biblical worldview grid. Learning to see and be patterned by Biblical symbols and habits will give us the perspective we need to evaluate our world, acquire wisdom, and begin to think how to reshape the world and make it more pleasing to God. Quite clearly, no society can be shaped on a Christian base without the restoration of symbols. We have to give new direction to our culture, and to do that we need to revive our symbols. People understand this instinctively, even if they do not understand it intellectually. Thus, we have movements in conservative Churches to go "back to the confession," and among political conservatives to go "back to the Constitution."

Such movements can be of help, but they can also do harm, and even become idolatrous. This is for two reasons. First of all, history never repeats itself. Man-generated symbols (i.e., the Westminster Confession of Faith, the Belgic Confession, or the U.S. Constitution) have power over the minds of men for a season only. Because God has ordained that men will grow, whether they want to or not, men always outgrow their symbols. We can never outgrow God's symbols, but we do outgrow our own. To attempt to return to earlier symbols, without recasting them, is a rejection of maturity.

Moreover (still on point one), no living man can ever really understand the meaning of an old symbol. No living Presbyterian, no matter how strict and conservative, thinks like the men of the Westminster Assembly. And this is not just true in minor matters, but in major ones as well. The Westminster Confession expressed the Biblical faith in certain terms, in a certain way, against certain errors, at a certain time. It is one of the finest Church Confessions ever written, and should be studied by every theologian. Our long-term goal, however, must be to produce a new Confession that will embrace the greatness of the older documents, and transcend it. Thus, such symbols as constitutions must be administered by living courts from generation to generation. As a result, the constitutions change, until they are no longer functional. The U.S. Constitution is an example. There came a time when the continual interpretation and application of the Constitution by living men gave way to perversion and ignoring of the Constitution. The Constitution no longer has the same power in the minds of men as it did when it was written, and it can never again have such power. It can, of course, continue to function as the foundation of our laws, provided we understand that it inevitably will be reinterpreted from generation to generation, though hopefully within Christian parameters.[8]

The second problem with trying to revivify old symbols is that such an attempt can become idolatrous, if it says that the mainspring of human society lies in man-made symbols, instead of in God's symbols. It is idolatrous to say that restoring the U.S. Constitution is more necessary to social renewal than restoring the sacraments. The key to social renewal, to cultural reformation, to Christian reclamation, then, is this: We must restore the primary special symbols: Word, Sacrament, Persons. That is because only the primary special symbols transcend history, and thus only they can form the wellspring of historical progress.

Conclusion

Practically speaking, does this mean to stop singing in church any hymn more than a hundred or so years old? Stop reciting the Apostles' Creed? Stop using the Westminster Confession (or whatever)? Not at all. The principle of growth means we have to move on, but it also means we cannot move on until we understand our heritage. To try to generate good church music out of the meager vocabulary of American popular music is like trying to generate good theology out of the ideas heard on Christian radio and television. Christian theologians need to acquire familiarity with the whole of the Christian past, in constant contact with the primary special symbols, in order to move forward into new man-made theologies. Christian musicians must know all the music of the Christian past, in constant contact with the primary special symbols, in order to produce good contemporary Christian music.[9]

Thus, earlier man-generated symbols have great value to us, if we do not commit idolatry with them. The preacher must preach his man-generated sermons from the primary symbol (the Word) with an eye to the man-generated symbols of the past as well as the needs of the present. The liturgist must organize his man-generated expression of worship from the primary symbol (the sacraments) with an eye to the man-generated liturgies of the past as well as the needs of the present. The Christian must live his man-generated life out of the example of the primary Symbol (Jesus Christ), with an eye to the godly men of the past and present.

Moreover, at the general level we need a restoration of sight into God's created symbols. We need to learn again how to look at trees, stars, shrubs, grass, snakes, birds, flowers, emeralds, clothing, and all else — look at them with Bible eyes, not with the eyes of Western rationalism. When this has happened, Christians will once again take control of the arts and sciences, but not until then. General cultural renewal is impossible apart from recovering the symbolic worldview of the Bible.

Only then will we see renewal in the Church (the primary institution) and in society (secondarily). Judgment begins at the House of God. Restoration begins when men take His primary symbols seriously once again.

PART TWO

THE FEATURES
OF THE WORLD

Round each habitation hovering,
See the cloud and fire appear
For a glory and a covering,
Showing that the Lord is near;
Thus deriving from their banner
Light by night and shade by day,
Safe they feed upon the manna
Which he gives them when they pray.

—John Newton

THE WORLD AS
GOD'S HOUSE

Suppose we were going to build a house. What would be our
first step? Imagine that we bought some land, and then went out
and bought some materials. We all came out to the land one day
and started putting it together with no pre-arranged plan. We
started nailing boards together, pouring concrete, laying pipes,
and all the rest, according to our whims. What kind of building
would we erect, if we could get anything up at all?

Clearly something else is needed: a blueprint. We need to go
to an architect and have him draw up a blueprint, a model, for
us to work from. We also need to come up with a schedule of
what is done first, and what is done later. Then we can get
together and build the house properly. The Bible tells us that
man is God's image and workman, taking the raw materials of
the world and building civilizations from it. As a worker, man
needs a blueprint and a schedule; that is, he needs a worldview
and a philosophy of history. In general, these are provided by
the Scriptures: The Bible tells us what to do and how to do it in
the transforming power of the Spirit. In terms of a worldview
model, however, the Bible shows heaven as the blueprint for
earth. Heaven as a model for the earth is presented to us in
Genesis 1.

The Heavenly Blueprint

"In the beginning, God created the heavens and the earth,"
says Genesis 1:1.[1] This heaven is the "highest" or "third" heaven.
In Genesis 1:8, God created the "firmament" within the earth,
and called it "heaven." The stars were placed in this "firmament
heaven," and birds are said to fly in it (Genesis 1:17, 20). Thus,

neither the atmospheric heavens nor "outer space" were established until later in the week, and are actually part of the original "earth" of Genesis 1:1.

The heaven created in Genesis 1:1, then, is the special throne-house of God. "Thus says the LORD, 'Heaven is My throne, and the earth is My footstool'" (Isaiah 66:1; cf. Psalm 11:4; Matthew 5:34; 23:22; Acts 7:49). It exists (to use the language of science fiction) in another dimension from earth, infinitely near to us, yet also infinitely far away.

The Bible shows us quite a lot about heaven. In fact, if we do not understand heaven, we cannot do our work here on earth; for we pray, "Thy will be done on earth as it is in heaven." If we do not know what heaven is like, we cannot imitate it on earth. Thus the Bible frequently opens heaven to give man a view of what it is like. Ezekiel's visions of the divine Glory (Ezekiel 1:1ff.; 3:12ff.; 10:1ff.; 11:22ff.; 43:2ff.) are a good place to start. As we shall see, the "glory-cloud" of God is a picture of heaven; when it appears, we get a view of heaven.[2]

It is when heaven is opened that the Law of God is revealed. But more than that, the heavenly pattern Moses was shown on Mount Sinai included art, architecture, worship, and indeed all of life. The Tabernacle and the Temple were both architectural heaven-models.[3] Similarly, in the book of Revelation, John is shown how worship is conducted in heaven, as a model for earthly worship.[4] Thus, heaven is the model or blueprint for earth, though not in a simplistic sense. After all, the Tabernacle and the Temple were not identical. There is unity and diversity in man's imitation of heaven. Man is to labor to take the raw material of the earth and remodel it according to the heavenly blueprint: "Thy will be done on earth as it is in heaven."

This explains to us why God would initially create two different environments, rather than just one. Man was created to act as God's agent, His son, in the world. Man was going to be given the delightful task of transfiguring the world from glory to glory according to the heavenly model.

Glory and Heaven

The second verse of the Bible tells us that darkness was over the surface of the deep, and the Spirit was also hovering over the surface of the waters. While there is a "contest" between the dominion of darkness and that of the Spirit here on the first day, this is not a conflict between evil and good. Darkness was not an environment of evil, nor a symbol of sin, at this stage. Rather the idea is that the Spirit was beginning the work of glorifying the creation.

The hovering Spirit manifested the presence of the Triune God in creation. It is the Spirit who *proceeds* eternally from the Father and also from the Son (in two different ways, according to the properties of each spirating Person). Once the world has been created, it is the Spirit who *proceeds* out of eternity into time, and makes manifest the presence of the other two Persons. The Father and the Word send the Spirit into the creation as initial Light-bearer.

Genesis 1:3 records the creation of the cloud of glory, also called Shekinah Glory: "Let there be light." Light implies transmission from some source, with the possibility of shadowing. Moreover, the light was not constant, but alternated with darkness for three days before the creation of the sun. Thus, there had to be some local source of this created light, and it was not the sun.

As Meredith G. Kline has shown at length, the visible manifestation of God's throne-environment in the creation is always the work of the Spirit. Thus the hovering Spirit in Genesis 1:2 corresponds to the hovering cloud-chariot of God elsewhere in the Bible, as in Deuteronomy 32:10-11, where the glory of God hovered over Israel in the wilderness.[5] Until God spoke from His throne and said, "Let there be light," there was no visible manifestation of glory in connection with the Spirit.

When God's glory-cloud appears later in the Bible, we find that it consists of such basic heavenly phenomena as light, clouds, lightning, thunder, blue sky, and the like. Here in Genesis 1:2-3 is the explanation of this. God first created heaven, and then sent His Spirit to hover over the earth. Proceeding from heaven, the Spirit brought the heavenly pattern into the cosmos. With the creation of light, the Spirit manifested God's presence as a cloud of glory. In the design of God, this glory was reproduced in the firmament heavens made on the second day, and then was further reproduced in successive stages, on the earth. (See Diagram 4.1.) "The heavens declare the glory of God in the special sense that they are a copy of the archetypal Glory of God."[6]

Diagram 4.1
The Heavens and the Earth

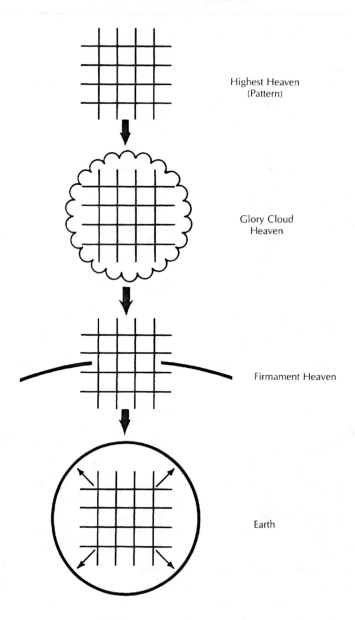

Highest Heaven
(Pattern)

Glory Cloud
Heaven

Firmament Heaven

Earth

When men saw the glory-cloud, they were seeing heaven, or at least a replica of heaven in the world. As Kline has noted, "The Glory-cloud was indeed the invisible realm of heaven appearing in a veiled visibility in the midst of earthly creatures."[7] The phenomena of the glory were heavenly phenomena. To see into the cloud was to see into heaven. Genesis 1 explains that the hovering Spirit proceeded from heaven to make this glory-light appear within the world. In this way, the Spirit brought a blueprint with Him, and began the work of shaping the world after the heavenly model.[8]

We pray "Thy will be done on earth as it is in heaven." Genesis 1 gives us the first fulfillment of this principle. As the light shone from the glory-cloud of God's heavenly throne environment, that environment began to be reproduced on the earth. God spent one week laying the initial foundations and showing man how to work. Just as man labors to make earth like heaven, so did God.

The Firmament-Heaven

After making light, God created a "firmament" to separate waters above from waters below (Genesis 1:6, 7). This firmament He called *heaven*. We now have two heavens, the one the dwelling place of God and the angels, made on the first day, and the second created *within the original earth* as a reminder of the original heaven. The fact that the word *heaven* is used for the firmament means that the firmament is analogous to the original heaven, and thus is symbolic of it. On the fourth day, God placed lights *in* the firmament-heaven, to be symbols and to act as clocks (Genesis 1:14-18). This means that the sun, moon, and stars are not part of the original heaven, but part of the original earth. The original earth of Genesis 1:1 is now being separated into the globe on which we live on the one hand, and upper waters and lights on the other hand. On the fifth day, God created birds to fly *on the face of* the firmament-heaven (Genesis 1:20).

What is this firmament-heaven? The related verb in Hebrew means "to stretch out, beat out, or flatten out." The idea is of a shell or surface cast over the earth.[9] Now as a matter of scientific fact, there is no hard shell around the earth, nor do birds fly inside a hard shell. We have here the language of visible appearance, not of scientific investigation. Thus, we need to see the language as pointing to a symbolic structure. The blue sky (firmament) is a symbolic boundary between waters above and waters below. Looking at the sky, we see an image of heaven. The things found in the sky — stars, birds — symbolize things found in heaven — angels (e.g., Job 38:7; Revelation 12:4; 18:2; John 1:32).

To paraphrase what Genesis 1 says about the firmament-heaven, we can say that God created the appearance of a shell to separate the (blue) waters above from the (blue) waters below. This shell symbolizes the boundary between heaven and the heavenly sea (Revelation 4:6) and earth. If we look up at this blue shell, it looks as if the "greater light and the lesser light" and the stars are fixed *in* the shell. As we look up, it appears that the birds fly *on the face of*, or in front of the surface of this blue shell. Neither the atmosphere nor outer space, however, but the shell itself is the firmament-heaven.

Why is this shell called "heaven"? Because the phenomena that appear in the sky are signs and symbols of things in the original heaven. Clouds remind us of God's glory-cloud. Rainbows remind us of the rainbow around His throne. Stars speak of angels. The sun speaks of Christ. The blue speaks of the heavenly sea before the Throne. And so forth. (Cf. Psalm 19:1; Daniel 12:3.)

The firmament is best situated to show heaven to us because it is the symbolic boundary between heaven and earth. It is as if the shell were translucent, and we can see dimly through it into heaven — through a glass darkly. Thus, when Moses and the elders ascended the mountain to eat with God, "they saw the God of Israel; and under His feet there appeared to be a pavement of sapphire, as clear as the sky [heaven] itself" (Exodus 24:10). The blue sapphire pavement is the firmament, which here becomes temporarily transparent enough to enable the elders to see the King of kings. The same picture is given in Ezekiel 1:22-26, where the cherubim are positioned just under the firmament, to carry out God's will in the world, while God is enthroned above the firmament-boundary.

What we have seen thus far is that heaven forms the model for the earth — socially, artistically, morally, spiritually, and in every other way. The Spirit initiated the task of shaping the earth after the heavenly model. But we have also seen that God set the sky within the earth as a symbol of His highest heaven. The creation of the firmament-heaven, visible to man, means in part that man, like the Spirit, will work at shaping the world after the heavenly model. The highest heaven is invisible to us, but the firmament-heaven gives us a visible blueprint.

The fact that the firmament-heaven contains images of heaven (stars, birds, rainbows) is delightful and wonderful, but it does not carry us very far in terms of a descriptive program. It is the Bible, God's Word, that is our primary blueprint. Since heaven is the blueprint, the Bible is a heavenly book. The Bible teaches this in imagery, for we read that the sky is like a scroll (Isaiah 34:4; Revelation 6:14). This relates to the very word *firmament*, which as we saw refers to something stretched or beaten out, like a scroll.

The primary passage that relates heaven to the Bible as our blueprint is Psalm 19. The first six verses of the psalm have to do with the heavens, which "are telling of the glory of God; and the firmament is declaring the work of His hands." Having celebrated the visible revelation of God's glory in the heavens, the psalmist then celebrates the Law-Word of God in verses 7-11. The relationship is clear: The "speech" that is poured forth from the heavens is found in the Bible.

Thus, in terms of the Biblical worldview, the blue sky and all that it contains are to remind us of God, of His Word, and of our wonderful project of "heavenizing" the earth.

Seeing God's Glory

When Israel came out of Egypt, they grumbled against Moses and Aaron because they did not have anything to eat. Moses and Aaron called the people together and told them that God would provide them heavenly bread, manna, and that

in the morning you will see the glory of the LORD. . . . And it came about as Aaron spoke to the whole congregation of the sons of Israel, that they turned toward the wilderness, and behold, the glory of the LORD appeared in the cloud (Exodus 16:7, 10).

They had seen this glory before. As they marched out of Egypt,

the LORD was going before them in a pillar of cloud by day to lead them on the way, and in a pillar of fire by night to give them light, that they might travel by day and by night. He did not take away the pillar of cloud by day, or the pillar of fire by night, from before the people (Exodus 13:21-22).

This was almost certainly only one pillar. During the day, the brightness of the sun hid the fire within, and Israel saw the cloud. At night, the fire shone through the cloud. Thus, they were given shade by day and warmth at night.

This glory-cloud settled over Mount Sinai.

And there were thunder and lightning flashes and a thick cloud upon the mountain and a very loud trumpet sound . . . and Mount Sinai was all in smoke because the LORD descended upon it in fire, and its smoke ascended like the smoke of a furnace, and the whole mountain trembled violently (Exodus 19:16, 18).

The One seated on His throne in the midst of this "portable heaven" then spoke the Ten Commandments to Israel (Exodus 20).

God told Israel to build a house for Him, a tent called the Tabernacle. Since the glory-cloud was God's portable heaven, and thus His house, we expect the Tabernacle to be an architectural replica of the glory-cloud of heaven. This is indeed what we find. Once the Tabernacle was completed, God moved into it; and His glory-cloud filled it, identifying with it: "Then the cloud covered the tent of meeting, and the glory of the LORD filled the Tabernacle" (Exodus 40:34).

Later on in history, God gave blueprints to David for a more permanent house for His Name, the Temple (1 Chronicles 28:19). Again, when the Temple, a model of God's heavenly house, had been completed, "the cloud filled the house of the LORD" (1 Kings 8:10).

Still later, when the Temple was about to be destroyed, God's glory appeared to Ezekiel in Babylon. God told Ezekiel that He was moving out of the Temple, and was going to reside in exile with His people (Ezekiel 8-11). Ezekiel was granted a vision through the blue firmament into the cloud, and what he saw was a chariot made of four cherubim with wheels, surrounded by a rainbow: God's portable throne (Ezekiel 1:4-28). Earlier, Isaiah had had a similar vision of God's heavenly, cloud-filled throne-room (Isaiah 6:1-4).

Last, but certainly not least, the apostle John was caught up into the cloud, and into heaven itself, where he stood on the firmament and saw the throne of God and all sorts of heavenly phenomena (Revelation 4-5).[10]

In Chapters 12-18 of this book, we shall examine these various heaven models in detail, because they were also pictures of the world. Remember, heaven is the model for the earth. Each of these symbolic pictures was given to teach the people of that time how they were to live and relate to God. Accompanying each visual blueprint were words from God, verbal blueprints. It was man's task to build the world, carrying it from glory to glory, and making it a fit house for God. God dwells in heaven, but He wants also to dwell on earth, when man has made it ready for Him. Heaven is God's throne-house, but potentially, so is the earth. The blueprint for God's earth-house is heaven.

Typology

The Greek word *typos* refers to an image impressed onto something else, for instance, wax.[11] It is the word used in Scripture for the imprint of God's heavenly pattern on the earth, and thus it is absolutely fundamental to a Biblical worldview.

In Acts 7:44 Stephen says, "Our fathers had the Tabernacle of testimony in the wilderness, just as He who spoke to Moses directed him to make it according to the pattern [type] which he had seen." Similarly, Hebrews 8:5, quoting Exodus 25:40, reminds us that Moses was told, "See that you make all things according to the pattern [type] which was shown you on the mountain."

As we have seen, there are a succession of such imprints. Each imprint is more glorious than the one before. Solomon's Temple was more glorious than the Mosaic Tabernacle. Ezekiel's visionary Temple (Ezekiel 40-48) was more glorious than Solomon's Temple. The New Jerusalem is more glorious yet. The study of how each of these models is transformed into the next, and the parallels between them, is part of typology.

Because all men are made in the image of God, all men bear His imprint. Every man is, thus, in one sense a type of every other man. More importantly, church leaders are to be types or models for kingdom citizens (Philippians 1:7; 1 Thessalonians 1:7; 1 Timothy 4:12; Titus 2:7; 1 Peter 5:3). In terms of a typological view of history, the kingdom of men in the Old Covenant was a type of the New Covenant (1 Corinthians 10:6, 11), and the first Adam was a type of the Last (Romans 5:14).

A great deal of nonsense has been published under the banner of typology; but in spite of this, the fact remains that typology is the fundamental Biblical philosophy of history.[12] Typology means that history is under God's control, not man's. It means that the successive stages of world history have meaning, a meaning related to the heavenly pattern and God's purpose to glorify man and the world progressively.

In an important study, Jean Daniélou has shown that the early Church Fathers regarded typology as central to their understanding of the Scriptures. It enabled them to answer both their Jewish and their Gnostic critics. Against the Jews, typology showed the superiority of the New Covenant over the old; against the Gnostics, typology showed that the Old and New Covenants both revealed the same truths.[13] The symbolic and typological approach of the Church Fathers is often confused with allegory, but Daniélou shows conclusively that the Fathers were well aware of the difference. The Fathers did indeed use the Bible allegorically to express what they intended to be a Christian philosophy, but

> this trend, strictly philosophical, is something quite different from typology. It goes back to Philo. In his *Treatise on Paradise*, Ambrose, who was much influenced by Philo, writes as follows: "Philo confined his attention to the moral sense, because his Judaic outlook prevented him from a more spiritual understanding" (IV, 25; C.S.E.L. 281, 21). *Spiritual* here denotes the Christological or typological sense, while *moral* implies philoso-

phical allegory. What Ambrose calls the moral sense is therefore something entirely different from typology.[14]

Eventually, however, "Christian philosophy freed itself from an allegorism which artificially tied it to the Bible, and became an independent approach."[15]

Herbert Schlossberg has written, "All idols belong either to nature or to history. The whole creation falls into these two categories, and there is no other place to which man can turn to find a substitute for God."[16] The Biblical symbolic worldview answers man's idols of nature. Only if we allow nature to point us to the Creator can we avoid idolatry. Just so, the Biblical typological worldview answers man's idols of history. God superintends history so that events of the past shed light on events of the future. The key to unlocking the meaning of history lies in the typological blueprint of heaven, as heaven progressively is impressed upon the earth, and as the Heavenly Man, Jesus Christ, is progressively impressed upon His people.[17]

Conclusion

When we step outside and look up, what do we see? We see the blue sky of day, and the black starry sky of night. We see clouds and heavenly fire (lightning). We see rainbows and falling stars. We hear thunder. The Bible tells us that these are not merely natural phenomena. They are pictures of heaven, revelations of God's glory, dimensions of His home. With new eyes, we can see this world also as God's house.

The spacious firmament on high,
With all the blue ethereal sky,
And spangled heavens, a shining frame,
Their great Original proclaim.
The unwearied sun from day to day
Does his Creator's power display,
And publishes to every land
The works of an almighty hand.

Soon as the evening shades prevail
The moon takes up the wondrous tale,
And nightly to the listening earth
Repeats the story of her birth;
Whilst all the stars that round her burn
And all the planets in their turn,
Confirm the tidings, as they roll,
And spread the truth from pole to pole.

What though in solemn silence all
Move round the dark terrestrial ball;
What though no real voice nor sound
Amid their radiant orbs be found;
In reason's ear they all rejoice,
And utter forth a glorious voice;
Forever singing as they shine,
"The hand that made us is divine."

—Joseph Addison

SUN, MOON, AND STARS

When twentieth-century people step outside and look at the sky, they see a huge atomic furnace burning hydrogen during the day, and a small planetoid reflecting the light of the sun at night. They also see other atomic furnaces that appear very small because they are so far away.

When twentieth-century people step back inside their homes and pick up the latest coffee table book of astronomy, they see color-enhanced photographs of distant galaxies, the Magellanic Clouds, and binary stars. They see speculative drawings of quasars, neutron stars, and black holes.

All these are wondrous things, and proper to study as part of God's universe. But if this is all we see, we are not getting the whole picture. If we look through new eyes, we shall see much more.

The Purpose of Heavenly Lights

The Bible speaks more of the purpose of the heavenly lights than it does of their constitution:

> Then God said, "Let there be lights in the firmament of the heavens to separate the day from the night, and let them be for signs, and for seasons [festival times], and for days and years; and let them be for lights in the firmament of the heavens to give light on the earth"; and it was so.
>
> And God made the two great lights; the greater light to govern the day, and the lesser light to govern the night; He made the stars also. And God placed them in the firmament of the heavens to give light on the earth, and to govern the day and the night, and to separate the light from the darkness; and God saw that it was good. (Genesis 1:14-18)

The first thing said about the astral bodies is that they are lights. We have seen that light is an aspect of God's glory-cloud, and it is as a reflection of God's glory that these heavenly bodies are made as lights. They represent glory, and so the Bible can say of the glorified saints that "the righteous will shine forth as the sun in the kingdom of their Father" (Matthew 13:43). Similarly, Solomon wrote, "Who is this that grows like the dawn, as beautiful as the full moon, as pure as the sun?" (Song of Solomon 6:10). Or as St. Paul wrote, "There is one glory of the sun, and another glory of the moon, and another glory of the stars; for star differs from star in glory" (1 Corinthians 15:41).

It is because the heavenly bodies show God's glory that we delight in looking at beautiful pictures of them in astronomy books. We live in a happy age, to have access to photographs of such wonders as the Ring Nebula, the Crab Nebula, and the great spiral nebula in Andromeda.

As lights, the astral bodies are glorious. But, *second, they were given for signs, or symbols*. As we have seen, all created things point back to God; but all things also symbolize particular things, and in this case, the astral bodies symbolize rulers and governors. The lights are positioned in the firmament, called heaven. Heaven rules the earth. Thus, those things positioned in the firmament symbolize rulers of the earth, as we shall see shortly.

Third, they are said to be for seasons, or, more literally, for festival times. This applied to the Old Covenant, which was regulated by these creational clocks. It was particularly the moon, regulator of months, that governed the Israelite calendar. The moon established which day was the first of the month, and which was the fifteenth. Such festivals as Passover, Pentecost, and Tabernacles were set on particular days of the month (Leviticus 23:5-6, 34; Numbers 28:11-14; 2 Chronicles 8:13; Psalm 81:3). The moon, of course, governs the night (Psalm 136:9; Jeremiah 31:35), and in a sense the entire Old Covenant took place at night. With the rising of the Sun of Righteousness (Malachi 4:2), the "day" of the Lord is at hand (Malachi 4:1), and in a sense the New Covenant takes place in the daytime.[1] As Genesis 1 says over and over, first evening and then morning. In the New Covenant we are no longer under lunar regulation for festival times (Colossians 2:16-17). In that regard, Christ is our light.

Diagram 5.1
Sun, Moon, Stars

If we compare Genesis 1:14 and 16 we see employed the literary device known as *chiasm*. A chiasm is a literary device in which parallel ideas or terms are presented in a sandwich form instead of normal parallelism; that is, ABCDDCBA instead of AABBCCDD. The use of chiasm, which helps bring out the particular symbolic associations of sun, moon, and stars:

> A 14. Let them be for signs
>   B 14. And for festival times
>   C 14. And for days and years
>   C' 16. The greater light to govern the day
>   B' 16. And the lesser light to govern the night
> A' 16. The stars also

The stars (A) are primarily associated with astral symbolism. The moon (B) is associated with appointed festivals, which began in the evening and were removed in the New Covenant. The sun (C) is associated with days and years.

Fourth, they are said to be clocks for days and years. Long before our mechanical clocks and watches were invented, people told time by the position of the sun, the occurrence of solar equinoxes and solstices, and the precession of the equinoxes. Particularly mentioned are days and years, which are regulated not by the moon but by the sun.

Fifth, they are said to rule over day and night, to govern time. Here again the emphasis is on rule. The astral bodies signified those who are glorified and exalted. While this is true of all the saints, it is also true of all human rulers as well. Revelation 1:20 says that the rulers of the church are like stars, and Jude 13 says that apostate teachers are "wandering stars." Long before this, in Genesis 37:9-10, Joseph had seen the rulers of his clan as sun, moon, and stars. We see this even today. The flag of the United States of America has fifty stars, for the fifty states of our nation. The flags of oriental nations include the rising sun. The flags of Near-Eastern countries feature a crescent moon. Sun, moon, and stars are symbols of world powers.

Sixth, they are associated with the heavenly host, the angelic and human array around the throne of God. This also follows from the fact that they are positioned in heaven. They represent the angelic host in Judges 5:20, Job 38:7, and Isaiah 14:13. They represent the human host of the Lord as well, as we see from the promise to Abraham in Genesis 15:5, reiterated in Genesis 22:17, 26:4, and Deuteronomy 1:10. Christians "appear as stars in the world in the midst of a crooked and perverse generation" (Philippians 2:15). The fact that Abraham's descendants were to be like stars implies that they would not only be positioned in the heavenlies (Ephesians 2:6), but also that they would be *rulers* over the gentiles.

Now, it is neither possible nor desirable to separate these aspects of astral symbolism. The sun, moon, and stars mark time as clocks. Since they mark time, they govern time. Positioned in the heavenlies, they signify governments, ruling day and night. Since they mark time, they can be seen to signify the duration of earthly governments, so that as we shall see the fall of sun, moon, and stars is a symbol for the fall of earthly governments.

Let us now look at these things in more detail.

The Sun

The sun, ruler of the sky and of the day, is used to symbolize the Lord in Psalm 84:11, "The Lord God is a sun and shield." Similarly, a familiar passage in Isaiah says,

> Arise, shine, for your light has come, and the glory of the LORD has risen upon you. For behold, darkness will cover the earth, and deep darkness the peoples; but the Lord will rise upon you, and His glory will appear upon you. And nations will come to your light, and kings to the brightness of your rising (60:1-3).

God is like the sun, and when He comes, He glorifies His people so that they also shine. So Deborah could pray, "Let those who love Him [God] be like the rising of the sun in its might" (Judges 5:31b), a prayer answered a few years later in Gideon, and then again in Samson, whose name means "Sun."[2] Psalm 19 reflects on this: The sun is like a bridegroom, like a strong man. The reference here, first of all, is to Samson, the bridegroom of Judges 14-15. But beyond this we see the Messianic Judge of all the earth, who is to come and bring His Word (vv. 7-11). When John saw that One, "His face was like the sun shining in its strength" (Revelation 1:16b).[3]

Night gives way to day, and this is an image of the coming of the Kingdom. If Nicodemus met with Jesus by night, this was in part a reflection of the condition of history at that point, for the whole Old Covenant is seen as nighttime. Malachi 4:1 says that a "day is coming," and goes on in verse 2 to predict that "the Sun of Righteousness will rise with healing in its wings." In this way, moon and sun are governors of time, of the Old Covenant and New Covenant; but they also symbolize the First and Last Adams, who are the real governors of these two eras.

Finally, we should note that in the Bible the sun can also symbolize counterfeit gods, those who falsely pretend to be the true Sun of Righteousness. The Pharaoh of Egypt claimed to be an incarnation of the sun, and thus it was appropriate that in the judgment of Egypt, God put out the sun for three days (Exodus 10:21-23).

The Stars

The prophets often see the "sun, moon, and stars" falling to the earth. One of the most frequently encountered mistakes in Bible prophecy today is the notion that this always refers to the end of the world at the Second Coming of Jesus Christ. Actually, though, this expression usually refers to the collapse of some particular nation.

Suppose we wrote a prophetic poem about the destruction of the United States, and included in the poem these lines:

> The sun was darkened, the moon eclipsed;
> The stars fell, they fell to the ground;
> Fifty in ranks, trampled under foot;
> Her rulers imprisoned, caged in darkness.

Let's analyze this section of our "poem." It has an ABBA structure, which (as we saw above) is a "chiasm." The first line, about the darkening of sun and moon, is explained by the last line about the imprisonment of our rulers. The second and third lines clearly refer to the defeat of the fifty states. This would be fairly obvious to us, would it not? Anyone who has had a high school class in literature could probably figure it out.

With this in mind, let us begin a survey of the Biblical passages that use sun, moon, and stars as symbols of rulers and times.

Abraham's Stars

In Genesis 15, when God cut the covenant with Abraham, He took him outside and told him to "tell" the stars, "if you are able to tell them; thus shall your seed be" (v. 5). Bible exegetes differ on exactly what Abraham was being asked to do. Generally it is assumed that he was being asked to count up the number of the stars, and that his descendants would be like the stars of the heavens for multitude, even as they would be like the sand of the sea. Some have pointed out, however, that the Hebrew verb translated "count" can also be translated "tell" in the sense of "evaluating" (Hebrew *saphar*, as in Psalm 56:8). This is not clearly the case, however, since the verb often just means "count up."

All the same, two alternative interpretations have been suggested. The first is that of M. Barnouin. Barnouin points out that the patriarchs in Genesis 5 and 11 lived lives of curious numerical lengths. Enoch, for instance, lived 365 years, the length of a solar year. Kenan lived 910 years, ten times a standard quarter year of 91 days. Lamech lived 777 years, which is the sum of the synodical periods of Jupiter (399 days) and Saturn (378 days) (Genesis 5:23, 14, 31). Is it possible that God was saying to Abraham that his seed would be like the great patriarchs of old, the faithful godly men who were blessed and preserved before the Flood, and in the years after the Flood?

Barnouin suggests that when Abraham looked at the stars, he was considering the planets and how they *govern time* (Genesis 1:14), and making an evaluation based on this. The years of the patriarchs corresponded to the time-governing periods of the planets and other heavenly bodies. Abraham's seed would be like this. They would be a heavenly people, gathered around God's heavenly throne. Their history would mark time.

Barnouin sees this fulfilled in the censuses of the book of Numbers, in which these same astral periods recur. In Numbers 1, all the men twenty and older were enrolled in the Israelite militia, God's army. As God's army, Israel was in one sense a "heavenly host," captained by the Lord of heaven. In this respect, they are spoken of as stars in Deuteronomy 1:10, and as a heavenly host they are commanded by an angel, the Angel of the Lord (Joshua 5:13-6:2; Exodus 23:20-21). Thus, it would not be surprising if the numbering of that heavenly host had some association with astral numbers. At any rate, Barnouin's thesis is a complex one, but certainly also a challenging one.[4]

The second alternative view of Genesis 15:5 relates to the constellations of the zodiac, and we shall defer consideration of it until after we examine Genesis 37:5-10.

To conclude our look at Abraham, let me point out that when God made the covenant with Abraham in Genesis 15, He did so by burying the sun and making it "very dark" (Genesis 15:17). This implies that if the "seed" is to be like the stars of heaven and dust of earth, it will have to be a new heavens and a new earth.

Joseph's Stars

When Joseph saw twelve stars bowing down before him, could this have been the constellations of the zodiac, and not individual stars? In this section, we want to focus on the *possibility* (please note) that the twelve signs of the zodiac *may* have been designed by God as twelve portraits of humanity, and that they *may* correlate with the twelve tribes of Israel (which clearly were twelve portraits of humanity).

This is not a new idea. Synagogues dug up in Israel have been found to have tiled mosaics showing the twelve signs of the zodiac, and Josephus relates this to the twelve tribes.[5] Before looking at this, however, let us get before us what the Bible says about the constellations.

The constellations are referred to several times in Scripture, without any implied criticism, simply as if they were part of the created order of things. An example is Job 38:31-33, where God says to Job,

> Can you bind the chains of the Pleiades, or loose the cords of Orion? Can you lead forth a constellation (or, the zodiac) in its season, and guide the Bear with her sons? Do you know the ordinances of the heavens, or fix their rule over the earth?

This is an interesting passage, for it speaks of the chains and cords of the astral signs. After all, everyone who has ever learned the constellations knows that they don't in the least resemble what they are supposed to look like. It takes a lot of imagination to tie together the stars in these symbols. Who, then, devised them in the first place? Who set up the chains and cords that bind them together? If they were set up by heathen Babylonian priests, why does God refer to them as if they were His creations?

Job 9:9, speaking of God's greatness, says that He "makes the Bear, Orion, and the Pleiades, and the Chambers of the South." It certainly seems that this verse says that God Himself designed the constellations. Amos 5:8 says the same thing: "He who made the Pleiades and Orion . . . the LORD is His name." It might be argued that God made the unnamed stars, and men designed the constellations, but I find that to be a strained interpretation. It seems to me that Job and Amos would in that case just have said that God made the stars, and left it at that. To say God made the constellations certainly implies that He designed them.

Another avenue of evidence points in the same direction. Psalm 147:4 says that God "counts the number of the stars; He *gives names* to all of them" (emphasis added). Similarly, Isaiah 40:26 encourages us to lift up our eyes "and see who has created these stars, the One who leads forth their host by number, He *calls them all by name*" (emphasis added). Does the Bible tell us any of these names? It would seem so, as we have seen: Bear, Orion, Pleiades, etc. Maybe, of course, the constellations are not what Psalm 147:4 and Isaiah 40:26 are talking about. Maybe these verses are just talking about individual stars, in which case we simply don't know any of their names. Maybe. But again, this is not the simplest and most obvious interpretation. Comparing Scripture with Scripture, it seems that God named the constellations.

Some passages allude to the misuse of the constellations by idolaters. Second Kings 23:5 refers to apostate Israelites who burned incense to Baal, the sun and the moon, and the constellations. Similarly, Isaiah 13:10a, speaking of the destruction of Babylon, says that "the stars of the heaven and their constellations will not flash forth their light." It is likely that the constellations are included in this judgment because of their misuse in Babylonian astrology.

With this in mind, let me lay out a series of propositions. *First*, it appears that God designed the major constellations, both those of the zodiac and the circumpolar ones (Bear and Serpent, Job 26:13). It seems that this is part of what Genesis 1:14 means when it says God made the stars as signs.

Second, clearly the Bible is opposed to the *abuse* of the constellations for idolatrous or astrological purposes, to tell fortunes and the like (Deuteronomy 18:9-13; Isaiah 8:19-20; 44:24-25; 47:8-15).

Third, I know of no evidence to support the notion that the precession of the equinoxes and the 2,000-year-long periods of time that they introduce (Age of Pisces, Age of Aquarius) are used by any Biblical passage to structure either history or prophecy. As a way of marking time, the precession of the equinoxes is part of God's universal clock system, but it seems to have no special symbolic significance.

Fourth, I find no Biblical evidence to support the popular notion that the twelve signs of the zodiac are a map of Bible history and prophecy, beginning with Virgo and ending with Leo. This has been the most common evangelical/fundamentalist use of the zodiac in popular literature. Abraham's analysis of the stars is explained this way: Abraham looked at the cycle of the constellations and received a picture of prophetic history and of the coming Redeemer.[6] I can find, however, no foundation for this approach to the zodiac in Scripture.

Fifth, it is a fact, however, that the four faces of the cherubim in Ezekiel and Revelation correspond to the four central constellations in the zodiac, and to the four tribes of Israel that were positioned north, south, east, and west of the Tabernacle in the wilderness (Numbers 2:1-34). The Lion is Leo, Judah (Genesis 49:9). The Bull is Taurus, Ephraim (Deuteronomy 33:17). The Man is Aquarius, Reuben, "unstable as water" (Genesis 49:4). The Eagle is Scorpio, Dan. (This last identification is more difficult until we understand two things. First, Scorpio was also drawn as an Eagle in the ancient world, according to R. H. Allen.[7] Second, the scorpion is linked with the serpent, and Dan is the serpent [Genesis 49:17; Luke 10:17-19].)

With this paradigm in mind, it is possible to draw a diagram of the twelve tribes in the wilderness, and link the other tribes with the other zodiacal signs by going to the right and left of each of the four major (cherubic) signs. A correlation of these signs with the prophecies of Jacob and Moses in Genesis 49 and Deuteronomy 33 would prove most interesting, but we have no time for it here.[8]

In conclusion, when Joseph saw the sun, moon, and eleven stars bowing down to him (Genesis 37:5-10), what do you suppose the "stars" were? It seems most likely that they were the twelve signs of the zodiac. It would be interesting to take the twelve tribes of Israel, and the preeminent symbols associated with each by Jacob and Moses, and study them as "humanity in twelve dimensions," both as revelations of sinful Adam and as adumbrations of Christ. Such a study might shed light on the relationship between the twelve tribes and the zodiac.

Prophetic Stars

Let us now briefly survey the passages where sun, moon, and stars are used in a prophetic-symbolic sense. A failure to understand the symbolic nature of these passages has led a few popular writers to assume that such expressions as "the sun turned to sackcloth and the moon to blood" can only be understood as referring to the collapse of the physical cosmos. Nobody takes these verses literally, after all. The question is, to what kind of event does this symbolic language refer? For modern man, it seems that it can only be speaking of the end of the natural world. For ancient man, it was indeed the end of the "world" that such language indicated, but not the "world" in our modern scientific sense. Rather, it was the end of the "world" in a sociopolitical sense.

For instance, Isaiah 13:9-10 says that "the day of the LORD is coming," and when it comes, "the stars of heaven and their constellations will not flash forth their light; the sun will be dark when it rises, and the moon will not shed its light." It goes on to say in verse 13, "I shall make the heavens tremble, and the earth will be shaken from its place at the fury of the LORD of hosts in the day of His burning anger." Well, this certainly does sound like the end of the world! *But*, if we read these verses in context, we have to change our initial impression. Verse 1 says, "The oracle concerning Babylon which Isaiah the son of Amoz saw," and if we read on, we find nothing to indicate any change in subject. It is the end of Babylon, not the end of the world, that is spoken of. In fact, in verse 17, God says that he will "stir up the Medes against them," so that the entire chapter is clearly concerned only with Babylon's destruction.

If we read Biblically, this won't seem so strange. What verse 10 is saying is that Babylon's lights are going to go out. Their clocks are going to stop. Their day is over, and it is the Day of Doom for them. And, since these astral bodies symbolize governors and rulers, their rulers are going to have their lights put out as well.

The "heavens and earth" in verse 13 refer to the socio-political organization of Babylon. The "heavens" are the aristocracy, roughly speaking, and the "earth" are the commoners.

We find the same kind of thing in Ezekiel 32. In verses 7-8 of that chapter God declares,

> And when I extinguish you, I will cover the heavens, and darken their stars; I will cover the sun with a cloud, and the moon shall not give its light. All the shining lights in the heavens I will darken over you and will set darkness on your land.

The end of the world? Yes, indeed, but not for everybody. What ancient people might God be speaking of in using this language? The idea in the Babylon oracle was that the astral bodies would not shine forth any light. Here the idea is that they will be covered over. God's glory-cloud will interpose itself between this nation and the heavenly lights. While God's glory-cloud shines brightly for His people Israel, it is dark and foreboding to His enemies, with the result that they are in darkness when He appears to them. These people experienced this once before. Their whole land was darkened; and when they pursued the Israelites, God's cloud came between them and Israel and put them in darkness (Ezekiel 32:2; cp. Exodus 10:21-23; 14:19-20).

Similar language is used prophetically concerning Israel, but with a twist. It is in the prophecy of Joel that we find this most clearly set out. Joel begins by reminding Israel of a recent plague of locusts. In his first chapter, he describes the horrors of the locust invasion. Then, in Chapter 2, he threatens the people with another locust plague, this time an invasion by human locusts. Such an invasion will be a manifestation of "the day of the LORD," that is, the day of judgment (2:1).

The expression "day" of the Lord refers to the rising of the sun—the sun of God's searching light that shows up sin and brings judgment, the sun of God's blazing heat that destroys sin.

Yet for Israel, this "day" will be a "day of darkness and gloom, a day of clouds and thick darkness" (2:2). The metaphor is mixed, but apropos: When God brings His *day*, and evaluates their sin, He will cast them into *darkness*.

Accordingly, when God's locust army comes to judge Israel, "before them the earth quakes, the heavens tremble, the sun and the moon grow dark, and the stars lose their brightness" (2:10). This is a reference to the collapse of Israel as a body politic. After all, Abraham had been told that his seed would be like the stars of the heavens. It is possible that the quaking of the earth refers to the Israelite citizenry, the trembling of the heavens to the Levites and priests (since the Temple was a symbol of heaven), and the darkening of the astral bodies to the royal court and other rulers in Israel.

If the people repent, however, God will return to them, and restore them (2:12ff.). God promises them a great future. He promises them the coming of the Holy Spirit.

> And it will come about after this that I will pour out My Spirit on all mankind, and your sons and daughters will prophesy [fulfilling Numbers 11:17], your old men will dream dreams, your young men will see visions. And even on the male and female servants I will pour out My Spirit in those days" (Joel 2:28-29).

We know from Acts 2:16-18 that this was fulfilled at Pentecost.

"And I will display wonders in the sky and on the earth" (2:30). This is connected with Pentecost, and was, therefore, a warning to the Jews of Peter's day. Wonders in the sky and on the earth is what is foretold. In reverse order (chiasm), first we read of the earth: "Blood, fire, and columns of smoke." These are the phenomena of war. There will be war. There will be yet another invasion. This was fulfilled when the Romans invaded Palestine and destroyed Jerusalem, A.D. 66-70.

Wonders in the sky are also foretold: "the sun will be turned into darkness, and the moon into blood, before the great and awesome day of the LORD comes" (2:31). What is of interest here is the expression "moon into blood." In a solar eclipse the sun turns black, and in a lunar eclipse the moon turns red. Thus, not merely a general darkening but an *eclipse* of powers is spoken of here. But more than that, the turning of the moon to "blood" points, I believe, to something particularly Jewish: the sacrificial system. If they will not accept the blood of Jesus Christ, the final Sacrifice, then they themselves will be turned into blood. They will become the sacrifices. That is what the prophesied war is all about. That is what the destruction of Jerusalem in A.D. 70 was all about.

But Joel is issuing a warning. Those who listen can escape.

> And it will come about that whoever calls on the name of the LORD will be delivered; for [just as Obadiah has already told you] "on Mount Zion and in Jerusalem there will be those who escape" [Obadiah 17], as the LORD has said, even among the survivors whom the LORD calls (2:32).

Just as Isaac escaped death on Mount Moriah, because of the substitute ram that God provided (Genesis 22:13), so those who trust in the Lamb of God will escape the destruction of Jerusalem in A.D. 70. Such is Joel's warning, reiterated by Peter on the day of Pentecost.

It is also reiterated by John. Prophesying of this same event, the destruction of Jerusalem, John writes,

> And I looked when He broke the sixth seal, and there was a great earthquake; and the sun became black as sackcloth made of hair, and the whole moon became like blood; and the stars of the sky fell to the earth, as a fig tree casts its unripe figs when shaken by a great wind (Revelation 6:12-13).

The fig tree is a standard symbol for Israel, especially in this context (Matthew 21:19; 24:32-34; Luke 21:29-32). Both sackcloth and blood remind us of the Levitical system, the blood for sacrifices, and the sackcloth for the mourning associated with leprosy and uncleanness.[9]

In this way, the astral symbols are given peculiar coloring depending on the context. The Babylonians worshipped the stars, and so they are extinguished. The Egyptians worshipped the sun, so God darkens it. The Jews continued to maintain the sacrifices, so the moon is turned to blood.

To round out this discussion, we need only look at two more passages, briefly. After promising the coming of the Spirit and the judgment upon apostate Israel in Joel 2, God goes on to say in Chapter 3 that He will shake down all the nations of the world, and bring them to their knees. Speaking of the nations, He says that "the sun and moon grow dark, and the stars lose their brightness" (Joel 3:15).

Speaking of the same event, our Lord said that "immediately after the tribulation of those days, the sun will be darkened, and the moon will not give its light, and the stars will fall from the heaven, and the powers of the heavens will be shaken" (Matthew 24:29; cf. Mark 13:24-25; Luke 21:25). This is not a reference to the destruction of Jerusalem, because it comes *immediately after* that event. It is rather a reference to the shaking of the nations (Haggai 2:6-7; Hebrews 12:26). We notice that the language of blood is absent. It is simple extinction of these lights that is prophesied.

Failure to take careful note of context has misled some expositors into thinking that Matthew 24:29 is speaking of the destruction of Jerusalem; but as we have seen, it cannot be. This is particularly clear in the parallel account in Luke 21, where we read that the Jews

> will fall by the edge of the sword, and will be led captive into all the nations; and Jerusalem will be trampled underfoot by the Gentiles until the times of the Gentiles be fulfilled. And there will be signs in sun and moon and stars, and upon the earth dismay among nations, in perplexity at the roaring of the sea and the waves, men fainting from fear and the expectation of the things which are coming upon the inhabited earth; for the powers of the heavens will be shaken (Luke 21:24-26).[10]

In conclusion, the symbolism of universal collapse — the extinction of sun, moon, and stars — has reference to the fall of nations and empires. In the Old Testament, it was used for Babylon, for Egypt, for Israel, and for the nations in general. In the New Testament, it was used for Israel and also for the nations in general. At the destruction of Jerusalem, the Jewish sun went into black eclipse, mourning in sackcloth, and the Jewish moon went into red eclipse, the blood-red of sacrifice. Immediately after the destruction of Jerusalem, God began shaking down the nations, darkening their suns and moons, and replacing them with the light of the Sun of Righteousness, whose rising brings healing in His wings (Malachi 4:2).

Conclusion

God's skies are friendly skies. He made the sun, moon, and stars. If some people have perverted these into false religions, such as astrology, this need not cause Christians any alarm. When we view the skies through new eyes, we are free to learn the constellations as Biblical symbols and become at home in the night sky.

I wish to stress one point that has emerged from our survey of astral symbolism. We have seen that the expression "stars of the heavens" and "powers of the heavens" often refer to human governors. This means that the expression "heaven and earth" can *sometimes* refer to the body politic. The expression "new heavens and new earth," while it can refer to a transfigured cosmos, can also refer to a new order on the earth: new rulers and new people. We shall come back to this in the latter part of this book, when we examine the succession of worlds in the Bible.

Glorious things of thee are spoken,
Zion, city of our God;
He, whose word cannot be broken,
Formed thee for His own abode.
On the Rock of Ages founded,
What can shake thy sure repose?
With salvation's walls surrounded,
Thou may'st smile at all thy foes.

—John Newton

ROCKS, GOLD, AND GEMS

I have seldom lived in large cities, and thus have not often been privileged to visit museums. I recall my frustration on one occasion, however, when I visited an exhibit of precious gemstones. I did not get to see very much of it, because the room was so crowded with people peering through the glass at these pieces of rock. In another room there was an exhibit of rocks that glowed with peculiar colors under ultraviolet light. One had to stand in front of a window to see these, and again it was difficult to work one's way through the crowd.

I don't suppose my experience is particularly unique or worth recounting, except that it is a telling example of the fact that people, for some reason, like to look at certain pieces of rock.

The Bible has a lot to say about stones and rocks, and more than we might think about gold, gems, and precious stones. These are given us as emblems of God and His glory; and since men are made in God's image, they also speak of men.

The Rock of Ages

The best way to begin a study of this it to look at God, the Rock of our salvation. The key passage to begin with is Deuteronomy 32, which might be called the Song of the Rock, though it is usually called the Song of Moses because Moses wrote it. You remember that when Israel came out of Egypt, the Israelites were thirsty, and God told Moses to strike the rock to give them water. God's cloud sat upon the rock; and when Moses brought the rod of judgment down on the rock, it passed through the cloud. In this way, God told the people that He would take upon Himself the judgment that they deserved, and that when He did

69

so, living water would be given to them. Thus, God told them
that He was their Rock, and that He would give them water
(Exodus 17:2-6). Naturally, when God the Rock made covenant
with Israel, He wrote it on stone (Exodus 24:12).

For years after that, Israel wandered in the wilderness. This
wilderness was full of rocks and huge stones. They were all
around Israel as she traveled, and they surrounded the people as
they gathered to Moses to hear the song of Deuteronomy 32.

> I proclaim the name of the Lord,
> Ascribe greatness to our God!
> The Rock! His work is perfect,
> For all His ways are just;
> A God of faithfulness and without injustice,
> Righteous and upright is He
> (Deuteronomy 32:3-4).

In other words, God is constant and unfailing to His people. Like a rock, God does not change from day to day, from
time to time.

> But Jeshurun grew fat and kicked—
> You are grown fat, thick, and sleek—
> Then he forsook God who made him,
> And scorned the Rock of his salvation.
> They made Him jealous with strange gods,
> With abominations they provoked Him to anger. . . .
> You neglected the Rock who begot you,
> And forgot the God who gave you birth
> (Deuteronomy 32:15-16, 18).

Moses told them that God would forsake them if they turned
to other "rocks":

> How could one chase a thousand,
> And two put ten thousand to flight,
> Unless their Rock had sold them,
> And the Lord had given them up?
> Indeed their rock is not like our Rock.
> Even our enemies themselves judge this
> (Deuteronomy 32:30-31).

The gods of other nations are like little rocks without much to them. Israel would be foolish to forsake the True Rock, because in time God would destroy these pebbles.

> And He will say, "Where are their gods,
> The rock in which they sought refuge?"
> (Deuteronomy 32:37)

When Samuel was born, his mother Hannah celebrated God as her Rock: "There is no one holy like the Lord, Indeed, there is no one besides Thee, nor is there any rock like our God" (1 Samuel 2:2).

David also celebrated God as his Rock:

> The Lord is my Rock and my Fortress and my Deliverer; my God, my Rock, in whom I take refuge. . . . For who is God besides the Lord? And who is a Rock, besides our God? . . . The Lord lives, and blessed be my Rock; and exalted be God, the Rock of my salvation (2 Samuel 22:2-3, 32, 47; cf. 2 Samuel 23:1-5).

The Psalter abounds in references to God as our Rock:

> To Thee, O Lord, I call;
> My Rock, do not be deaf to me (Psalm 28:1).

> Incline Thine ear to me, rescue me quickly;
> Be Thou to me a Rock of strength,
> A stronghold to save me.
> For Thou art my Rock and my Fortress (Psalm 31:2-3).

> I will say to God my Rock, "Why hast Thou forgotten me? Why do I go mourning?" (Psalm 42:9)

> O come, let us sing for joy to the Lord;
> Let us shout joyfully to the Rock of our salvation
> (Psalm 95:1; cf. also 61:2; 62:7; 71:3; 89:26; 92:15; 94:22).

Isaiah also delights to call God the Rock of Israel:

> For you have forgotten the God of your salvation
> And have not remembered the Rock of your refuge
> (Isaiah 17:10).

Trust in the Lord forever, for in God the Lord, we have an everlasting Rock. (Isaiah 26:4; cf. 30:29; 44:8)

We can summarize what the Bible says about God as our Rock by taking note of five things. First, the rock points to *strength*. A rock is hard and firm, and if it is a large rock, it is pretty much unbreakable.

Second, God presents Himself as a rock to hide in, a *fortress*. God put Moses in the cleft of a rock to protect him from God's consuming glory (Exodus 33:22); and since this rock is said to be a place "next to Me," commentators have often associated it with Jesus Christ, our Protector.

Third, God as Rock points to *judgment*. If a large rock falls on you, you are crushed, and just such a judging rock is God. Jesus called Himself "the Stone which the builders rejected," and said that "every one who falls on that Stone will be broken to pieces; but on whomever it falls, it will scatter him like dust" (Luke 20:17-18). Falling on the Stone and being broken is an image of salvation, but the Stone falling on you is an image of judgment. Along these lines, we remember that the prescribed method of execution in the Bible was by stoning (Deuteronomy 13:10, etc.). Daniel's vision of world history saw the Kingdom of Christ as a "stone cut without hands" that would strike and shatter the kingdoms of the world (Daniel 2). In an ambiguous passage, the saints are said to rejoice when they dash the children of Babylon against the rock (Psalm 137:9)—but in the light of Luke 20:18, does this point to destruction or salvation? Since the Church has always seen the waters of baptism as waters of judgment unto salvation, baptismal fonts have often been made of stone.

Fourth, God as our Rock is the *foundation* of His house, His Kingdom. The wise man builds his house on this Rock (Matthew 7:24-25). Christ is chief Cornerstone, and we are all living stones (Ephesians 2:20; 1 Peter 2:6).

Fifth, a mighty rock gives *shade*, a picture of God's provision and protection. We have seen that God's glory-cloud gave shade to Israel in the wilderness (Isaiah 4:6; 25:4). A large shade-giving rock is like this cloud, in shape and function.

God's people, as His images, are also like rocks. God is the Great Rock, and we are little rocks. We have already mentioned how we as living stones are built on God as our foundation, His living temple. Isaiah 32:2 speaks of how Christians minister to one another as rocks, "Each will be like a refuge from the wind, and a shelter from the storm, like streams of water in a dry country, like the shade of a huge rock in a parched land."

The best known passage that speaks of this is Matthew 16:18, "And I say to you that you are Peter, and upon this Rock I will build My church." The name Peter means rock, but it is not the same as the word for the Rock upon which Christ builds His church. That second word means "great rock" or "bedrock, foundation." Thus, Peter is a little rock, a "chip off the True Rock," as it were.[1]

The Stones of Havilah

The first stones mentioned in the Bible are those of Havilah, a land downstream from Eden.

> Now a river flowed out of Eden to water the garden; and from there it divided and became four rivers. The name of the first is Pishon; it flows around the whole land of Havilah, where there is gold. And the gold of that land is good; the bdellium and the onyx stone are there (Genesis 2:10-12).

Eden is the land of food, and the outlying lands are lands of other raw materials. The Bible conceives of commerce between these lands, so that those of Adam's descendants who lived in Eden would have to engage in trade with those who had moved downstream to Havilah. In this way, precious stones would be brought from Havilah back to Eden to adorn the sanctuary.

When Israel came out of Egypt, she sojourned in the land of Havilah while the Tabernacle and the High Priest's garments were made (Genesis 25:18). Here in this land of rocks were made many items of gold and onyx. Indeed, the only reference in the Bible to the onyx stone, outside of Genesis 2, is in connection with the High Priest's garments. The shoulder stones of the "ephod" were made of onyx, and had the names of the twelve tribes put upon them (Exodus 25:7; 28:9-12).

No one knows what bdellium is supposed to be. The only other reference to it in the Bible is Numbers 11:7, where we are told that manna was the color of bdellium. Since manna was white (Exodus 16:31), the bdellium was also white. Notice that Israel only ate manna while she was in the wilderness of Havilah, the land of bdellium.[2]

Gold is much more familiar to us. More than any other metals, gold and silver show forth the glory of God. In every time, in every clime, in every land and nation, gold and silver come to be regarded as valuable. There are two points to be made concerning this.

First of all, gold and silver, especially gold, are heavy. The Hebrew word for "glory" literally means "heavy." A few years ago, in American slang anything that was impressive was "heavy," and this reflects a sound linguistic instinct. Part of the attractiveness and glory of gold, then, lies in its weight.

Second, not only is gold heavy, it is also radiant and shining. God's glory appears as a flaming fire and a burning furnace, and gold more than any other mineral ties into the human tendency to appreciate this glory. The walls of the Tabernacle and Temple were both lined with gold, creating a golden glory environment all around. Similarly, the fiery tree or lampstand in the Tabernacle—an abiding replica of the burning bush—was made of gold, as were many other items.

Stones of Fire

Let us turn our attention now to precious stones. They are, after all, the glory-stones. We enjoy looking at them in coffee table books. We make jewelry out of them. We pay high prices for them, not because they are rare (after all many other minerals are much rarer), but because they are beautiful and thus highly prized.

In Ezekiel 28:13-14, we find a description of the "King of Tyre":

> You were in Eden, the garden of God;
> Every precious stone was your covering:
> The ruby, the topaz, and the diamond;
> The beryl, the onyx, and the jasper;
> The lapis lazuli, the turquoise, and the emerald;
> And the gold, the workmanship of your settings
>   and sockets,

Was in you.
On the day that you were created they were prepared.
You were the anointed cherub who covers;
And I placed you.
You were on the holy mountain of God;
You walked in the midst of the stones of fire.

Some commentators have suggested that the "King of Tyre" is Lucifer (because he is called a cherub), and others have pointed to Adam (because of Eden). In light of the context, however, we should see this "King of Tyre" as the High Priest of Israel. Israel was the true head of the nations, spiritually speaking (Genesis 12:3; Deuteronomy 28:13). Tyre had been allied spiritually with Israel in David's time, and thus had recognized the High Priest as her ultimate earthly spiritual leader; indeed, Tyre had helped build the Temple (2 Samuel 5:11-12; 1 Kings 5:1-18; 9:10-14; 2 Chronicles 8:2; Psalm 45:12). Tyre, living downstream from "Eden" in "Havilah," assisted Solomon in getting gold for the Temple (1 Kings 9:26-28). Tyre had provided these "Havilah" raw materials in exchange for table provisions from the Edenic "Foodland" of Israel, thus providing a snapshot of how the priestly nation was to interact with other converted nations (1 Kings 5:9-12).

Now, however, Tyre had broken faith, and thus the Lord made a long prophecy against her and her prince (Ezekiel 26-28). This apostasy did not occur in a vacuum, however. As Ezekiel had already shown at length (Ezekiel 1-23), it was Israel's apostasy that had misled the nations. It was the High Priest, the spiritual King of Tyre, whose sin had ultimately caused the Prince of Tyre to go astray.

Now with this background we can understand better the imagery of Ezekiel 28:13-14. Eden, the garden of God, is the land of Israel, and most particularly Jerusalem (Ezekiel 31:8-9, 16; 36:35). The covering of precious stones is the breastpiece of the High Priest, described in Exodus 28:15-21. The High Priest was the cherubic guardian of the Temple, and his failure to maintain God's holiness had led both Israel and her ally Tyre into sin. The holy mountain is Mount Moriah, the Temple site. We notice that the gemstones are called "stones of fire" (vv. 14, 16). This is because these stones house fire. If you have a diamond ring, hold it up. Notice the fire within? Each of these stones is a tiny image of God's glory, His fire. The High Priest, whose chest was covered with such fiery stones, thus had his own personal glory-cloud, an image of God's.

It is because gemstones so pointedly reflect God's glory that we regard them as beautiful. It is written on the heart of man to appreciate glory, and it takes a great act of the will to pervert this attraction. We delight in a beautiful sunset, in the sound of rushing water, and in gemstones, because each of these images the very glory of God Himself. Fallen man may not want God, but he does want God's glory.

Not only can we see gemstones as frozen pieces of glory, but we can also see them as frozen pieces of the rainbow. The rainbow is, of course, a manifestation of glory, being made of light and all colors. It appears in the heavens, like the glory of God, and the Bible shows it encircling God's throne.

The rainbow first appears in the familiar passage Genesis 9:12-16, where God put His warbow in the sky, and said, "When the bow is in the cloud, then I will look upon it, to remember the everlasting covenant between God and every living creature of all flesh that is on the earth" (Genesis 9:16). It is nice for us to look at rainbows and be reminded that God will never again destroy the earth with a Flood, but it is far more important for God to be "reminded" when He sees it. Of course, God does not need to be reminded of anything, but He has chosen to do things this way for our comfort.

But does God only see this rainbow when it rains? No, because God is always surrounded by His glory-cloud, and thus He always sees the rainbow. When Ezekiel saw God's glory-chariot, he wrote that "as the appearance of the rainbow in the clouds on a rainy day, so was the appearance of the surrounding radiance. Such was the appearance of the likeness of the glory of God" (Ezekiel 1:28). Similarly, when John stood before God's throne, he saw that "there was a rainbow around the throne, like an emerald in appearance" (Revelation 4:3). John compared the rainbow to a gemstone. Finally, in Revelation 10:1, John had a vision of the exalted Christ, and described him as "another strong Angel coming down out of heaven, clothed with a cloud; and the rainbow was upon His head, and His face was like the sun, and His legs like pillars of fire." The rainbow around His head means that Christ looks through it to see the world, always reminded of the Noahic covenant.

The rainbow encircles God's throne, but so, too, do the gemstones. In Revelation 21 we have a vision of the New Jerusalem, the city built around God's throne (Revelation 22:1). Jerusalem is an architectural replica of God's glory-home:

> The foundation stones of the city wall were adorned with every kind of precious stone. The first foundation stone was jasper; the second, sapphire; the third, chalcedony; the fourth, emerald; the fifth, sardonyx; the sixth, sardius; the seventh, chrysolite; the eighth, beryl; the ninth, topaz; the tenth, chrysophrase; the eleventh, jacinth; the twelfth, amethyst.[3] And the twelve gates were twelve pearls; each one of the gates was a single pearl.

In other words, the city was encircled with gemstones: stones of the land for Israel, and pearls from the sea for Gentiles.[4] These foundation stones have already been associated with the names of the Apostles (Revelation 21:14), just as the High Priest's twelve stones had written on them the twelve tribes of Israel. Thus, these stones represent people. (See also Isaiah 54:11-12.)

We are God's house of gemstones. The righteous people in the Church are likened to gemstones by Paul in a famous temple passage:

> According to the grace of God which was given to me, as a wise masterbuilder I laid a foundation, and another is building upon it. But let each man be careful how he builds upon it. For no man can lay a foundation other than the one which is laid, which is Jesus Christ. Now if any man builds upon the foundation with gold, silver, precious stones, wood, hay, straw, each man's work will become evident; for the day will show it, because it is revealed with fire (1 Corinthians 3:10-13a).

Paul is writing to pastors, who will continue building the house whose foundation he has already laid. Paul says that the Church is built up of saints, who are like gold, silver, and gemstones, but also includes Satan's agents, who are like wood, hay, and stubble. God puts the wicked into the Church so that they may catch on fire, and turn the Church into a refining furnace to purify His people.

Conclusion

God does not want ugly brown stones adorning the walls of His house. He wants lovely, pure stones, glorious stones of fire, chips of frozen rainbow. He wants a people of peace, a rainbow people, who respect the Noahic covenant and thus love His world and will not destroy it. Christians are the rainbow warbow of the Prince of Peace, bringing peace to the world of humanity in the Gospel.

But also, the fact that the High Priest carried the gemstones on his heart means that we as God's gemstones are always next to the heart of Christ. We may feel like ugly gray rocks that have been cast aside; but we know in faith that God carries us on His heart, and we are of infinite value to Him.

Fulfilled is all that David told
In true prophetic song of old;
How God the nations' King should be,
For God is reigning from the tree.

O tree of beauty, tree most fair,
Ordained those holy limbs to bear;
Gone is thy shame, each crimsoned bough
Proclaims the King of glory now.

Blest tree, whose chosen branches bore
The wealth that did the world restore,
The price of humankind to pay,
And spoil the spoiler of his prey.

O cross, our one reliance, hail!
Still may thy power with us avail
More good for righteous souls to win,
And save the sinner from his sin.

—Venantius Fortunatus (1-3)
and Anonymous (4)
Translation: *The Episcopal Hymnal*, 1940

TREES AND THORNS

Trees arrest our attention in the earliest chapters of the Bible; we are told not only that the Garden of Eden was planted with all kinds of trees, but that there were two special trees in its center, the Tree of Life and the Tree of the Knowledge of Good and Evil. Adam's interaction with these two trees almost doomed humanity, had not the Shoot of Jesse come to die on the Tree of the Cross. As a result, God's people can be replanted, and flourish "like a tree firmly planted by streams of water, which yields it fruit in its season, and its leaf does not wither" (Psalm 1:3).

The trees of Eden are said to be good for food, but also delightful to look at (Genesis 2:9). In other words, in terms of their appearance they were glorious. Lovely trees are, then, but one more emblem of the glory of God in the world.

Because of man's sin, however, the ground would yield ugly thorns as well as splendid trees (Genesis 3:18). Though this is not explicitly said, the symbolic structure of Genesis 3 and 4 makes it plain that man, himself made of earth, would yield sons who are like trees and thorns; and thus we have a tree, Abel, and a thorn, Cain. The Bible continues to picture the unrighteous as thorns, as in Judges 9:14-15. Such bramble-men imposed their curse on our Lord when they gave Him a crown of thorns (Matthew 27:29).

Trees as Provision

As we noticed, Genesis 2 speaks of trees as providing both food and beauty. In terms of food, we can look back at Genesis 1:29, where God had said, "Behold, I have given you every plant yielding seed that is on the face of all the earth, and every tree in which is the fruit of a tree yielding seed; it shall be food for you." These two categories of food plants were established on the third day of creation, when God said, "Let the earth sprout grass, herbs yielding seed, fruit trees bearing fruit after their kind" (Genesis 1:11). Although there are other things we eat as well, such as leaves and tubers, the Bible takes special notice of grain (seed) and fruit. Grain and fruit are processed into bread and wine. Melchizedek gave bread and wine to Abram (Genesis 14:18). Joseph encountered a baker and a cupbearer in prison, and eventually he replaced them both (Genesis 40; 41:53-57; 44:2-5).[1] This, of course, carries over into the bread and wine of Holy Communion.

After the fall of man, plants provided not only food but also medicine. The Bible signifies this by saying that fruit is for food, and leaves for healing:

> And by the river on its bank, on one side and on the other, will grow all kinds of trees for food. Their leaves will not wither, and their fruit will not fail. They will bear every month because their water flows from the sanctuary, and their fruit will be for food and their leaves for healing (Ezekiel 47:12; cf. Revelation 22:2; Psalm 1:3).

In terms of Biblical symbolism these trees are the saints, fed by the spiritual waters of the sanctuary, and healing the nations of the world by the Gospel.

Genesis 2 says that trees provide beauty; and after the fall, part of that beauty is shade from the burning sun. The Bible refers to this in several striking symbolic passages. In Ezekiel 17:23, Israel is pictured as a great tree whose shady ministry attracts the birds of the nations:

> On the high mountain of Israel I shall plant it, that it may bring forth boughs and bear fruit, and become a stately cedar. And birds of every wing will dwell under it; they will dwell in the shade of its branches.

The cedar here is Israel, because the Temple on Mount Moriah was made of cedar wood (1 Kings 6). The birds are the nations. Jesus repeated this parable in Matthew 13:31-32, but spoke of a mustard tree, showing that the kingdom was going to shift from the Old Covenant cedar to a new planting (cf. Mark 4:30-32; Luke 13:18-19).

In Jonah 4, Assyria is pictured as a suddenly sprouting plant that would provide shade for Israel. Jonah had been reluctant to preach to Nineveh, fearing that God would convert those people and thereby raise them up as a powerful nation. He knew that Israel deserved judgment, and that God had threatened to take the Gospel to another nation, thereby raising it up as a weapon to punish Israel (Deuteronomy 32:21). Sure enough, the people of Nineveh repented at the preaching of Jonah, and Jonah was horrified. In spite of her sins, Jonah loved wayward Israel and hated to see the Gospel taken from her to the Gentiles (compare Paul, Romans 9-11). Jonah went outside the city to wait and see what God would do.

> So the Lord God appointed a plant and it grew up over Jonah to be a shade over his head to deliver him from his discomfort. And Jonah was extremely happy about the plant. But God appointed a worm when dawn came the next day, and it attacked the plant and it withered. And it came about when the sun came up that God appointed a scorching east wind, and the sun beat down on Jonah's head, so that he became faint and begged with all his soul to die, saying "Death is better to me than life" (Jonah 4:6-8).

The plant represented Assyria. Its sudden sprouting represented the conversion of Assyria. Such a converted nation would be sure to bless Israel, in terms of the Abrahamic covenant (Genesis 12:3), and thus would provide shade for Jonah (Israel). In time, however, the serpent would attack the roots of Assyria, and that nation would apostatize, and would indeed become a threat to Israel, as Jonah had feared. Israel would experience the scorching heat of God's wrath.[2]

God did promise to restore Israel, however. The promise was made through Hosea, and again employed *arboreal*, or treelike, imagery:

> I will be like the dew to Israel; he will blossom like the lily and he will strike his roots like the cedars of Lebanon. His shoots will sprout, and his beauty will be like the olive tree, and his fragrance like the cedars of Lebanon. Those who live in his shadow will again raise grain, and they will blossom like the vine. His renown will be like the wine of Lebanon. O Ephraim,

what more have I to do with idols? It is I who answer and look after you. I am like a luxuriant cypress; from Me comes your fruit (Hosea 14:5-8).

It is interesting to note the Temple imagery that comes through here, because the olive, cypress, and cedar were the three woods used in the Temple, while the bronze pillars and bronze sea were decorated as lilies (1 Kings 6; 7:19, 26). Note also again the association of grain (bread) and the vine (wine).

We should also note that God compares Himself to a tree here. The Bible does not refer to God as a Tree as often as it does to God as a Rock, but this is one instance of it. The shade of the tree canopy recalls the shade of God's glory-cloud (Isaiah 4:5-6) and the shade of the mighty rock. As we shall see, the tree in the Bible is a common picture of a ladder to heaven, with the glory-canopy at the top.

In summary, the primary aspects of the tree to which the Bible calls attention are food and medicine, beauty and shade. The picture of the blessed and happy Israelite is found in 1 Kings 4:25, "So Judah and Israel lived in safety, every man under his vine and his fig tree."

God Manifest at Trees

At first glance there do not seem to be many "arboreal theophanies" — appearances of God in or at trees — in the Bible, but there are more than we might think. The key that unlocks this imagery is found in Exodus 3:1-5:

Now Moses was pasturing the flock of Jethro his father-in-law, the priest of Midian; and he led the flock to the west side of the wilderness, and came to Horeb, the mountain of God. And the Angel of the Lord appeared to him in a blazing fire from the midst of the bush; and he looked, and behold, the bush was burning with fire, yet the bush was not consumed. So Moses said, "Let me turn aside now, and see this great sight, why the bush is not burned up." When the Lord saw that he turned aside to look, God called to him from the midst of the bush, and said, "Moses, Moses!" And he said, "Here I am." Then He said, "Stop coming near here; remove your sandals from your feet, for the place on which you are standing is holy ground."

There are several important things to notice here. *First*, this takes place on God's mountain. We have already taken note of the prophecies of Ezekiel and Hosea concerning God's planting a tree on His mountain, and we have associated this with the wood of the Temple. There are typological parallels between those later statements and this event.

Second, the burning fire in the bush is to be correlated with the burning fire of God's glory-cloud as it later appeared on this same mountain at the time of the giving of the law (Exodus 19:16-18; and cf. Genesis 15:17). It is God's glory that is in the midst of the bush (Deuteronomy 33:16).

Third, the environment around the bush is said to be holy ground. This is only true of God's sanctuary. Later, Mount Sinai will be holy ground, and then the Tabernacle and Temple precincts. These things stand in a typological line: The burning wooden bush of glory on Mount Horeb becomes the burning glory atop Mount Sinai (same mountain), then the glory-cloud inside the wooden Tabernacle, and then the glory-cloud inside the wooden Temple on Mount Moriah (Zion).

Thus, God reveals Himself in connection with trees and wood frequently in the Bible, because the Tabernacle and the Temple, made of wood, are themselves arborescent theophanies. As we have already mentioned, and as will become clearer as we proceed, the Tabernacle and Temple are actually symbols of God's host gathered around Him. Trees stand for people, and thus the wood of the Tabernacle and Temple stand for people. The gold overlay on this wood means that God's host is glorified.

God's cloud is made up of His heavenly host around Him. God's people are like stones of fire arrayed as a rainbow around Him. Now we see that God's people are also like a planting of trees around Him. With this in mind, we can understand one more dimension to the burning bush. The bush represents Israel in the furnace of Egyptian affliction, an affliction actually caused by God's refining fire. The fire of God's glory would purify them in the furnace of Egypt (cf. Exodus 3:7).

Once we see that wood cut from trees can represent God's presence among His people, we can see Moses' and Aaron's rods as arboraceous manifestations of God's glory and power, particularly of the arm of God (plagues: Exodus 4:2-5; 7:10-12, 15, 17,

20; 8:5, 16; 9:3, 8, 15, 22-23; 10:12-13; Red Sea: Exodus 14:16, 21, 26; water from the rock: Exodus 17:5-6; Numbers 20:8-9; defeat of Amalek: Exodus 17:11; Aaron's rod blossoms: Numbers 17). The hyssop branch, so often used in bringing cleansing, resurrecting water to those symbolically dead in uncleanness, should also be associated with God's power (Exodus 12:22; Leviticus 14:4, 6, 49-52; Numbers 19:6, 18; Psalm 51:7; Hebrews 9:19).

We can mention also the use of oil from trees, especially olive oil, in connection with God's glory manifestation. All the furniture of the Tabernacle was anointed with special olive oil (Exodus 30:22-33), and olive oil was burned to provide the glory-light in the Tabernacle lampstand (Leviticus 24:1-4; Zechariah 4:3, 11-12). The holiest parts of the Temple were made of olive wood (1 Kings 6:23, 31-34), and the New Covenant involves a rejection of Mount Zion and a shift to the Mount of Olives (Zechariah 14:4; Matthew 24:3; 26:30; Acts 1:12).[3]

But most interesting is the institutionalized burning bush: the golden lampstand in the Tabernacle and Temple.[4] The lampstand was a stylized almond tree that burned with fire (Exodus 25:31-40; 37:17-24). We can hardly avoid the connection with the burning bush. The word for the shaft of the lampstand is literally "reed." Such reeds represent people, as in 2 Kings 18:21, Isaiah 36:6, and Ezekiel 29:6-7, all of which refer to Pharaoh, since Egypt was a land of reeds. A reference to the lampstand as an image of people is found in a famous verse, Isaiah 42:3, "A bruised reed He will not break, and a dimly burning wick He will not extinguish."

The idea of a "dimly burning wick," of the lampstand about to go out, occurs elsewhere in the Bible. Just before the Tabernacle was destroyed, we find that "the lamp of God had not yet gone out, and Samuel was lying down in the temple of the Lord where the ark of God was" (1 Samuel 3:3). Shortly after this event, the "lamp" of God's revelation dwindled further as the Ark was captured and the High Priest died.

David and his heirs, God's oil-anointed kings, are spoken of as lamps that need to be sustained (2 Samuel 21:17; 1 Kings 11:36; 15:4). Given the connection between lamps and trees, we also find David's line spoken of as a tree, the root and Shoot of Jesse (Isaiah 4:2; 6:13; 11:10, 12; Jeremiah 23:5; 33:15; Zechariah

4:3, 6-10, 14; Ezekiel 17:22-23; Romans 15:12). The Messiah is the True Lampstand. He is the very Word of God, the Tree of Life, the Lamp to our feet (2 Samuel 22:29; Psalm 119:105).

Trees as Ladders to Heaven

Having seen God manifest in connection with trees, and the Messiah as a Tree of Life, let us look now at trees as ladders to heaven. We can easily visualize a tree as a ladder to heaven, with the bottom as the beginning of the ladder, the trunk as the ladder proper, and the leafy crown on top as the glory-cloud of heaven. Is this a *Biblical* image, however, or is it just one that we have dreamed up?

Clearly it is Biblical. The place to begin is with the most famous counterfeit tree-ladder, found in Daniel 4. There Nebuchadnezzar had a dream of himself as a Tree of Life.

> The tree grew large and became strong, and its height reached to the sky, and it was visible to the end of the whole earth. Its foliage was beautiful and its fruit abundant, and in it was food for all. The beast of the field found shade under it, and the birds of the sky dwelt in its branches, and all living creatures fed themselves from it (Daniel 4:11-12).

God ordered that this presumptuous Tower of Babel Tree be cut down, with only a stump remaining (Daniel 4:14-15). This meant that Nebuchadnezzar would be bestially insane for seven years, to teach him not to play god (Daniel 4:16, 20-33).

Just as the Tower of Babel was a counterfeit ladder to heaven, so Jacob's visionary ladder was the true one (Genesis 28:12-17). Babylon means "gate of heaven," and at the foot of Jacob's ladder was the true gate of heaven (v. 17). Just so, if Nebuchadnezzar's ladder tree was a counterfeit, there must also be a true ladder tree. That true Ladder is the Messiah. Jesus said to Nathaniel, "You shall see the heavens opened, and the angels of God ascending and descending upon the Son of Man," referring to Jacob's vision (John 1:51). But also, in context, Jesus stresses that Nathaniel has been sitting under a fig tree (John 1:48, 50). The fig tree, a symbol of Israel as God's priestly nation, is correlated with the ladder of heaven, with the True Israel, Jesus Christ.

I need to mention something briefly here that we shall take up in more detail later. Altars and pillar stones are also ladders to heaven. This is because they are miniature holy mountains, and the holy mountain is a ladder to heaven. The Tower of Babel, a ziggurat, and the pyramids of Egypt were counterfeit holy mountains. The holy mountain has God's glory at the top, the glory-heaven. The altar and pillar represent this (see Diagram 7.1). We shall come back to this in detail later. I mention it now to point up the association of altars and trees in the patriarchal era. Abram built a worship altar, a ladder to heaven, at Shechem, and this is associated with a tree (Genesis 12:6; 35:4; Joshua 24:25; Judges 9:6). The same is true of Abram at Mamre (Genesis 13:18; 14:13; 18:1), at Beersheba (Genesis 21:33), and of Jacob at Bethel (Genesis 28:18, 22; 35:7, 8, 14). These were terebinth oaks, trees that had massive trunks and huge cloud-like canopies. (Also note that God fed Elijah under a broom tree, and from there led him to the holy mountain Horeb, 1 Kings 19:4, 5, 7.)

The gate, or entry court, of the city was the place where the law courts were held (Deuteronomy 17:5; 22:15, 24; Ruth 4:1, etc.). The gate or forecourt of the Tabernacle was where God executed judgment upon the animal substitutes in the sacrificial system (Leviticus 1:3, etc.); and as we shall see later on, this area was the foot of the symbolic holy mountain, and thus the bottom of the ladder, the gate of heaven. The association of the gate, then, is with judgment.

We find the same association with trees. As a ladder to heaven, the base of the tree is the gate. Thus, Deborah set up her chair of judgment at the Palm Tree of Deborah (Judges 4:4-5). Joash the Abiezrite held court and conducted false worship at an oak (Judges 6:11, 12, 19, 21, 30-32). Saul held court at a pomegranate tree (1 Samuel 14:2) and at a tamarisk tree (1 Samuel 22:6).

Of course, there were plenty of counterfeit ladder trees, and the Bible condemns false worship when conducted under leafy trees (Deuteronomy 12:2; Isaiah 57:5-7; Jeremiah 2:20; 3:6; 17:2). But these are only counterfeits of the truth.

In this connection it remains only to note that since both altars and trees are ladders to heaven, a tree can be an altar. The

Diagram 7.1
Ladders to Heaven

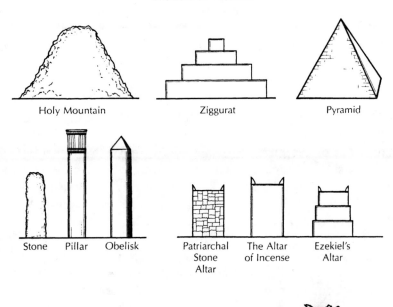

Holy Mountain   Ziggurat   Pyramid

Stone   Pillar   Obelisk

Patriarchal   The Altar   Ezekiel's
Stone   of Incense   Altar
Altar

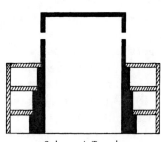

Solomon's Temple
Cross section, front view

Palm Tree

Terebinth Tree

illustration of this is the cross of Christ, whose four extremities correlate to the four horns of the altar. As blood was put on the four horns of the altar (the four corners of the earth), so the blood of Christ was on the four ends of the cross (head, hands, feet). The cross is our altar, and our ladder to heaven.[5]

God's Grove

We have noted that God's people are spoken of as trees. Genesis 2 sets up the connection by saying that both men and trees come out of the ground (Genesis 2:7, 9). We have mentioned already such passages as Psalm 1 and Judges 9, where trees symbolize men. An interesting sidelight on this symbolism is provided in Mark 8:24, where the blind man healed by our Lord initially saw men as trees walking.

Trees represent men, and trees are found in association with men. Such associations often convey imagery to us, and so let us briefly trace this imagery as it appears in Scripture. To begin with, of course, is the Garden of Eden, a planting of trees and also the first planting of humanity. Cast from Eden, man could only expect the scorching sun; it is a sign of God's blessing whenever we find the righteous dwelling at groves of trees.

In the Patriarchal era, the tree that stands out is the terebinth or oak.[6] Abraham in particular is pictured dwelling among oaks (Genesis 12:6; 13:18; 14:13; 18:1, all mistranslated "plain" in the A.V.; and cf. Genesis 35:4, 8). When Israel entered the land, she was reminded that she was but following in the footsteps of Abram, who had lived at the oaks of Moreh (Deuteronomy 11:30).

In the Mosaic era, while other trees are mentioned from time to time, the tree that seems to stand out is the palm. God's placing of Israel in the land of Canaan is repeatedly spoken of in Edenic terms as His "planting," His grove of trees (Exodus 15:17; Numbers 24:6; 2 Samuel 7:10; Psalm 44:2; 80:8-12; Isaiah 5:2, 7; 60:21; 61:3; Jeremiah 2:21; 12:10; 24:6; Amos 9:15). This grove of human trees around God's arboraceous footstool—for the Ark was made of wood overlaid with gold—was celebrated annually at the Feast of Tabernacles, when Israel was commanded:

> Now on the first day you shall take for yourselves the foliage of
> beautiful trees, palm branches, and boughs of leafy trees and

willows of the brook; and you shall rejoice before the LORD your God for seven days. . . . You shall dwell in booths [tabernacles] for seven days; all the native-born in Israel shall dwell in booths [tabernacles] (Leviticus 23:40, 42).

Of course, the Tabernacle itself was built of boards (acacia wood this time) and pillars covered with gold, a symbol of God's glorified human host (Exodus 26:15-25, 32, 37; Galatians 2:9; Revelation 3:12). The Divine Forester not only plants His trees, but also planes them, fitting each into His house. It was no accident that our Lord was a carpenter. He is both planter and harvester-builder, both Alpha and Omega, both the Creator of history and the Governor of destiny.

When Israel came out of Egypt, she encamped at Elim, "where there were twelve springs of water and seventy date palms" (Exodus 15:27; Numbers 33:9). In my opinion, the twelve springs here stand for the twelve tribes, and the seventy palms for the seventy nations of the world (Genesis 10), who are to be fed by Israel. It was Israel's mission to give grace to the world, a mission she generally failed to carry out.

Such spiritual water would grow new palms to replace the old. The first city destroyed by Israel in Canaan was Jericho, known as the City of Palm Trees (2 Chronicles 28:15; Judges 1:16; 3:13). Once the counterfeit City of Palm Trees was destroyed, God began to grow His own. Fittingly, Deborah judged Israel under a palm tree (Judges 4:5). When finally grown, the true City of Palm Trees was the Temple, which was frescoed with palms all around inside, representing God's arboreal host (1 Kings 6:29; Ezekiel 41:18-20; Psalm 92:12-14; cf. Psalm 52:8).

If the palm predominated during the Mosaic era, the cedar comes to the fore during the Davidic. The palm trees carved in the Temple were carved out of cedar wood. Cedar predominated in the Temple, as the second most holy wood (1 Kings 5-7). The most holy wood was the olive, used for the most holy places, and the least holy was the cypress, used for the outer areas.[7] We have already taken note of Ezekiel 17, which prophecies concerning the Davidic house in cedar terms. The Davidic covenant itself can be associated with the cedar, while the Temple and Palace complex is associated with cedar, olive, and cypress.

With the destruction of the Temple, the Kingdom moved into a period of outward humility, but inward glory (see Chapter 16). The myrtle tree receives notice during the post-exilic period. God had prophesied renewal in terms of the myrtle (Isaiah 55:13), and Nehemiah added it to the list of trees used for the Feast of Tabernacles (Nehemiah 8:15). Zechariah saw Israel as a myrtle grove (Zechariah 1:8-11), and it is doubtless no accident that Queen Esther's original Hebrew name was Myrtle (Hadassah; Esther 2:7).

In the New Covenant we have another shift. Jesus repeated the parable of the cedar tree from Ezekiel 17, but transferred it to the mustard, a tree without any Old Testament associations (Matthew 13:31-32; Mark 4:30-32; Luke 13:18-19). This must have offended His first audience, for they would have taken it as a deliberate assault on their hopes for a revived Davidic monarchy. Jesus was announcing that His Kingdom would be of a different sort, as different as the humble mustard from the mighty cedar. We have mentioned already Jesus' shift from cedar to olive, the most holy wood. Thus, mustard and olive seem to be preeminently associated with the New Covenant.

Of course, none of these images is exclusive. Throughout we find references to vine and fig tree, as well as to many others. (See Diagram 7.2.)

Diagram 7.2
Kingdom Wood

Period	Arboreal Imagery
Eden	Trees of Life and of the Knowledge of Good and Evil
Noah	"Gopher" wood for the Ark
Abraham	Terebinth or Oak trees
Wilderness	Acacia for the Tabernacle
Settlement	Palms
David	Cedar
Temple	Olive, Cedar, Cypress
Kingdom	Fig
Restoration	Myrtle
New Covenant	Mustard, Olive

Conclusion

Certainly the Bible enables us to view trees through new eyes! But this is not really new for Christians. Each year, most Christians set up a tree in their homes. The Christmas tree has its origins in the medieval paradise tree, decorated with apples, and the North European Christmas light, a treelike stand decorated with boughs and candles.[8] The stylized fruits (balls and ornaments) of our Christmas tree, and its electric lights, still speak of glory and beauty, and point us to the nativity of Christ, the Tree of Life.

All things bright and beautiful,
All creatures great and small,
All things wise and wonderful,
The Lord God made them all.

Each little flower that opens,
Each little bird that sings,
He made their glowing colors,
He made their tiny wings.

He gave us eyes to see them,
And lips that we might tell,
How great is God Almighty,
Who has made all things well.

—Cecil Frances Alexander

EIGHT

BIRDS AND BEASTS

When God created the world, he set up the animals as man's particular zone of dominion. God said,

> Let Us make man in Our image, according to Our likeness; and let them rule over the fish of the sea and over the birds of the heavens and over the cattle and over all the earth, and over every creeping thing that creeps on the earth (Genesis 1:26).

Again God said to humanity,

> Be fruitful and multiply, and fill the earth, and subdue it; and rule over the fish of the sea and over the birds of the sky, and over every living thing that moves on the earth (Genesis 1:28).

We notice what God did not say. He did not say, "Rule over the soil, the moon and planets, the grass, trees, and herbs." These seem to be taken for granted. If man rules over the highest aspect of creation, the things made at the end of the week, it stands to reason that he will rule over the lower aspects, in some sense.

Part of man's peculiar domination of the animals lies in the fact that only animals can be helpers to man. Pigs can help man hunt for truffles, and oxen can pull man's plows. Dogs can guard man's home, and cats can cleanse his house of vermin. This particularly close association of men and animals is seen in Genesis 2, where God used the animals to teach Adam of his need for helpers. God said, "It is not good for the man to be alone; I will make a helper suitable for him" (Genesis 2:18). God chose to bring the animals and birds before Adam for him to name or describe. These animals were indeed helpers, and Adam could see that, but they were not helpers fitted to him.

95

Under the instigation of Satan, part of the animal kingdom rose up against human dominion. The serpent's seduction of Eve and Adam in Genesis 3 is the story that tells of this. After the fall of man, all animals have the potential of becoming man's enemy. Even the peaceful ox, if it rises up and gores a man, is counted an unclean animal (Exodus 21:28-29).[1] Thus, it would be necessary for the Seed of the woman to exert dominion over the rebellious animals, by crushing their head, their leader (Genesis 3:15).

A marvelous picture of this is given in Daniel 7, where the Son of Man, the Seed of the woman, takes dominion over the four beasts of the sea. The sea represents the Gentiles, and the four beasts represent the idolatrous nations of the world: the lion-eagle is Babylon; the bear is Persia; the leopard is Alexander's Greece, and the nightmare beast is Rome. The Son of Man, however, takes dominion over them all, subduing Satan's beasts permanently. Just so, Mark tells us that Jesus "was in the wilderness forty days being tempted by Satan, and He was with the wild beasts . . ." (Mark 1:13a).[2] With these remarks we have arrived at a discussion of the symbolism of animals, and so to that subject we must now turn.[3]

Animals as Symbols

The Bible presumes an analogy between men and animals from the beginning. Animals image human life more closely than do any other of the other aspects of the creation. This is especially true of land animals, which were made on the same day as man. In Genesis 2, we find that God brought animals to Adam to name, or describe. Adam gave names to them, and in the process noticed that all the animals came in sexual pairs. He might have reasoned from this that he was simply different from the animals in this regard. Instead, however, he rightly observed that if animals had mates, he should also (Genesis 2:18-20). This reasoning could only take place on the basis of a perceived analogy.

Let us now briefly overview the ways in which the Bible sets forth animals as imaging human life. Elijah Schochet has provided a fine introduction to our present considerations, and his remarks are worth reprinting in full.

Scripture depicts God with strikingly concrete imagery. He is described in varying contexts as a father, husband, judge, king, warrior, winnower, husbandman, smelter, builder, teacher, healer, harvester, giver of rain, leader of the blind, wayfarer and stranger, as well as the shepherd of a flock. It is therefore not surprising to find God also portrayed with imagery drawn from the world of fauna.

> As an eagle that stirreth up her nest,
> Hovereth over her young,
> Spreadeth abroad her wings, taketh them,
> Beareth them on her pinions. (Deuteronomy 32:11)

> I bore you on eagle's wings. (Exodus 19:4)

> He will cover thee with His pinions,
> And under His wings shalt thou take refuge. (Psalm 91:4)

God is also depicted as a lion, as a leopard, and as a bear lying in wait for its prey (Isaiah 31:4; Hosea 5:14; 11:10; 13:7; Lamentations 3:10); and the wrath of the Lord is compared to that of a she-bear bereaved of her cubs (Hosea 13:8; 2 Samuel 17:8; Isaiah 59:11). In Balaam's orations, God is to Israel "like the lofty horns of the wild ox" (Numbers 24:8; 23:22). Now clearly, God is not being compared to the animals themselves. It is rather the *deeds* of God that are described and compared to the deeds of specific animals in particular circumstances.

Similarly, Israel is portrayed as being an unfaithful wife, a wild vine, God's servant, God's beloved, a bride, a vineyard, as well as, from the world of fauna, sheep, a wild ass, well-fed stallions, fatted cows of Bashan, a turtledove, an untrained calf, and a worm (Micah 2:12; Jeremiah 2:24; 5:8; Amos 4:1; Psalm 74:19; Jeremiah 31:18; Isaiah 41:14). By means of such concrete imagery the concept of God and His covenant with Israel was related to the life experiences of the Israelites, notably those embodied in the world of nature.[4]

God groups animals with men in certain special ways that indicate a closer analogy between men and animals than between men and any other aspect of the earthly creation. Both men and animals stand under the penalty of capital punishment for murder (Genesis 9:5). More specifically, as regards the cattle, both were to keep the sabbath (Exodus 20:10; Deuteronomy 5:14); both were under the blessing and curse of the covenant (Leviticus 26:22; Deuteronomy 28:4); and the firstborn of both belonged to God. Additionally, the entire logic of the sacrificial system depends upon analogy between men and animals.[5]

The Mosaic revelation contains numerous laws concerning animals, such as that ox and ass are not to be yoked together, and that the ox is not to be muzzled while it treads. Commenting on such laws, Paul writes, "God is not concerned about oxen, is He? Or is He speaking altogether for our sake? Yes, for our sake it was written" (1 Corinthians 9:9-10). In other words, all the animal laws are really concerned with human life. Not muzzling the laboring ox (Deuteronomy 25:4), in context (25:5-10), means that the levir (brother-in-law) is entitled to benefit from the property of the child he rears for his deceased brother, during the years of the child's minority. Paul applies this to pastors who care for the Church while Christ is in heaven (1 Corinthians 9:10; 1 Timothy 5:18).

In fact, if we press Paul's language, these laws did not concern animals at all, but were "altogether"[6] concerned with human beings. Does this mean that the Jews never needed to keep these laws as they pertained to animals, but only as they pertained to people?[7] Or does Paul's "for our sake" refer to the New Covenant believers and mean that while the Jews were to keep the "letter," Christians only need to be concerned with the human dimension? Or is Paul's "altogether for our sake" only a hyperbole of comparison? It is hard to know. One thing is clear: The primary focus of the animal laws in the Mosaic revelation is the symbolic and human dimension. According to Paul, God is not particularly concerned with whether or not we yoke oxen with asses, but He is concerned with whether or not Christians marry unbelievers.

Not all animals symbolize the same things about God and man. The Scriptures help us in seeing the precise ways in which certain animals image the life of man, both positively and negatively. This is particularly in evidence in poetry and proverbs.

Poetic allusions often emphasize the close similarities between humans and animals. When Jacob blesses his sons, he compares Judah to a lion's whelp, Issachar to a large-boned ass, Dan to a serpent in the path, Naftali to a hind let loose, and Benjamin to a wolf that raveneth. Balaam's orations compare Israel to a "people that riseth up as a lioness, and as a lion does he raise himself up," and David, in his moving eulogy, laments Saul and Jonathan as being swifter than eagles and stronger than lions. Shimei son of Gera, who curses David, is deemed a "dead dog," and Hazael modestly refers to himself as a dog, one clearly unworthy of greatness. (Genesis 49:9-27; Numbers 23:24; 24:9; 2 Samuel 1:23; 16:9; 2 Kings 8:13.)[8]

There is little need to expand on this point, however, since the book of Proverbs is familiar to all readers. It is well known that the Bible draws comparisons between human beings and animals, and in particular regards.[9] There is one special way in which some animals represented human beings, and that was in the sacrificial system. Only five animals were eligible for sacrifice in Israel: the ox, the sheep, the goat, the dove, and the pigeon. There were other animals that were clean, and might be eaten, such as deer, gazelle, and chicken, but only these five might be sacrificed (Genesis 15:9, and contrast Genesis 8:20; Leviticus 4:1–5:10; Deuteronomy 14:4-5).

Animals found their way into the imagery of the Temple (though not of the Tabernacle). Twelve bronze bulls symbolizing Israel supported the bronze sea in the Temple courtyard (1 Kings 7:25), and lions and oxen were engraved on the ten bronze water chariots (1 Kings 7:29). The choice of lions and oxen arises from the fact that they are the two animal faces of the cherubim (Ezekiel 1:10; 41:18-19).

The Categories of the Animal World

Genesis 1 provides us with six categories of animals. In terms of the wider world, there are (1) the winged fowl, (2) the great monsters of land and sea, and (3) the fish of the sea. In terms of the land, there are (4) the wild animals, (5) the creeping things, and (6) the domestic animals (cattle).

The *great monsters* are occasionally mentioned in the Bible, some of them by name: Leviathan, Rahab, Behemoth (Job 26:12-13; 40:15-24; 41:1-34; Psalm 91:13; 148:7). From what the Bible says about them, these are evidently what we today call dinosaurs.[10]

Birds are associated with the "heavens above." Thus, they are frequently symbols of spirits, clean or unclean. The dove can symbolize the Spirit of God, Who hovered over the creation in Genesis 1 and over our Lord at His baptism (Matthew 3:16). The dove's flying over the waters of the Flood while it receded is an image of a new creation (Genesis 8:8-12). Unclean birds can thus be associated with the demonic realm (Revelation 18:2; Isaiah 34:8-15).

Fish are associated with the "waters under the earth." In Biblical imagery, the seas are generally the world of the Gentiles. Israel is a people of the land, and throughout the Old Testament, the important people of God were farmers and herdsmen, not fishermen. Jonah traveled by sea to get to Gentile Nineveh, and Gentile Tyre is pictured as a vast ship of state sailing on the seas (Ezekiel 27:25-36). In the New Covenant, however, all is changed. The Apostles were largely fishermen. Jesus fed the crowds with fish. Paul carried the Gospel abroad over water. All this indicates a shift from land to sea, from Israel to the nations.

Domestic animals are those that live with men, and thus are somewhat dependent on man for life. They are man's closest helpers, and most closely image the life of man. Cats and dogs and sheep and cattle and horses are much more "human" than are armadillos, possums, and bears. Such domestic animals come to represent Israel, God's domestic people.

Wild animals are those that live by themselves, without man's help. Such wild animals often represent Gentiles, especially converted and ennobled Gentiles, who may not live in Israel, but who are still admirable.

Finally, the *creeping things* are those that live in the dirt. After the ground was cursed, these came to be associated with the serpent, and with evil men (Genesis 3:14, 15, 17).[11]

Clean and Unclean Animals

What was it that made some animals clean and others unclean during the Old Covenant? Some have suggested that it was the food value of their meat, but this cannot be so. The distinction between clean and unclean was known before the Flood, when men apparently did not yet eat meat. After the Flood, God gave Noah permission to eat the flesh of *all* animals, without restriction as to kind (Genesis 9:3-4). It was only with the Mosaic covenant that the unclean animals were declared inedible.[12]

The distinction between clean and unclean animals, then, must be symbolic. Here again, we must be careful. It was not the overall lifestyle of these animals that made them clean or unclean. The Bible has many fine things to say about the eagle. "As would be expected, the eagle's regal appearance and superior power are frequently emphasized. The Bible describes the impressive sweep of its wings in flight, its awesome speed, and its characteristic manner of swooping down to attack its victims."[13] Indeed, one of the faces of the cherubim is that of an eagle. Yet the eagle is an unclean animal. The same is true of the lion; indeed, Christ is the Lion of the tribe of Judah. Yet the lion is unclean. The eagle and lion are every bit as unclean as dogs and pigs, concerning both of which Scripture has nothing good to say. And, unclean though the serpent is, it is used on one occasion to describe the tribe of Dan in a "flattering metaphor."[14] The clean goat is every bit as disgusting in its habits as the unclean pig.

What this means is that we have to be extremely precise in determining exactly what made clean animals clean, and unclean animals unclean. It is not their general habits. It is not information from poetry, prophecy, or proverbs. It is, rather, the precise details given in Leviticus 11 and Deuteronomy 14. The lion was unclean, resembling the Satan-possessed nations in only one respect: He does not have split hooves and does not chew the cud. Apart from this consideration, he is a fine and noble beast.

In fact, the primary feature of clean animals is their feet, in one sense or another. To understand this, we must bear in mind that the ground was cursed under the Old Covenant (Genesis 3:17). Men normally wore shoes, and it was ceremonially important to wash the cursed soil off one's feet before entering a house (Genesis 18:4; 19:2; 43:24; Judges 19:21; Luke 7:44; John 13:3-15). Holy ground, where the curse was removed, required men to go barefoot (Exodus 3:5; Joshua 5:15).

Bear in mind that animals are symbols of men. We find that clean land animals wear "shoes," while unclean land animals do not. Clean land animals also chew the cud, traditionally regarded as an image of meditating on God's Word (e.g., Psalm

1:2; 119:103; Jeremiah 15:16). To be clean, an animal must both chew cud and wear proper shoes (hooves that are split) perhaps so that the animal can "distinguish" between the things with which he comes in contact, and so that he can travel on high places: the holy mountain (Leviticus 11:2-8, 27; Psalm 18:33). Fish must also be shod. In their case, it means having scales. Scales are like armor that keeps the fish from contact with his environment (cp. 1 Samuel 17:5). The clean fish must also have fins, enabling him to make purposeful movement through the water. The man of God, symbolized by the clean fish, does not drift with the tide (Leviticus 11:9-12).

Clean birds are those that are careful and particular about where they land—where they put their feet (Genesis 8:9). Unclean birds will land on anything, especially on rotting carcasses (Leviticus 11:13-23).

Finally, animals that swarm around in the dust and that invade homes are unclean. They attack the woman's domestic environment, spreading death to her kitchen utensils. The woman is at enmity with them (Genesis 3:15; Leviticus 11:29-38).

All unclean animals resemble the Serpent in the Garden. They are boundary transgressors who break into the domestic garden and bring death. They crawl in the dust. They eat dust. In these ways they image the life of the Serpent—but in only these ways. The unclean lion, as we have seen, is also a noble and mighty beast.

In the New Covenant, of course, this distinction is removed (Mark 7:19; Acts 10-11). Christ has cleansed the world, once and for all.[15] We can go barefoot in the dirt, and wear shoes to church. We can eat the flesh of any animal we desire. We don't need to break kitchen utensils when we find a dead lizard or mouse lying on them (Leviticus 11:32-35).

Conclusion

As we look at the world through new eyes, we must be careful not to bring the clean/unclean distinction into play, since we now live in the New Covenant. All the same, the meaning of that distinction is still relevant. We need to be careful to walk in the ways of righteousness and meditate on God's word. We need to avoid the environment of the serpent.

In other regards, however, the Bible enjoins us to observe the animal world carefully, for God created it as a living parable of human life. By studying the ways of the animals, we come to understand more and more what it means to be true human beings, images of God in His world.

Let us, the Cherubim mystically representing,
And unto the Life-giving Trinity
    the thrice-holy chant intoning,
All cares terrestrial now lay aside,
That we may raise on high the King of all,
Like Conqueror on shield and spears,
By the angelic hosts invisibly upborne.
Alleluia!

                The Cherubimic Hymn[1]

NINE

ANGELS

The song quoted on the opposite page is a hymn of the Eastern churches, sung at the beginning of the communion liturgy. It asserts that believers in the New Covenant are like the angels who guard the throne of God. When Adam rebelled and was cast from Eden, cherubic guardians were appointed in his place; but with the coming of the Son of Man, the keys of the Kingdom are returned to human guardians.

We have seen that heaven is a model for the earth. Since angels are the original host of heaven, it is reasonable to infer that angels are, in some senses, models for humanity. To help us come to grips with this, it is useful to reflect on the creation and purpose of angels.

The Heavenly Host

When were angels created? Because angels are associated with stars throughout the Bible (Job 38:7; Isaiah 14:13; Revelation 12:4), it might seem that angels were created on the fourth day, along with the stars. In the New Covenant, however, men are also associated with stars (Philippians 2:15; Revelation 1:20 — that the stars are men here is proved by the fact that the same right hand that upholds the stars also upholds the man John, Revelation 1:16, 17). Men were created the sixth day, not the same day as stars. Thus, the fact that angels are associated with stars does not serve to indicate which day they were created.

It is most likely that they were created in Genesis 1:1, right along with the heavens and earth, in one act. This is indicated by what God says to Job in Job 38:4-8. In verse 4, God refers to the actual creation of the earth itself: "Where were you when I laid the foundation of the earth!" He goes on in verses 5 and 6 to refer to the work of six days, the work of shaping and structuring: "Who set its measurements, since you know? Or who stretched the line on it? On what were its bases sunk?" Finally, referring to the angels, God says: "Or who laid its cornerstone, when the morning stars sang together, and all the sons of God shouted for joy?" (verses 6b and 7). The cornerstone is the first part of the foundation, so that by returning to the cornerstone at the end of His list, God returns to the initial act of creating the earth. The angels were present to praise at that moment.

From this we can reasonably *guess* (without being dogmatic about it, obviously) that God created heaven and the angels instantly, and then created the primordial earth. Thus, Genesis 1:1 says, "heaven and earth," not vice versa, indicating not only that heaven is a model for the earth, but that it was made first.

Angels were created a host, but not a race. Angels do not marry, and new angels do not emerge as time goes along. All the angels were created mature at one instant of time. Thus, angels did not emerge from formlessness, emptiness, and darkness.

It is quite otherwise with man. Being of the earth, earthy (1 Corinthians 15:47), man is built up over time. The womb is empty until it is filled with a new man. During the nine months of pregnancy, the new man is in darkness, and is moving from (relative) formlessness to form, as Psalm 139 says,

> Thou didst form my inward parts; Thou didst weave me in my mother's womb. . . . My bones were not hidden from Thee, when I was made in secret, skillfully wrought in the depths of the earth. Thine eyes have seen mine unformed substance (vv. 13-16).

While the Hebrew words used in Psalm 139 are not the same as those used in Genesis 1:2, the general idea is the same.

Yet it is the destiny of this *race* of men to mature into a holy *host*. Thus, the armies of God are spoken of as His host; and enlistment into that host at the age of twenty (Numbers 1) is an indication that a certain stage of maturity has been reached. Moreover, the fact that men are to mature from glory to glory (2 Corinthians 3:18), becoming ever more glorious in time, while the angels were created glorious at the outset, again indicates that the angelic host forms a picture of the goal of human maturation: from fetal "formlessness" to "angelic" glory. Thus,

Jesus affirms that men, in their transfigured glory, are "like the angels in heaven," and "neither marry nor are given in marriage" (Matthew 22:30). Note that men are not said to *become* angels (contrary to popular mystical presentations, such as the film "It's a Wonderful Life"). Rather, men become *like* the angels.

In one sense, maturation in glory can never end, either for angels or for men, since there are always new depths and heights to God for us to appreciate and reflect. In another sense, however, there is a point at which maturity is reached; and in that sense angels serve as models for men.

Thus, the original creation purpose of the earth was to grow into heaven-likeness, and for man was to grow into angel-likeness. This natural process of growth and development, built into the Old Creation, was forever wrecked by the rebellion of man. As a result, the process of maturation took the world downhill in the direction of wilderness degradation (Genesis 4-6), and man into the likeness of beasts and creeping things (Romans 1:23; Psalm 135:18; 49:12).

In the New Creation, inaugurated at the Resurrection of Jesus Christ, the world and humanity are restored to their original program. The developmental processes of the Old Creation are reestablished in the Spirit, on the basis of the heaven-attainment of Christ.

Cosmic Controllers

Angels run the world for God. This is one of the most difficult aspects of the Biblical worldview for modern men to understand, and so we should take a closer look at it. The modern view of the world is that the cosmos is run by natural forces, sometimes called natural laws. The expression "natural law" is a holdover from earlier, more Christian times. The notion of a "law" requires a personal lawgiver, and also a personal agent to obey the law. What modern people mean by "natural law" is better termed "natural forces."

At this point, most modern people are deists. They believe that God created the universe (billions of years ago), winding it up like a clock, and then leaving it to run itself. Occasionally God interferes in these natural processes, and they call this a "supernatural" event, or a "miracle."

This is not the Biblical view. Christianity teaches that God is intimately active in running His universe *all the time*. He is not an "absentee landlord." There are no impersonal natural forces at "work" in the cosmos. Bavinck writes that

> after the creation of the world God did not leave the world to it-self, looking down upon it from afar. The living God is not to be pushed to one side or into the background after the creation issues from His hand.[2]

From the Biblical perspective, a miracle occurs when God does something differently from the way He usually does it. As Auguste Lecerf has written,

> The constant relations which we call natural laws are simply "divine habits": or, better, the habitual order which God im-poses on nature. It is these habits, or this habitual process, which constitute the object of the natural and physical sciences. The miracle, in its form, is nothing but a deviation from the habitual course of natural phenomena, provoked by the inter-vention of a new factor: an extraordinary volition of God.[3]

Poythress goes straight to the heart of the matter:

> The Bible shows us a personalistic world, not impersonal law. What we call scientific law is an approximate human description of just how faithfully and consistently God acts in ruling the world by speaking. There is no mathematical, physical, or theoretical "cosmic machinery" behind what we see and know, holding everything in place. Rather, God rules, and rules consistently.

> A miracle, then, is not a violation of a "law of nature," and not even something alongside laws of nature, but is the *operation* of the only law that there is — the Word of God. What God says is the law (see Psalm 33:6).[4]

The Bible tells us that God actively "works all things after the counsel of His will" (Ephesians 1:11). In a particular way con-cerning the Church it can be said that "there are varieties of effects, but the same God who works all things in all" (1 Corin-thians 12:6). It is true of all men, however, that "in Him we live *and move* and have our being" (Acts 17:28).

The theological doctrine that God works along with all things is known as the doctrine of *Divine Concurrence*. It means, according to Louis Berkhof,

> (1) That the powers of nature do not work by themselves, that is, simply by their own inherent power, but that God is immediately operative in every act of the creature. This must be maintained in opposition to the deistic position. (2) That second causes are real, and not to be regarded simply as the operative power of God. It is only on condition that second causes are real, that we can properly speak of a concurrence or cooperation of the First Cause with secondary causes. This should be stressed over against the pantheistic idea that God is the only agent working in the world.[5]

Thus, it is God who makes it rain and snow (Psalm 104:13; 147:8, 16); God who causes grass to grow (Psalm 104:14; 147:8).

God usually does things the same way, and this enables us to go about our business in the world with confidence that the gravitational constant, for instance, will not change. The gravitational constant and coriolis force and other "forces" that are described by natural science are actually regularities that God has imposed upon Himself and His angelic agents. The covenant regularities of our present world were set up after the Flood, according to God's promise in Genesis 8:22, "While the earth remains, seedtime and harvest, and cold and heat, and summer and winter, and day and night shall not cease."[6] This poetic statement sums up the natural world, and says that as regards nature God will not change the fundamental way He does things until the end of the world. From a Christian standpoint, the study of the "laws of nature" is a study of the terms of the Noahic covenant.

Let me give an illustration that has been helpful to me in thinking about this. According to Joshua 5:12, God gave manna to Israel for forty years in the wilderness. This manna was found on the ground every morning except the Sabbath. There was twice as much on Friday morning. It rotted if it was kept overnight, except Friday night (see Exodus 16). Also, Deuteronomy 29:5 says that during the forty years in the wilderness their clothes and shoes did not wear out.

Now, imagine a child growing up in this situation. Let us assume that this child was born while Israel was encamped at Sinai. For nearly forty years, these are the only conditions he has ever known. If this man were a scientist, he might come up with some scientific "natural laws." For instance, he might believe that it is a law of nature that while some fabrics wear out, fabrics worn by human beings do not. While some leather objects wear out, shoes worn by human beings do not. Perhaps this is because human beings have a "restraining aura" around themselves that prevents wear. He might also formulate a "natural law" that says that the gravitational and tidal forces of the sun and moon prevent the fall of manna every seven days, while providing a doubling of manna the day before. Concentrations of "cosmic rays" cause the quality of the manna provided on the day before the cessation to be different, more "concentrated," so that it lasts twice as long without rotting.

It is easy for us to see that these explanations would not be valid. Our present world order, however, is the same. The "laws" that govern natural processes are actually just God's current ways of doing things.

This brings us to the involvement of angels in running the natural world. It is in the area of weather that the Bible shows angels running the world. The passages that show this are in Psalm 104 and the book of Hebrews. Speaking of God, the Psalmist says:

> He lays the beams of His upper chambers in the waters; He makes the clouds His chariot; He walks upon the wings of the wind; He makes the winds His messengers, flaming fire His ministers (Psalm 104:3-4).

The author of Hebrews explains that these are references to angels, "And of the angels He says, 'Who makes His angels winds, and His ministers a flame of fire'" (Hebrews 1:7).

This means that at least sometimes angels are involved in running the weather, and carries with it an implication that angels run other things in the world also. God, of course, is *concurrently* running the world, but angels are also involved, at least sometimes. Thus, for instance, if you pull the watch off your arm and drop it into your lap, what causes it to fall? And to fall at a rate we can describe by a "gravitational constant"? Well, first of all, the eternally active God caused it to go down at that rate, according to His provisions in the Noahic covenant. Second, it is likely that gravity-angels either pulled or pushed it down at that rate.

We need to face the fact that this way of thinking seems "primitive" or "childish" to us, but that is only because of the secular propaganda we have absorbed. God's world is a friendly world, run by Him personally and by His angels. Investigations of "natural" processes are really investigations of how God's stewards run His house.

Before the rise of modern secularism, Christian theologians spoke more freely about this kind of thing. Let me just call attention to some of John Calvin's remarks on the prophecy of Ezekiel. Calvin takes note of the fact that the angelic cherubim who drive God's cloud-chariot have four faces: the faces of man, eagle, ox, and lion. Calvin does not hesitate to say that:

> by these heads all living creatures are represented to us: for although trees, and the sea, and rivers, and herbs, and the air, and stars, and sun, are parts of the universe, yet in living beings there is some nearer approach to God, and some clearer display of His energy: for there is motion in a man, in an ox, in an eagle, and in a lion. These animals comprehend within themselves all parts of the universe by that figure of speech by which a part represents the whole. Meanwhile since angels are living creatures we must observe in what sense God attributes to angels themselves the head of a lion, an eagle, and a man: for this seems but little in accordance with their nature. But He could not better express the *inseparable connection which exists in the motion of angels and all creatures.* We have said that angels are not called the powers of God in vain: now when a lion either roars or exercises its strength, it seems to move by its own strength, so also it may be said of other animals. But God here says that the living creatures are in some sense parts of the angels though not of the same substance, for this is not to be understood of similarity of nature but of effect. We are to understand, therefore, that while men move about and discharge their duties, they apply themselves in different directions to the objects of their pursuit, and so also do wild beasts; *yet there are angelic motions underneath, so that neither men nor animals move themselves, but their whole vigor depends on a secret inspiration.*[7]

As the Nicene Creed says that the Holy Spirit is the "Lord and Giver of life," so Calvin seems to have felt that life and energy were communicated to men and animals by the angelic agents of the Spirit. Calvin's interpretation of Ezekiel 1 may not be correct at this particular point, but his overall worldview is in accord with the Bible's.

Angels and Men

Now that we have a fuller understanding of the service of angels, we can see once again how they model life for humanity. We are to do God's will on earth as it is done in heaven, to act in this world as heavenly people. The angels — perfect servants of God — are thus models for us.

There are three particular things the Bible shows angels doing as models for us. First, the Bible shows angels praising God, ascribing holiness to Him, around His throne. The seraphim of Isaiah 6 sing "holy, holy, holy" to Him, as do the cherubim in Revelation 4. When the cherubim start up this chant, the twenty-four angels of the second rank take it up, and also worship God (Revelation 4:8-11).[8] In Revelation 4, humanity is absent, still excluded from heaven. In Revelation 5, however, we watch the Son of Man, the Lamb of God, ascend to the throne next to His Father. Now at last the redeemed multitude also can join the heavenly choir. The cherubim and twenty-four chief angels begin a new song (Revelation 5:8-10), which is taken up by the whole angelic host (Revelation 5:11-12), and finally by humanity and all creation (Revelation 5:13-14).

Second, these praises constitute the hymnic throne of God. The cherubim form His throne in the Tabernacle, as He sits on their outstretched wings with His feet on the Ark, the footstool (1 Samuel 4:4; 2 Samuel 6:2; 2 Kings 19:15; Isaiah 37:16; Psalm 80:2; 99:1).[9] When this throne becomes His chariot, we find again that He is seated above the wings of the cherubim (1 Chronicles 28:18; Ezekiel 1:4-28). Just so, God is enthroned on the praises of Israel (Psalm 22:3; 148:13), and His throne was carried on the shoulders of the Levites (Numbers 4:15; 7:9; 2 Samuel 6:3-7, 13). God's hosts thus labor for Him as His servants. By holding Him up, they proclaim Him King.

Finally, the cherubim guard the heavenly throne of God, and kill those who defile His holiness. Originally, man was given this task on earth (Genesis 2:15), but Adam allowed the serpent to take possession of his heart and was defiled. Thus, the cherubim also guarded the portal of the earthly throne (Genesis 3:24; Leviticus 10:1-2; 2 Chronicles 26:19). When the Tabernacle was set up, a curtain of cherubim separated the throne from the rest of the tent (Exodus 26:31). The outer areas, however, were guarded by armed Levites, who were to keep away sinful encroachers on pain of death (Numbers 18:3).[10] With the coming of the New Covenant, the keys of the Kingdom were returned to humanity, since a Son of Man had become guardian of Eden once more (Matthew 16:19; Acts 2:3; 5:1-11).

Conclusion

The angelic host models the Church. As angels bear the throne exalted, so the Church in her preaching and life proclaims and exalts her King. As angels guard the throne, so the Church through her discipline guards God's holiness. As angels worship at the throne, so the Church worships her Lord in sacrament and liturgy. And beyond this, angels also model for us our work in the world. As angels delight to work and run God's world for Him, so should we, for in His service is perfect freedom.

PART THREE

THE TRANSFORMATION OF THE WORLD

Batter my heart, three person'd God; for you
As yet but knocke, breathe, shine,
   and seeke to mend;
That I may rise, and stand,
   o'erthrow mee,'and bend
Your force, to break, blowe,
   burn and make me new.
I, like an usurpt towne, to'another due,
Labour to'admit you, but Oh, to no end,
Reason your viceroy in mee,
   mee should defend,
But is captiv'd, and proves weake or untrue.
Yet dearly' I love you,'and
   would be loved faine
But am betroth'd unto your enemie:
Divorce mee,' untie,
   or breake that knot againe,
Take mee to you, imprison mee, for I
Except you enthrall mee, never shall be free,
Nor ever chast, except you ravish me.

—John Donne
"Holy Sonnets" No. 14

TEN

BREAKING BREAD: THE RITE OF TRANSFORMATION

In the preceding chapters we have investigated the fundamentally revelatory or symbolic view of the world presented by the Bible. We have inspected some of the fundamental items of "furniture" in God's world-house. Now we need to put all these pieces together into a worldview, and show how God has acted to bring His world from glory to glory through the transforming process of history. In the present chapter we shall look at the process of transformation. In Chapter 11 we shall look at man, who is God's primary agent for transforming the world. Then in Chapter 12 we shall begin our study of the design of the world, as God originally made it, and as He has acted to transform it.

The Bible opens with a Garden and closes with a City. This simple observation points to the meaning of history, of process, of change, of time. Something has happened during the years between Genesis 1 and Revelation 22, and that something is the work of glorification. The world, created good, has been transformed or transfigured. The potential has become actual. The raw material has been worked into art.

Man is God's agent for the glorification of the world. Man is positioned between heaven and earth. He started out at the apex of the pyramid, the holy mountain. There he was able to see into heaven, to perceive the heavenly pattern, and then bring it down into the world and transform the earth. "Thy will be done on earth as it is in heaven." Just so, Moses was shown the pattern on the mountain, and then he built the Tabernacle on the plain (Exodus 25:40). Just so, Jesus ascended to a mountain to speak the Sermon on the Mount, giving the pattern of the Kingdom to His disciples.

The labor of glorification takes nature and turns it into culture. Henry Van Til has written that culture "is the activity of man as image-bearer of his Creator in forming nature to his purposes."[1] The natural glories of the Edenic world are reworked by man into the cultural glories of the New Jerusalem.

Since this is man's task, to dress the Garden as well as to guard it (Genesis 2:15), we can expect God to give direction as to how to go about it. We find those directions in Genesis 1.

The Five-Fold Pattern of God's Work

God could have made the world instantaneously, or He could have done it over the course of six billion years. He could have taken six seconds, or six millennia. The fact that He chose to take six days is significant, for His sole revealed purpose in doing so was to set a pattern for His image. This is stated in Exodus 20:10-11, where man is told to work six days and rest on the seventh, because that is what God did. The world was designed for man; and God's actions in building up the world are prototypes of human actions in continuing to build up and glorify the world, transforming the raw materials of Eden and Havilah into the perfected beauty of New Jerusalem, from glory to glory. Man's work of re-creation follows the pattern of God's original work of creation.

God's original creation of the heavens and the earth out of nothing obviously cannot be imitated by man. From that point on, however, God acted in ways that man can copy. He brought light to darkness, gave form to the shapeless, named the unnamed, apportioned the restructured world to various kingdoms, etc. Man copies these acts of illuminating, restructuring, naming, distributing, etc. For reasons that will become clear as we proceed, let us synthesize the material in Genesis 1:2–2:4 into a five-fold sequence of actions.[2]

First, God took hold of the creation. I believe we can see this expressed by the phrase "And God said." The Word of God is the member of the Divine Trinity who acts in the world to restructure it according to the plan of the Father and under the hovering guidance of the Spirit. We see this in Proverbs 8:30, John

1:3, 10, and Hebrews 1:2, 3. The Father plans; the Son executes. The Son comes to do the will of the Father. Thus, the Word of God is the "hand" of God; and accordingly, the glorified Son is seated at the right hand of the Father. Man images this aspect of the Divine work when he lays hold on any created thing, to begin to work with it.

Second, God restructured the creation. This is particularly in focus in the first three days of the creation, during which God *separated* light from darkness, waters above from waters below, and land from sea. The world, which was already glorious in that it reflected God's glorious Person, was rendered even more glorious in the course of time by being broken down and restructured. Men continually and inescapably image this action of God. If I remove a book from my shelf, I have broken down the original form of my room and restructured it. If I dig up ore from the ground, and heat it so as to separate gold from dross, I am restructuring. This act of restructuring is what we generally think of as work in the strict or narrow sense.

Once things have been broken apart and restructured, they are different from what they were before. New names are needed. "Gold ore" is transformed into "pure gold" and "dross." Thus, we see God giving new names to the products of His labors on the first three days of creation: day, night, heaven, earth, seas. Similarly, we give names to the new things we bring forth—whether we produce a child, a work of art, or a new street.

Third, God distributed His work. This is particularly in view in the last three days, during which God gave the firmament to the sun, moon, stars, and birds, the sea to fishes, and the land to animals and men. This act of distribution follows naturally upon work in the strict sense. After I have made something, I can do one of three things with it. I can keep it for myself (as God kept the sabbath time for Himself, and as He temporarily reserved the fruit of the Tree of Knowledge of Good and Evil); I can give it away; or I can trade it for the work of someone else (barter or sale).

When you buy something, you almost always get directions to go with it. When you give something to someone, you usually provide some instructions along with the gift: "Let me show you how to work this thing." Thus, as He distributed the world, God gave commands to fish, birds, beasts, and men. These were to be the rulers of the world, and they were under His orders. Thus, God's Word is always simultaneously both promise and command, both the grant of His Kingdom and rules to obey concerning it (cf. Genesis 1:28-30).

Notice that the order is gift and then rules, promise and then law. God gives the Kingdom, and then gives us rules to live by. The order is never Law and then Gospel. God's Word comes to us first as a Tree of Life, giving us grace, and then afterwards as a Tree of Knowledge of Good and Evil, giving us rules.

Fourth, God evaluated His work. This is noted in the text where it says, "God saw what He had made and it was good," and in 1:31: "God saw all that He had made and it was very good." Initial evaluation is preliminary to consumption or full enjoyment. Before eating there is tasting. Thus, when mother makes a soup and distributes a bowl to each member of the family, the first taste elicits an evaluation. "Well, how do you like it?" That question comes not at the end of the meal, but after the first taste or so.

Fifth, God enjoyed His work. God's sabbath rest on the seventh day was not apart from the creation, but in it. God's temple, where He rested enthroned, was always set up in the world — for instance, in the midst of the Israelite camp, or in the center of the land. Having tasted His work and found it good, God relaxed and enjoyed it. Similarly, if the soup is good, we enjoy a whole bowl of it, and maybe a second.

These five simple actions are very ordinary, and are inescapable. It is, or should be, encouraging and invigorating to realize that the imaging of God is not focally the performance of great, heroic acts, but the carrying out of very ordinary activities. For instance, for me to give you a glass of water means:

1. I take hold of a glass in the cabinet, and take hold of the faucet.

2. I restructure the cabinet by removing the glass. Just as God separated the waters from the waters by putting "firmament" between them, so I separate one glass from the rest, putting space between them. Also, I separate water from the pipe into the glass, dividing water from water. I

probably won't rename it, but my mind will recognize that "empty glass" has become "filled glass."

3. I distribute the glass of water to you, and I may say, "Drink up."

4. You evaluate the water. It might taste bad if the faucet had not been used for a week and I failed to run the water out of the pipe first, or it might taste fine.

5. Assuming your judgment is that the water is good, you enjoy it by drinking more of it.

Such simple, mundane actions constantly and unavoidably imitate God's actions in the building of the world. Every calling in life, indeed every action in life, thus has immeasurable dignity.

The Six-Fold Pattern of Man's Work

Because all men, Christian and apostate, thus constantly imitate God in their work, it cannot be in the area of works that the final distinction between the righteous and the wicked is found. Rather, it is the attitude or faith that accompanies these works that makes the difference. In the truest Biblical sense of the word, this attitude is "piety," the religious sense that accompanies our actions. This requirement of right faith or piety is set out in Genesis 2 and 3, and is seen in that God required an additional step in the performance by man of this sequence of actions. That additional step is the *giving of thanks*, a conscious act of self-submission to God, affirming that He is the One who set up the conditions for human labor, and affirming that He does all things well. The act of thanksgiving is placed immediately after the first step of "taking hold," before the act of "restructuring." While all our actions are to be pervaded by a spirit of thanks, an act of thanks is at least sometimes to be performed at this point in the sequence.

What is thanksgiving? It is a rendering of praise and an affirmation of dependence upon someone else. A person does not thank himself—that would be absurd. Thus, God did not thank Himself when He made the world. When, however, I thank you for something, I am acknowledging that you have done something for me (acknowledging dependence) and expressing gratitude (not resentment).

Romans 1:21, speaking of all men and thus pointedly of Adam and Eve, says "for even though they knew God, they did not glorify Him as God, or *give thanks*." Man was created on the sixth day of creation week. He was made in the middle of the day, after the animals. Before that first day was over, God brought various animals to Adam for Adam to name. The next day was the sabbath, the time when Adam was to come before God and give thanks, glorifying God as God.

It is important to reflect on what it meant for Adam to name the animals. These were not new names resulting from a work of restructuring. Rather, Adam was coming to grips with things the way they already were. To put a name on something is a way of laying hold on it. We cannot deal with things we cannot name. Thus, it was not labor in the strict sense for Adam to name the animals. Adam was simply taking hold of the creation.[3]

Before beginning to work with the creation, Adam was to give thanks to God, affirming His sovereignty. Adam was not to give thanks to God empty-handed. Rather, it was with God's creation in his hands that Adam was to render thanks to God. This involved the dedication of his *future* works to God. Thus, Adam's future works would involve moving the creation from glory to glory, by restructuring and redistributing it. Adam's six-fold rite for life, thus, was as follows:

1. Adam was to lay hold on the cosmos.

2. Before working with it, Adam was to give thanks to God for His gift of the cosmos.[4]

3. Adam would then break down and restructure that portion of the cosmos within his grasp. He would give new names to the results (e.g., Genesis 4:17).

4. Adam would then distribute his works to others. A tithe (10 percent) would be given to God, on the sabbath day of judgment, for God's evaluation. The rest Adam would either keep for himself or distribute to others through giving or trading. Just as directions for use accompany things we buy today, so Adam would have given directions to those who received his gifts or bought his wares.

5. Adam's works would then be evaluated. Adam would evaluate his own works, and so would other people. That portion given to God would be evaluated by Him, the part for the whole.[5]

6. The works of the unfallen Adam would be enjoyed by all, particularly by God, for whom they would be a savor of sweet incense.

There are two aspects of this I should like to call attention to. The first is that this process takes place in time. Thus, what is "good" at an early stage of history may not still be "good" later. A drawing by a child may be evaluated "very good" by adults, but the same crudities from the hand of an adult would not be given the same evaluation. It is important to affirm the eschatological character of the good, because it helps to explain the fact that the products of human work do not endure.

It also explains why each stage of the Old Covenant was good and wonderful at the time, but yet needed to be superseded later on. The New Testament speaks disparagingly of the Old Covenant, using such phrases as "weak and worthless elementary principles" (Galatians 4:9), "milk for babes" (Hebrews 5:13), and the like; but only in comparison with the New Covenant. In 1400 B.C., the Mosaic Covenant was the most wonderful thing in the world (Deuteronomy 4:6-8). But what is good for a child is not necessarily still good for an adult, and it is perverse to cling to childish things (Galatians 4:1-11; 1 Corinthians 13:11).

The second aspect of this, which also pertains to the fact that human works do not in themselves endure, is that man's six-fold action is an act of glorification. Man is God's agent for the glorification of the world. The world was created glorious, but is to become more glorious progressively under the hand of man. "Glory" is a difficult concept to describe, but clearly it has to do with the revelation of God. We know that God is fully revealed, and thus fully glorified, in all that He has made. Yet, the work of man is to reveal God even more, and bring Him even more glory. This is a theological paradox, called sometimes the "problem of the full bucket." If God is fully glorious, how can the creation add to His glory? If God is fully revealed in creation (Romans 1:19-20), how can He become more fully revealed? This is a mystery, but it is also clearly the truth.

The progressive revelation and glorification of God in history does not take place by a process of unveiling what is hidden, but by transforming what is already revealed. This is the mystery of time, of growth, of history. It means something amazing, however: that even in the simplest of human actions, God's glory can be enhanced and His Person revealed more fully.

This second aspect also gives perspective to the transitory nature of human works. The great paintings of the Reformation era are darkening and cracking with age. Many have been destroyed in wars. Of Bach's five great Passions, only two are extant. All our works are like castles of sand. Thus, it is sometimes argued that human work in the creation has meaning only in that it trains men: Adam himself is progressively transformed and glorified through the six-fold action. While this touches an important truth, the problem is with the word "only." By itself, the notion that human labor exists only to train men reduces the value of work only to the subjective dimension. The objective foundation needed is the confession that human labor, if it is ultimately worthwhile, progressively reveals and glorifies God. Even if the artifact does not itself endure, like the crude sketches of a child, the revelation of God and glorification of the creation is cumulative.

Corruption and Restoration

Unfortunately, this process of glorification was corrupted. The sin of Adam lay precisely at the second step of his rite. He refused to give thanks to God, because he could not do so. With the forbidden fruit in his hand, Adam could not give praise to God. Thus, Adam's original sin entailed (among other dimensions) the failure to glorify God as God (by restructuring the creation along His desired lines), and the failure to give thanks (by expressing dependence upon God and gratitude for what God had given him). Thus, the six-fold action designed for man's good was corrupted. In Cain we see this fleshed out.

1. Cain laid hold of the creation to restructure it into the city of man.

2. Cain did not give thanks, or express dependence and gratitude, to God or to anyone else.

3. Cain restructured part of the land of Nod into a wicked city, naming it Enoch (Genesis 4:17).

4. Cain distributed his work to his son, Enoch, and to his heirs. In so doing, he became their law-giver.

5. God came down to evaluate the works of men, and found them evil (Genesis 6:3,5; cf. 11:5).

6. God resolved the situation by bringing judgment on them and thereby "rested" (Genesis 6:7; cf. 11:8; Deuteronomy 28:63; Psalm 2:4).

Thus, instead of progressively glorifying the world, man's labors progressively degraded it. Instead of a process of glorification, we have a process of debasement (though restrained by "common grace," the crumbs that fall to the "dogs" from the Lord's Table; Matthew 15:26-27). Instead of a paradoxical increase in the revelation of God, we have an equally paradoxical obscuring of that revelation (yet God continues to be fully revealed!).

Unless arrested, this process of debasement would lead to the destruction of the world. God's promise after the Flood, however, was that never again would He permit the process to go that far. Rather, in man's youth God would intervene to set things right (Genesis 8:21). That restoration, of course, entailed the whole work of Jesus Christ, especially His death under God's wrath as a substitute for our sins, and His resurrection as the inauguration of the transfigured Kingdom of God.

In practical terms, Jesus set at the center of His Kingdom a rite designed to restructure our thinking, and reset our course along the true lines of our calling. He did this by establishing the ritual of the Lord's Supper, or Holy Communion, which ritual restores us to the holy six-fold action:[6]

1. Jesus took bread; and took the cup after He Himself had sipped from it.

2. Jesus gave thanks for the bread and the wine.

3. Jesus restructured the bread by breaking it. In terms of the Old Covenant sacrificial system, when the sacrifice was slain and divided into pieces, the blood was always separated from the flesh (Leviticus 1:5, 9). Thus, Jesus gave them the wine in an act separate from His giving the

bread, and it should be partaken of in a separate act. Jesus gave new names to the products of His actions, calling the bread His body, and the wine His blood.

4. Jesus distributed it to all present, giving them a command to do this as His memorial.

5. They all tasted of it. "O taste and see that the Lord is good" (Psalm 34:8). All but one evaluated it as good. Judas evaluated it as bad (assuming for the sake of argument that Judas was still present when the Lord's Supper was instituted, a disputed point).

6. (After Judas left) the godly disciples remained with Jesus, enjoying His fellowship and teaching for a time (John 14-17).

The performance of this weekly rite in worship is the heart of liturgical piety, and this is seen in both major sections of the worship service. The six-fold performance in the Eucharist, the Holy Communion, is obvious; but it is also performed in the Synaxis, the service of the Word. In virtually every kind of church, regardless how non-liturgical it may seek to be, during the time of proclamation the Word is first read, then thanks is offered, and then the Word is preached. Thus, the rite as applied to proclamation is this:

1. The reader lays hold of the Word, reading a portion or portions of it without comment.

2. Thanks is offered for the Word, and a request that the Spirit bless the exposition of it.

3. The Word is broken down and restructured in the preaching of it. Preaching expounds the text using different words from what are found there — new names as it were; and in that preaching. . . .

4. The Word is distributed to the people listening, as God's command for living. The Word provides both promise and law, both a description of Kingdom privilege and an outline of Kingdom duties.

5. The people evaluate what they hear. By that I do not mean to imply that the people are obligated to pass some kind of professional judgment on the sermon, but that inevitably

they will evaluate what they hear. The people are com-
mended if they evaluate carefully (Acts 17:10-11).

6. Assuming they find it good and profitable, the people will
take the message and inspiration with them as they leave,
and integrate it into their lives, finding enjoyment therein.

Not only is the performance of the rite in worship the heart
of liturgical piety, but it also restores us to true practical piety.
Jesus gives us the pattern we are to follow in all of life. Because
of His work we can, in Him, lay hold on the fallen creation (no
matter how perverse it has become), give thanks for it, and go to
work on it, restoring and transforming it progressively to the
glory of God.

By transforming (in a mystery) bread into His body, Jesus
provides a paradigm for the entire nature of the Kingdom. The
Church is also called Christ's body, which means that as men are
brought into the Church, this is parallel to the transformation of
bread into Christ's flesh. Men are broken, cut in half by the covenant Word (Hebrews 4:12), and restructured into the body of
Christ.[7] Eve (the Bride) is cut off from her one-flesh relationship
with Adam and restructured into one-body (by the Spirit) with
the New Adam. The fallen first creation, whether bread or people, is transfigured by death and resurrection into union with
Christ. Indeed, since all things are in Christ, not only men but
also the entire cosmos is progressively transformed by being
restructured (repositioned) into the "cosmic body" of Christ
(Colossians 1:17-23).

Thus, the structure of liturgical piety and of practical piety is
the same: the six-fold action. The redemptive key to both is
thanksgiving in Christ. Liturgical piety serves practical piety by
(a) setting the basic pattern in the Lord's Supper, and (b) transferring men into union with Christ and then sending them out to
transform the world after that same image.

The distinction between the Christian and the rebel thus lies
at the point of thanksgiving. It is not possible to take hold of the
world with the intention of sinning and still give thanks to God
for it. A man cannot load a gun intending to murder his boss,
and then give thanks to God for it.

The Centrality of Worship

Worship, then, trains us in the proper mode of dominion. Without God's rite to repattern us, we would go out and work with the world after the fashion of Cain, and take it and ourselves down a course of degradation. In worship, however, we are repatterned to a true approach to the world. For this reason, the historic liturgies of the church have stressed the giving of thanks. In this way, the church serves to transform the world.

The Eucharistic liturgy that grew up rapidly and organically around the basic six-fold rite of the Supper (and "eucharist" means "thanksgiving") stressed thanksgiving. This is still seen in any liturgical church today. The following, or something like it, is found in the worship of all the historic Churches that have preserved the old catholic liturgical forms. This example is drawn from within the Western tradition.

At the beginning of the communion service, after the *sursum corda* ("Lift up your hearts," an ascent into heaven for worship), the minister says, "Let us give thanks unto the Lord our God," to which the people reply, "It is fitting and right to do so."

Continuing, the minister prays, "It is truly fitting, right, and salutary that we should at *all* times and in *all* places give thanks unto You," affirming that thanksgiving must characterize all that we do and not just the central act of worship. "Therefore, with angels and archangels, and all the company of heaven, we laud and magnify Your glorious name," he says, whereupon follows the *sanctus*, the angelic "Holy, holy, holy."

The eucharistic prayer that follows includes thanksgiving as well, with such words as, "Remembering therefore His salutary precept, His life-giving suffering and death, His glorious resurrection, ascension, and enthronement, and the promise of His coming again, we give thanks to You, Almighty God, not as we ought but as we are able."

After the Lord's Supper, the minister exhorts the congregation, "O give thanks to the Lord, for He is good," to which the people reply, "And His mercy endures forever." There follows another prayer of thanksgiving: "We give thanks to You, Almighty God, that You have refreshed us with this life-giving gift. . . ." The service closes with the *benedicamus*, the minister calling, "Bless we the Lord!" and the congregation shouting, "Thanks be to God."

In this way, worship keys the believer into the proper frame of mind for all of life. Since men continually and unceasingly are engaged in acts of restructuring, distributing, and evaluating, it would be impossible to try to sort out every action in life and engage in a particular act of thanksgiving at the appropriate spot in the sequence. We do not ordinarily stop to give thanks, for instance, when we get a glass from the cabinet, to return to the example used above. All the same, there are certain specific times in the day when, according to the consensus of Christian wisdom of all ages, it is appropriate to stop and give thanks. The most obvious of these is mealtime. After the food has been set on the table (so that we visually "take hold" of it), we offer thanks, and then get to work eating it (restructuring, appreciating, etc.). Similarly, first thing in the morning, as we lay hold on the day's chores and events, we give thanks. Public meetings used to begin with prayer, before getting down to work. In this way, the simple six-fold rite is applied constantly in daily life, and in this way the Kingdom comes.

The stress on thanksgiving in liturgical piety is thus the key to practical or vocational piety. In the early Church, all life was thus worship, either the special worship of the rite, or the general worship of thanksgiving in all of life (1 Thessalonians 5:18). This worship-centered piety was the characteristic of the earliest Church. It must become ours today.

Conclusion and a Qualifying Addendum

While it would be interesting and valuable to trace out many more examples of how men are to transfigure God's world through the six-fold pattern, our main concern in the present book is with God's own actions. At each stage of Biblical history, God lays hold of an existing deteriorating situation, breaks His people down through a death-resurrection transition, and re-establishes them with a renewed covenant. Each time God does this, He brings in a new covenant, a new stage of history, a new *world model*. We shall trace this pattern in Chapters 12 through 18. By becoming familiar with how God acts, we shall become

much better able to understand what is going on in our world at
the present time.

My analysis of the activity of work and of covenant-making
into five or six steps originally grew out of the observations of
Dom Gregory Dix on the four-fold action of the eucharist, as I
mentioned above.[8] I am not, however, arguing that this is the
only useful or Biblical way to break down the sequence.

In my initial study, I did not relate this sequence to covenant-
making or covenant-renewal in worship, but simply to the relationship between worship and work (the six-fold action of worship restoring us to a properly thankful attitude in our work).[9]
There is, however, a clear correlation between the five stages of
God's work of creation and the aspects of God's covenant-
making, which can also be grouped in a set of five.[10]

Students of the nature of the covenant and of covenant-
making in the Bible have divided the sequence in various
ways.[11] We can say that in its fullest manifestations, God's covenant with man, which we can illustrate from the Mosaic covenant, entails the following steps and aspects:

1. Announcement of God's transcendence; His laying hold
   on the situation (Exodus 2:24-25; 20:3).

2. Declaration of God's new Name, appropriate for the new
   covenant being installed (Exodus 3:13-15; 6:2-8; 20:2a).

3. Statement of how God brought His people from the old
   covenant and world into the new one (Exodus 20:2b; Deuteronomy 1:6-4:40).

4. Establishment of the new covenant order, especially the
   governmental hierarchies thereof (Exodus 18:13-27; Deuteronomy 1:9-18).

5. Appointment of new names for the new finished product
   (Genesis 1:4-5, 6-8, 9-10; at Moses' time the new name was
   "children of Israel").

6. Grant or distribution of an area of dominion to the covenant
   steward or vassal (Exodus 3:8; Deuteronomy 1:19-12:31).

7. Stipulations concerning the management of this grant (Exodus 20-23; Deuteronomy 5:1-26:19).

8. Statement of the terms by which God will evaluate man's
   performance: promised blessings and threatened curses
   (Exodus 23:25-33; Deuteronomy 27, 28).

9. Placement of witnesses to report to God on man's behavior (Exodus 23:20-23; Deuteronomy 4:26; 30:19).

10. Arrangements for the deposition of the covenant documents (Exodus 40:20; Deuteronomy 31:9-13).

11. Arrangements for succession of covenant vice-regents (Deuteronomy 31:7, 14, 23; Deuteronomy 34).

12. Artistic poems and hymns that encapsulate the covenant, and that are to be taught to succeeding generations (Deuteronomy 31:14–33:29).

We could probably come up with other aspects as well, depending on how much detail we wished to go into.

This covenant order can be helpfully and Biblically grouped in more than one way. It is possible and desirable to see the sequence as proceeding from God's sovereign *Control* (1-3), to manifestations of God's sovereign *Authority* (4-7), and culminating in revelations of God's sovereign *Presence* with His people (8-12).[12] It is also possible and desirable to see the sequence as having five aspects:[13]

1. God's transcendence (1, 2).

2. New order and hierarchy (3-5).

3. Stipulations (6, 7).

4. Sanctions (blessings and curses) (8, 9).

5. Succession arrangements (10-12).

In the present study, which is concerned with how God institutes His new Kingdom progressively in history, we shall basically be concerned with four steps or stages:

1. God's announcement of His intention, including His judgment of the old world.

2. The exodus of God's people to a new world.

3. The establishment of God's people in the new world.

4. The history (and decline) of the new world.

We shall reserve a full discussion of this sequence, however, for Chapter 13, because before we begin to look at history, we need to take a closer look at man and at the world.

The Lord at first did Adam make
Out of the dust and clay,
And in his nostrils breathéd life,
E'en as the scriptures say.
And then in Eden's paradise
He placéd him to dwell,
That he within it should remain,
To dress and keep it well.

"Christmas Eve," traditional English carol[1]
stanza 1

MAN: THE AGENT OF TRANSFORMATION

Man is the crown and captain of creation. Celebrating man's exalted position, the psalmist sings,

> When I consider Thy heavens, the work of Thy fingers, the moon and the stars, which Thou hast ordained; what is man, that Thou dost take thought of him? And the son of man, that Thou dost care for him? Thou hast made him a little lower than God, and dost crown him with glory and majesty! Thou dost make him to rule over the works of Thy hands; Thou hast put all things under his feet (Psalm 8:3-6).

The Bible affirms the greatness of man in his very creation, for God said,

> Let Us make man in Our image, according to Our likeness; and let them rule over the fish of the sea and over the birds of the heavens and over the cattle, and over every creeping thing that creeps on the earth (Genesis 1:26).

A survey of Genesis 1 will show us the great things that God had already done, and that His image would also grow to do. God had given structure to a formless world, and filled an empty world. He had organized the oceans and the lands, and established ecologies. Such things as these would man, ruler of creation, also do.

God's intentions for man are set out in Genesis 2:15, "Then the Lord God took the man and put him into the Garden of Eden to cultivate (serve) it and to guard it." There are two tasks here, and we shall call them man's kingly (or basilic) and priestly (or hieratic) tasks. It is significant that man's prophetic task is not mentioned here. Service is the essence of man's kingly task, and guarding is the essence of his priestly task, as we shall see. Man's understanding of these two duties was to be progressive. Though made "like God," man was to become more and more like God through a process of growth and maturation in His image.

Man as King

First, God brought animals to the man to see what he would name them. Man would learn from the animals and acquire wisdom from them. Acquiring knowledge and wisdom is the first part of man's kingly function. It is his *scientific* task to understand the world before working with it.

Solomon is the great example of a king in the Bible, and we are told of his wisdom as he investigated the creation: "And he spoke of trees, from the cedar that is in Lebanon even to the hyssop that grows on the wall; he spoke also of animals and birds and creeping things and fish" (1 Kings 4:33). An example of how Solomon "named" the animals, and learned from them, is in Proverbs 6:6: "Go to the ant, O sluggard, observe her ways and be wise." Another example is Proverbs 30:24-28:

> Four things are small on the earth,
>   but they are exceedingly wise:
> The ants are not a strong folk,
>   but they prepare their food in the summer;
> The badgers are not a mighty folk,
>   yet they make their houses in the rocks;
> The locusts have no king,
>   yet all of them go out in ranks;
> The lizard you may grasp with the hands,
>   yet it is in kings' palaces.[2]

Once man has begun to understand the world, he can begin working with it. Building on his scientific task, thus, is his *aesthetic* task of beautifying the world, advancing it from glory to glory. Here again Solomon is the great example, as his beautiful temple and palace show.

As we have seen, working with the creation is always analogous to working with human beings, for the things in the creation are images of men. Moses and David, for instance, became leaders of men by first being shepherds of flocks; and Jesus learned leadership by working with recalcitrant wood as a carpenter. Adam was actually told to "serve" the Garden, and the word used is the same as that used for slavery in the Bible. Service to the creation would teach him how to serve his wife, his children, and other men.

True kingship is by service, and is never apart from service. Jesus said that

> those who are recognized as rulers of the Gentiles lord it over them; and their great men exercise authority over them. But it is not so among you, but whoever wishes to become great among you shall be your servant; and whoever wishes to be first among you shall be slave of all. For even the Son of Man did not come to be served, but to serve (Mark 10:42-45).

The lives of Joseph and Daniel and others show that it is through humble service that God's people become rulers. The lives of Saul and David show that if a man forgets to be a servant after he becomes a lord, he will lose his kingdom.

After all, the purpose of rule is not domination but glorification. If my goal is to glorify and beautify my wife, I will not abuse her. If my goal is to transfigure and exalt my neighborhood, I will not destroy it. If my goal is to "Jerusalemize" and "heavenize" my land, I will not pollute it.

God had an ulterior purpose in having Adam name the animals. From his examination of them, Adam realized that none of these animals was a helper peculiarly suited to him. For that, he would need another human being.

Now that Adam realized that human society was necessary, God acted to provide it. In accordance with the creation pattern, God sovereignly *took hold* of Adam and put him to sleep.[3] Then God divided Adam by removing flesh and bone from his side, and *restructured* humanity into male and female. When Adam awoke, God *distributed* the woman to him. Adam gazed upon her and gave her a positive *evaluation*: "This at last is bone of my bones and flesh of my flesh!" (Genesis 2:23). Finally, Adam expressed that this condition would continue, that the situation was at *rest*, "For this cause a man shall leave his father and his

mother and cleave to his wife; and they shall become one flesh"
(v. 24).

At this point it will be well to note that the act of making a new
creation is simultaneously an act of generating a new covenant.
Marriage is a covenant, according to Malachi 2:14. Covenant-
making in the Bible entails dividing and restructuring, and that
is what we have seen here. In the remainder of this book we shall
look more fully at God's acts of restructuring and initiating new
covenants in history. The point here is that human society is organized by covenant, by acts of separation and restructuring.

Eve is now part of the Garden, and it will be Adam's task to
guard her as he guards the Garden. This brings us to his priestly
task.

Man as Priest

Systematic theologians generally locate man's priestly work
in the area of worship. As the Presbyterian Westminster Shorter
Catechism puts it, "Christ executeth the office of a priest, in His
once offering up of Himself a sacrifice to satisfy divine justice,
and reconcile us to God; and in making continual intercession
for us" (Question 25). Without contradicting the insights of systematic theology, our purpose here must be to uncover the Biblical imagery surrounding the priesthood.

Just as man's kingly task proceeds from scientific examination to aesthetic transformation, so his priestly task has two
stages. First of all, as a priest, man establishes or recognizes pre-
existing boundaries, and then he acts to guard those boundaries.
Adam was to recognize the boundaries of God's holy Garden,
just as he recognized the names of God's animals. Then Adam
was to protect those boundaries against invasion.

In human society, it is actually a priestly task to establish and
enforce boundaries. In the Church, those boundaries are established by baptism and safeguarded by excommunication. In the
state, which also has a priestly role, the boundaries are political
and are safeguarded by military force. Property boundaries are
established by covenanting acts among people in society, and are
safeguarded by the state using police powers.

Preeminently, of course, the priest guards the house of God.
The most elaborate picture of the measuring function is found in

Ezekiel 40 and following, where a man with a measuring rod measures off the new Temple of God. For the most part, however, the Bible shows the priests guarding God's holy boundaries. They determined who was clean and who was unclean, and thus who could approach God's Tabernacle (Leviticus 11–15). They challenged sinners who dared to transgress His threshold, as Azariah confronted King Uzziah (2 Chronicles 26:16-23).[4] Primarily, though, the priest guarded God's throne by leading the people in worship. People who truly worship God will not disobey Him. Thus, the systematic theologians are right to say that the priest's primary task, in one sense, was to offer sacrifice to God by leading men to become living sacrifices.

Just as God brought animals to Adam to teach him about society and his kingly task, so also He brought an animal to Adam to teach him about holiness and his priestly task. The serpent or dragon was the most beautiful and wise of all the beasts of the field. He was doubtless one of the "great monsters" created on the fifth day. Indeed, the use of the word "create" in Genesis 1:21 points to an especially wondrous work.[5] With God's permission (cf. Job 1, 2), Satan used the dragon to challenge Adam and Eve.

The assault was directly against the woman. Since it was Adam's task to guard the Garden and all within it, he should have guarded her. Instead he stood by and let her fall. (Genesis 3:6 says that he was "with her" during the discussion.) He failed to guard the Garden, and admitted the enemy.

We noted above that the priest's primary means of guarding is through worship. What should Adam have done? He should have led Eve away from the serpent to the Tree of Life.[6] There he would have led her in rendering obeisance to the Lord of Life, admitting his own need for life from God. He would have taken the fruit and given it to her (as Jesus, the New Adam, feeds His Bride). In this way, Satan's designs would have been thwarted.

Instead, however, Satan was given access to the Garden. By receiving food from Satan, Adam and Eve acknowledged him as their priest. They were disqualified from guarding the Garden, and new cherubic guardians were set up in their stead (Genesis 3:24).

During the Old Covenant, God set aside men to fulfill the office of priest in a special way. These men led others to the door of the Garden (Tabernacle, Temple, etc.), but not inside. The priests themselves could only go into the Holy Place, not into the Most Holy. Only the High Priest could enter there, and only once a year (Leviticus 16). These exclusions pointedly reminded the people that access to the Garden had been lost due to sin, and only the work of the Messiah would give them renewed access.[7] Until that time, the priestly boundaries would be guarded primarily by cherubim, and only in limited ways by human priests.

Man as Prophet

One thing that emerges from all this is that God was acting to provoke human growth and maturation. Adam grew to understand his need of a wife, and then was married. Adam was to grow to see his need for a robe of authority, and then he would be given it.[8]

This is most clearly seen if we examine what the Bible means by man as prophet. Here again we have to sidestep the traditional definitions of systematic theology, which, while not wrong in themselves, do not go far enough in uncovering the Biblical-theological motifs involved. The Westminster Shorter Catechism, to return to the example used earlier, says that "Christ executeth the office of a prophet, in revealing to us, by His word and Spirit, the will of God for our salvation" (Question 24). This is true, but there is more to being a prophet.

The full meaning of prophet is council member, a member of God's Divine Council. Originally, that Council consisted of three persons, the Father, the Word, and the Spirit. Man, created in the image and likeness of God, was created to be a council member (though clearly below God in the hierarchy). Cast out of Eden, man was cut off from the Council. Under the Old Covenant, only a few men were ever permitted, and then only temporarily, to function as Council members.

Abraham Heschel has written,

> The prophet claims to be far more than a messenger. He is a person who stands in the presence of God (Jeremiah 15:19), who stands "in the council of the Lord" (Jeremiah 23:18), who is a participant, as it were, in the council of God, not a bearer of dispatches whose function is limited to being sent on errands. He is a counselor as well as a messenger.[9]

Amos 3:7 is worthy of citation on this point: "Surely the Lord God does nothing unless He reveals His secret counsel to His servants the prophets."

Understanding that the prophet is someone God consults with shows us why Adam had no "prophetic task" in the Garden. He had not yet matured to the point of being made a Council member. He was a priestly guard and a kingly shepherd, but not yet a prophetic counselor. I believe that Adam would have become a prophet by eating of the Tree of Knowledge.[10]

Certain Old Testament saints stand as striking examples of Council member/prophet. One is Abraham. When God was about to destroy Sodom, He asked Himself, "Shall I hide from Abraham what I am about to do?" (Genesis 18:17). God proceeded to tell Abraham His plans, and asked Abraham what he thought. The remainder of the story is familiar to everyone. Abraham gave his advice and counsel to God, though always in a deferential manner, respecting the hierarchy. It is in the light of this that we can understand Genesis 20:7, where God told Abimelech regarding Abraham: "Now therefore restore the man's wife, for he is a prophet, and he will pray for you, and you will live." As a Council member, Abraham the prophet could bring petitions before the Council.

The second great example is Moses, who is the exemplary prophet of the Old Covenant (Numbers 12:6-8), and the greatest before John the Forerunner. Moses not only received information from the Council and passed its decisions on to the people, as he ascended and descended Mount Sinai, he also actively argued before the Council when he felt it necessary, even "changing God's mind" on occasion (Exodus 32:7-14, 30-35; Numbers 14:13-19).

This is not the common idea of what a prophet was. There is no ranting and raving here. Nor is the prophet simply someone soberly possessed by God so as to become His mouthpiece. Rather, it is as a Council member that the prophet announces the Council's decisions to the people.

Vandervelde sums it up:

> [The prophets] are not only privy to the divine council (1 Kings 22:19-23; Isaiah 6:1-5), they are participants in God's plans. When God announces judgment, the prophet is not afraid to

challenge God. Amos asks God to forgive Israel, because Jacob is so small (Amos 7:2). As Heschel aptly puts it, Amos does not say, "Thy will be done," but "Thy will be changed." And in the case of Amos the Lord concedes. He repents: " 'It shall not be,' said the Lord" (Amos 7:3). The pivotal role of the prophet as one who stands in the council of the Lord and who becomes a partner in the unfolding of God's covenant plans of judgment and salvation is crucial for understanding the way in which the New Testament people as a whole may be considered prophetic people.[11]

John the Forerunner was the greatest prophet of the Old Covenant, according to the testimony of Jesus, yet the least in the heavenly kingdom of the New Covenant would be greater than he (Matthew 11:7-14). As a Council member, John was privy to more information than any other prophet ever had been (John 1:33), yet matters were not completely clear even to him (Matthew 11:3). Living under the Old Covenant, before the veil was torn and heaven reopened, John's access to the Council was limited and partial.

It would not always be so, however. God had given Joel to prophesy that when the New Covenant arrived, everyone would be made full-time Council members:

> And it will come about after this that I will pour out My Spirit on all flesh; and your sons and daughters will prophesy, your old men will dream dreams, your young men will see visions, and even on the male and female slaves will I pour out my Spirit in those days (Joel 2:28-29).

Not just men but women also; not just adults of full strength but also youths and the aged; not just free but also slaves; not just Israel but all flesh — all would be privileged to sit with the Council. All would have a voice in the decision-making processes, though each according to his station.

Jesus prophesied the same:

> No longer do I call you slaves; for the slave does not know what his master is doing; but I have called you friends, for all things that I have heard from My Father I have made known to you (John 15:15).

The King's Friend was his closest privy counselor (1 Kings 4:5; 2 Samuel 15:32 — 17:15; 1 Chronicles 27:33), which explains the full depth of the statement that Abraham was God's Friend (James 2:23; 2 Chronicles 20:7; Isaiah 41:8; Genesis 18:17). In the New Covenant, all are made King's Friends by baptism.

There is an historical progression, thus, in the Scripture. We see this in an interesting note in 1 Samuel 9:9, "Formerly in Israel, when a man went to inquire of God, he used to say, 'Come, let us go to the seer'; for today's prophet was formerly called a seer." A seer was not a Council member. He was one who knew God's will and proclaimed it, but without being consulted. At the time of the inauguration of kingship in Israel, there was simultaneously an elevation of the seer to prophet.

This historical progression in Israel shows the pattern of maturation for the individual as well. In the area of prophecy, men go from being hearers of God's Word, to seers who explain God's Word, and finally to prophets who are consulted by God. God hears the prayers of all, of course; but in the fullest sense, being a prophet is a privilege of maturity.

In the area of kingship, men start out as students, learning about the world. Then they become warriors, fighting for God by serving others. In Israel's history, this corresponds to the period of the Judges. Finally they become kings, giving direction to human life and society.

Finally, in the area of priesthood, men start out as followers, led to worship by the priests of the church. They can then become deacons (Levites), who assist in leading men before God. Finally, they can become elders, or priests in the fullest sense.

It is the destiny of all redeemed men to become prophets, priests, and kings in the fullest sense, though not all serve in official capacities in church or state.

Conclusion

Man was designed by God to be His agent for the glorification of the world. As men matured in their tasks, however, they themselves would also grow from glory to glory, as prophets, priests, and kings. Though sin sought to wreck God's design, through Jesus Christ we have been put back on track. May God raise up a generation of mature Christians who can see the world as it truly is, and serve it according to His will.

Let all the world in every corner sing,
    "My God and King!"
The heavens are not too high,
His praise may thither fly;
The earth is not too low,
His praises there may grow.
Let all the world in every corner sing,
    "My God and King!"

Let all the world in every corner sing,
    "My God and King!"
The Church with psalms must shout;
No door can keep them out;
But, above all, the heart
Must bear the longest part.
Let all the world in every corner sing,
    "My God and King!"

                —George Herbert
                "Antiphon I"

T W E L V E

EDEN: THE WORLD OF TRANSFORMATION

What was the world like when God finished making it? What was the design of the "raw-material cosmos" over which man was to take dominion? In this chapter it will be our concern to get before us the original Biblical world model. In succeeding chapters we shall study the transformations through which God and man put the world.

Before we begin, let us take an overview of the nature of Biblical world modeling. The Bible provides us with a number of world models, some very simple, and some very elaborate and complex. Fairly simple world models are provided by the three decks of Noah's Ark, the three zones of Mounts Sinai and Zion, and possibly the three zones of Ezekiel's stepped altar. Much more complex world models are provided by the Tabernacle and Temple.

The Bible uses forty-eight verses to describe the world in Genesis 1:1 – 2:17. By way of contrast, the world symbolically described in Ezekiel 40 – 48 occupies 260 verses, while the world of Solomon's Temple takes 346, and the world of the Mosaic Tabernacle runs to a conservative 1,140 verses.[1] We can also note that the description of New Jerusalem, also a world picture, takes twenty-four verses.

Why so many verses for the Tabernacle and the Temples? Because these images speak simultaneously of many things, and in much rich detail. The Tabernacle and Temple, being God's palaces, were symbols of heaven; and since heaven is the model for the earth, they were also models for the earth. Beyond this, when we put them together with their precincts and surrounding areas, the whole constituted a heaven and earth model. As heaven, as earth, and as both together, they were images of God's house. Since the human person is a temple and a tabernacle, they were also images of the individual human being (1 Corinthians 6:19; 2 Corinthians 5:1). The human community is also a temple and a tabernacle, so that they were images of the body politic as well as of the human individual (1 Corinthians 3:10-17). Because of this, they portrayed the True Man, Jesus Christ, as well as His Church (John 2:19).

We shall expand on all this as we proceed, but it is necessary for us to take note of it here as we begin. Some matters that are relatively obscure in Genesis 2 are made clearer by comparison with later world models (always bearing in mind that the later models are more glorified than the earlier ones). The four rivers that flowed out of Eden are simply a curiosity, for instance, until we associate them with the four corners of the earth, and the four corners of the altar, and the four corners of the cross. Thus, even in our initial study of the first world, we shall draw on later world models to help us understand the images presented compactly in Genesis 1 and 2.

The Three-Decker Universe

Bearing in mind that the Bible generally uses the language of appearance in describing the world, we can see the proper sense in which the Bible presents a triple-decker universe. The second commandment prohibits bowing before any image made in the likeness "of what is in heaven above or on the earth beneath or in the water under the earth" (Exodus 20:4b). This three-part cosmos is fundamental to Biblical imagery and symbolism.

In Genesis 1:9, we read that the waters were gathered "into one place." This seems to be a reference to the oceans of the world, which in fact are continuous with one another, so that all the continents are in reality large islands in this one vast ocean. Except for a few isolated lakes, all the bodies of water on the earth are one large sea, and so the "one" gathering can also be called "seas" (plural).

The sea level establishes the limit of the land. Thus, the sea is always "below" the land, and since the sea goes down and down, it clearly stretches into an abyss. Moreover, the land is clearly in a visual sense "founded" on the seas, "established" on the flood (Psalm 24:2). Suppose all the land of the earth were connected, so that the bodies of water were separated. In that case — a mirror image of the real world — we would say that the seas were borne up by the land. The reverse is the case, however: Each island of land, however large, is bounded by the sea. Thus, in *imagery* we have a three-decker universe: sea at the bottom, then land, and finally heaven. (See Diagram 12.1.) The three-decker world is referred to in Exodus 20:11, Psalm 146:6, Nehemiah 9:6, and Revelation 10:6. This visual three-decker world becomes a symbol for a three-decker moral world: hell, earth, heaven.

Diagram 12.1
The Three-Decker World

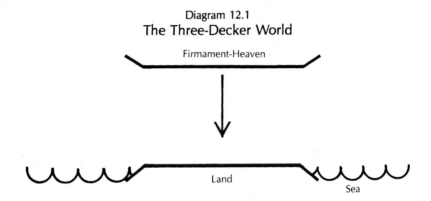

We have come to the wider symbolic structures established by the wording of Genesis 1. We saw that there are two heavens in Genesis 1: the highest heaven, created on Day One, and the earthly sky-heaven, the firmament, established on Day Two. The sky-heaven is an image, a symbol, a reminder of the highest heaven. By implication, the same thing is true of the sea, or abyss. The "deep," the "abyss" of the sea points beyond itself to The Abyss, the place where the devil and the wicked will spend eternity. This Ultimate Abyss did not yet exist in Genesis 1, however, because neither angels nor men had yet sinned, and that is why it is not mentioned in Genesis 1. Once the Ultimate Abyss was established, however, the ocean-abyss became an image, a symbol, a reminder of it, just as the sky-heaven is an image and reminder of the Ultimate Heaven.[2]

After the fall of man, the separation of land and sea becomes a common symbol for the separation of God's people and the ungodly nations of the world. The wicked are like the restless sea, while the righteous are given God's holy land to dwell in. As the chaotic sea tries constantly to eat the land, so the Gentiles try to invade God's land. In the Old Testament, the nations are frequently pictured in terms of the sea (cf. e.g., 2 Samuel 22:4-5; Psalm 65:7-8; Isaiah 5:30; 17:12-13; 57:20; Jeremiah 6:23; Daniel 7:2-3; cf. Luke 21:25; Revelation 13:1, 11). To protect His people, God at various times defeated the oceanic nations, and bounded them (Jeremiah 5:22; Psalm 74:13; Job 26:10-12).

It often is the "gathering of the sea into one place" that makes the "land" visible. When the wicked gather together against God and His people, He vindicates His people and defeats their enemies (Psalm 2). And notice the language of Revelation 20:8-9:

> [Satan] will deceive the nations which are in the four corners of the earth, Gog [Prince] and Magog [People], to *gather* them together for the war; the number of them is like the sand of the *sea*. And they came up on the broad expanse of the *earth* and surrounded the camp of the saints. . . . (italics mine)

God said in the beginning that it was "good" for sea and land to be separated (Genesis 1:10), and at the end, He will remove the ungodly human "sea" from the land, and put them into the Ultimate Abyss (Revelation 20:15).

Christians should not be worried when accused of holding to a "three-decker world model." There is nothing pagan or primitive about such a worldview. As a matter of simple observable fact, the sea lies below the land, and the sky is above the land. This simple observation is relatively meaningless, of course, until we see that the sky is an image of heaven, and reminds us of our calling to grow into the fullness of God's likeness and bring this world toward glory. Similarly, the sea has to do with life and potential. The Bible consistently speaks of water as life-giving, and it is water that feeds the plants, animals, and men in the land, enabling them to grow toward their heavenly calling.[3] Thus water undergirds the land, stimulating it toward perfection. Additionally, because of sin, the sea reminds us of the Abyss, the opposite of heaven, where impenitent sinners will reside forever.

The Four Corners of the Earth

One of the most familiar symbols of Scripture is that of the four corners of the earth. Isaiah 11:12 says that God will "gather the dispersed of Judah from the four corners of the earth," and Ezekiel 7:2 says that "the end is coming on the four corners of the earth." In Revelation 20:8 the wicked are gathered from the four corners of the earth.

To understand this imagery it is helpful to recall that the Bible pictures the world as a house:

> Where were you when I laid the foundation of the earth? Tell, if you have understanding, who set its measurements, since you know? Or who stretched the line on it? On what were its bases sunk? Or who laid its cornerstone? (Job 38:4-6)

The world is like a house, the firmament like its ceiling, and the mountains like the sky's pillars, so that the collapse of the mountains is associated with the rending of the firmament-ceiling (Isaiah 34:3-4; Revelation 6:13-14). As we have mentioned, the Tabernacle and Temple were world models, the world being conceived as a cosmic house.

A complementary image used in Scripture for the world is that of the altar. Altars must be made of earth (Exodus 20:24-25) and have four corners, and these figure the four corners of the earth (cp. Revelation 7:1 and 9:13). Thus, the fire on the bronze altar figured the judgment that must come upon the world; and the sacrifice spoke of the fact that the fire must come either upon a substitute, or upon humanity itself. In the same way, the incense burning on the altar of incense spoke of the universal duty and privilege of men to stand upon the world and pray to God. Thus, when the Bible speaks of the "four corners of the world," it reminds us of the world as house and altar. The house imagery sees the world as a container for men, while the altar imagery sees the world as a platform for men. Both images are used throughout Scripture. In terms of the world as house, judgment means the collapse of the house, the shaking of its mountain-pillars, the falling of its ceiling-stars, etc. In terms of the world as altar, judgment means fire falling upon the altar. Positively, the world is a house to be adorned and in which man worships, and also an altar on which man grows and upon which he offers himself and his faith-filled good works to God.

Not only is the Biblical, cosmic world four-cornered in a symbolic sense, so is the Biblical social world. Israelite society under the judges and kings had four *corners* or *cornerstones* at its top. These men were the supreme judge or king, and his three top advisors. This word occurs in Judges 20:2 and 1 Samuel 14:38, where it is translated "chiefs" (cf. also Isaiah 19:13; 28:16; Zephaniah 1:16; 3:6; Zechariah 10:4). Thus David had three mighty men, he being the chief corner (2 Samuel 23; 1 Chronicles 11). Similarly, Jesus had Peter, James, and John, who were the three corner pillars of the Apostolic Church (Galatians 2:9), remembering that Jesus was Himself the fourth and chief cornerstone of the new temple (Ephesians 2:20; 1 Peter 2:6).

This image of the four-cornered world takes its rise from the fact that four rivers flowed out of the Garden of Eden to water the whole world. They doubtless did not actually flow in four opposite directions; indeed, they all seem to have flowed south, as we shall see. Symbolically, however, they carried the Edenic pattern to the four corners of the earth. The task of Adam's descendants would be to follow the four rivers and carry with them the Kingdom pattern, extending it over the whole earth and bringing the world from primordial to eschatological glory.

The four rivers going to the four corners can and should be associated with the four faces of the cherubim (Ezekiel 1:10), the four sides of the camp of Israel (Numbers 2), and the four limbs of the cross.[4] It is a fundamental symbol of the world structure. (See Diagrams 12.2 and 12.3.)

North and South

Ancient man knew that the world was a sphere, and the Bible affirms, in Job 26:7, that God hung "the earth on nothing."[5] It is a fundamental mistake to assume that ancient or medieval world diagrams with four corners, or riding on the backs of elephants or bulls, were taken by educated people as literal pictures of the world. They were always understood to be symbolic. For in-

Diagram 12.2
The Four Rivers of the Garden of Eden

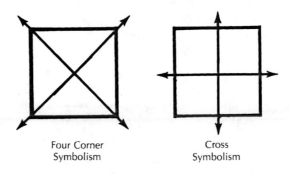

Four Corner
Symbolism

Cross
Symbolism

Diagram 12.3
The Israelite Camp (Numbers 2)

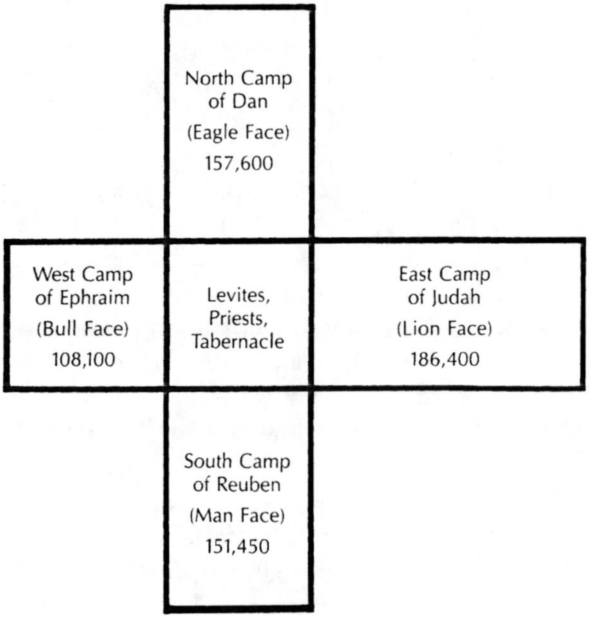

	North Camp of Dan (Eagle Face) 157,600	
West Camp of Ephraim (Bull Face) 108,100	Levites, Priests, Tabernacle	East Camp of Judah (Lion Face) 186,400
	South Camp of Reuben (Man Face) 151,450	

stance, the Biblical world picture says that the earth is founded upon the seas (Psalm 24:2) because the sea is below the earth, as we have seen.

All the same, we are given information in Genesis 2 that helps us ascertain roughly the geographical location of the land and Garden of Eden. Eden was a real place, though it was washed away in the Flood. We are told that the four rivers flowed out of the Garden and that they flowed south. The first river, Pishon, went to the land of Havilah (Arabia); the second, Gihon, to Cush (Ethiopia) and the third and fourth were the Tigris and the Euphrates. These names were probably put in by Moses when he put Genesis in its final shape, but they still tell us the locations to which these rivers initially flowed. The only way one river can break up into four streams and go to these four places is if it rises either in the north or the south. It seems most likely that the Pishon flowed down what is now the Jordan river valley toward Arabia, and the Gihon flowed down what is now the Nile, though in the opposite direction, toward Ethiopia. (Remember, the Flood drastically changed the world.)[6]

This hypothesis is lent credibility by the references to God's Kingdom in the far north. Psalm 48:2 says that Mount Zion is in the far north, but in fact Zion was located in southern Israel. The language must by symbolic, but of what? The throne of God is stated to be in the "north" in Isaiah 14:13, and God is said to come from the "north" in Job 37:22 and Ezekiel 1:4ff.[7] It is easy to trace a line back from the locations of these rivers to a hypothetical point of origin to the north, and that point turns out to be in Armenia. After the Flood, the Ark rested in Armenia, and this is the point from which the new creation spread out (Genesis 8:4). Since rivers flow downhill, Eden was clearly located on a height. This is consistent with the high mountains of the Armenian region, though of course the Flood may have changed the topography. (See Diagram 12.4.)

What emerges from this discussion, in addition to a possible location for the original Eden, is another symbolic picture. To the north is God's throne. In the center is where men live, and to the south is the outlying world.

This symbolic structure is picked up particularly in Zechariah 6. The north, God's throne, was corrupted by Satan

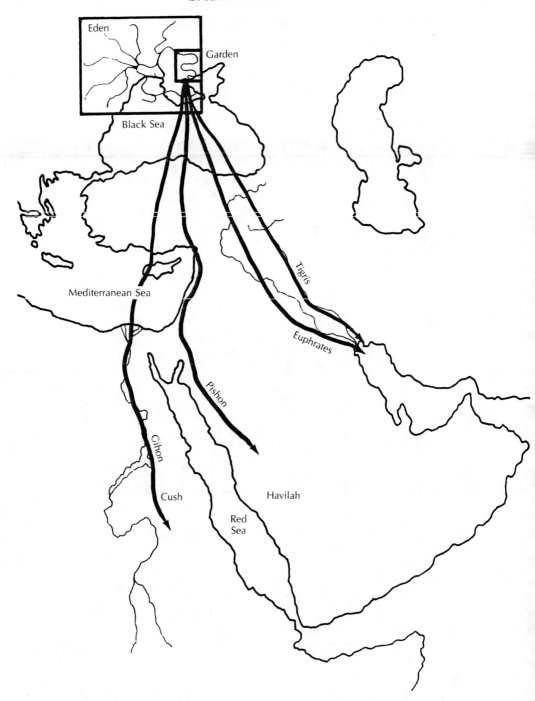

Diagram 12.4
Possible (Pre-Flood)
Location of Eden

when Adam turned the Garden over to him. The armies of God
in Zechariah 6 take judgment and then cleansing blessing to the
north, reestablishing it first. Judgment also proceeds to the
south, but without cleansing at this point in history.[8]

The Three Environments

The Bible tells us that God planted a garden in Eden, on the
east side of that land (Genesis 2:8). This establishes three environments on the earth: Garden, Eden, World. (See Diagram
12.5.) Men would proceed from the Garden and Home in the
north downstream toward the lands of the south. They would be
motivated to do so by the fact that there were good minerals in
the southern lands, as we are told that in Havilah (Arabia) there
were gold, bdellium, and onyx. Similarly, in another symbolic
picture, men would follow the four rivers out to the four corners
of the earth.

Diagram 12.5
Three Human Environments

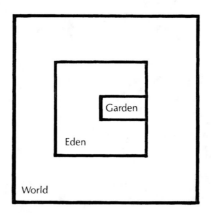

Let us consider the three environments. The land of Eden
would be Adam's initial home. It would be the place where he
slept, where his children were reared, and so forth. Home is
where man returns when his work is done.

The outlying lands, Havilah, Cush, and so forth, would be the place of man's labors. They figure the place where Adam did his work, wrestling joyfully with the world to make it more and more glorious. His sons would move downstream and set up new homes in these lands. Perhaps Cain would dwell with his family in Havilah, and Abel in Cush. There would be trade between the members of humanity, as each land's peculiar treasures were swapped for those of other regions.

And then there was the Garden. This was the sanctuary, the place where Adam would meet with God at the times of His appointment. Adam was created on the sixth day, and the next day was God's sabbath. Adam was to meet with God, but by the time God arrived, Adam was already in sin and had to be cast out. Nonetheless, the pattern was established. Had Adam not sinned, his sons would have set up Garden-sanctuaries in Havilah, Cush, and the other lands.

These three environments correspond to the three-decker world of Genesis 1, but on a lateral plane. The Garden-sanctuary is the contact-point with heaven. The homeland is to be related to the earth, and thus God's people Israel were given *land*. The outlying lands, reached by *rivers*, are to be associated with the sea, and thus the Gentile nations are pictured as the sea.

Each of these environments was to be patterned after heaven. Heaven is not only the pattern for the sanctuary and worship, it is also the pattern for home and homeland, and also for work in the world. (See Diagram 12.6.) Ultimately, the New Jerusalem is city and sanctuary and world all in one. This shows the "eschatological coalescence of culture and cult."[9] As long as we live in history, however, we can apply the words of Solomon in Ecclesiastes 3 to ourselves: For everything there is a proper time — a time to laugh and a time to weep, a time to worship in the sanctuary, a time to work in the world, and a time to relax at home. Thus, the three environments will continue to be distinct throughout history, and each is to be "heavenized" in a way peculiar to its nature.

Because of his sin, Adam was excluded from the Garden-sanctuary. It would not be until the Mosaic Covenant that men would be readmitted to the Garden, and then there were restrictions on who might enter. Sin did not stop with Adam; however,

Diagram 12.6
The Sequence of Creation

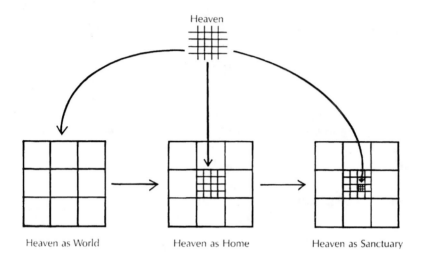

Heaven

Heaven as World   Heaven as Home   Heaven as Sanctuary

and Cain for his sin was excluded from the Edenic homeland as well (Genesis 4:16). At the Flood, because of the maturation of humanity's sin, mankind was excluded from the whole world, and a new world was begun.

When God made the world, He made the sea first. Then He drew out the land, and finally He planted the Garden-sanctuary. Just so, after the Flood, we read first of the Table of Nations (Genesis 10). Then we find the call of Abraham and the promise of the land (Genesis 12). With the Mosaic Tabernacle we have the erection of a provisional Garden-sanctuary. Only when the land is finally secured under David do we find the full establishment of a permanent Garden-sanctuary under Solomon: the Temple. Israel sinned, however, and Nebuchadnezzar came to destroy the Temple and Jerusalem (2 Kings 25:1-21). When the people continued in their rebellion they were all deported from the land into exile (2 Kings 25:22-26). Then God rebuilt the world, first converting the pagan nations and restoring them under Daniel (Daniel 4, 6), then returning the people to the land, and finally rebuilding the Garden-Temple under Haggai and Zechariah, Joshua and Zerubbabel (Haggai 1-2; Ezra 1-5).

Of course, regardless of where they lived symbolically, men always had access to God in heaven. Thus Noah worshipped God under the open sky, as did converted Gentiles of all ages. Abraham worshipped God in the land, as did all devout Jews. After Moses, the Israelites worshipped God in the courtyard of the sanctuary, the garden. Only the Aaronic priests, however, were permitted to worship God in the Tabernacle and Temple. All of this shows that the fullness of access to God was restricted until the coming of the Messiah.

In the New Covenant, men have immediate and full access to God in heaven. There are no longer any symbolic restrictions (Hebrews 7-10). Nonetheless, in the way of cultural movement, we find that when Christians first penetrate a pagan culture, they have to meet in homes and even catacombs. When the culture has been permeated by Christian influence, and becomes a Christian homeland, then the great and beautiful Garden-Churches (cathedrals) can be built. So it was with Rome. So it was with Europe. So it must be in our day.

Our cathedrals have been defiled, and our homes are under assault as officials of the secular humanist government seek to close down Christian schools and invade Christian homes. Thus, ours is not a day of cathedral-building, but a day of cultural permeation. Faithfulness must come first, and only then will glory come.

High Ground

Rivers flow downhill, which means that the Garden out of which they flowed was on high ground. Not the highest, however, because the river arose in the homeland of Eden, which means that the Garden was lower than other parts of Eden. This is, perhaps, not what we should expect; but it is reiterated in Psalm 125:2, "as the mountains surround Jerusalem, so the Lord surrounds His people," which draws on the fact that the mountains surrounding Zion were actually taller than she. Indeed, Mount Moriah, where the Temple was built, was lower than Zion proper, where the city of Jerusalem was built. In fact, as the waters in the Garden of Eden flowed from the Land of Eden, so the water used on Moriah flowed from springs on Zion.[10] Yet we are told that someday "the mountain of the Lord's house will be established as the chief of the mountains and will be raised above the hills" (Isaiah 2:2). What does this mean?

First, the true Mountain of God is in heaven, not on earth, and thus not approachable by man. It is always high, as the heavens are high above the earth.

Second, man's earthly sanctuary, while it starts high, is to grow and develop in glory during history. During the infancy of humanity, the sanctuary is protected with the swaddling clothes of the mountains roundabout (compare Galatians 4:1-7). Once maturity has been attained, then the holy mountain stands forth as the greatest of the mountains.

A third aspect of this prophecy is seen in that Jesus left Zion and Moriah behind, and transferred His Kingdom to the Mount of Olives, which was the highest mountain in the area.[11] Spiritually, though, the mountain of His Kingdom is a ladder to heaven, whose top breaks through the firmament to the Throne of God (Revelation 21:10; 22:1).

Mountain symbolism is found in all world religions. The Hindus had Mount Meru; the Japanese, Fujiyama; and the Greeks, Olympus.[12] It is also found throughout Scripture. Thus, Abraham offered Isaac on Mount Moriah (Genesis 22:2); Moses received the law on Mount Sinai (Exodus 19–24); Elijah defeated Baal on Mount Carmel (1 Kings 18) and received his commission renewed on Mount Sinai (1 Kings 19); Jesus preached His definitive sermon on a mount (Matthew 5), was transfigured on a mount (2 Peter 1:16-18), and gave his final, great commission on a mountain (Matthew 28:18-20).

Beyond this, we find that Christians "are the light of the world; a city set on a hill cannot be hid," a reference to Jerusalem on Mount Zion, and also a symbol of the righteous person (Matthew 5:14). Believers are God's people-mountain, and someday "the mountain of the house of the Lord will be established as the chief of the mountains, and will be raised above the hills; and all the nations will stream to it" (Isaiah 2:2). God's holy mountain grows until it fills the whole world (Daniel 2:34-35). This can be so because the mountain symbolizes not only the individual human person but also the Church:

You have come to Mount Zion and to the city of the living
God, the heavenly Jerusalem, and to myriads of angels in festal array, and to the church of the Firstborn who are enrolled in
heaven . . . (Hebrews 12:22-23a).[13]

The idea of a holy mountain is a place where men can meet
God, because the top of a mountain is nearest to heaven. This is
why Israel sacrificed on "high places." The image, symbolically,
is that of a pyramid, for a pyramid is but a stylized mountain.
The four sides, or the four edges, of the pyramid correspond to
the four rivers that flow out, taking God's kingdom influences to
all the earth. (See Diagram 12.7.) Man's position at the top of the
mountain enables him to see the heavenly pattern, and then
brings it down to the earth below, as did Moses.

Diagram 12.7
Eden in the World

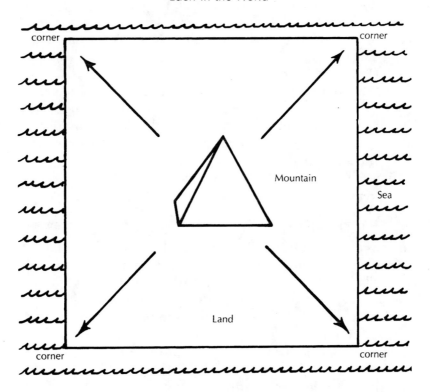

Thus, mountains and pyramids are ladders to heaven. (See Diagram 7.1, p. 89.) At the Tower of Babel, sinful man tried to build such a pyramid-ladder from the ground up, but God forbade it. The ground had been defiled by Adam's sin, since Adam was made of earth and his sin corrupted the earth. Thus, if there were to be a new ladder to heaven it would have to proceed from above to below. Jacob saw such a ladder in prophetic vision (Genesis 28:12). In fulfillment, the New Jerusalem came from heaven to earth, not vice versa, on the Day of Pentecost.

The New Jerusalem is a gem-studded pyramid overlaid on a mountain (Revelation 21:2, 10ff.). Unlike the holy mountains of the Old Covenant, the New Jerusalem is definitely (symbolically) on the highest of all mountains, because the apex of the pyramid reaches into heaven itself and the throne of God (Revelation 22:1); and it is from here that the restored rivers flow to bring life to the world.

Whence came these gems and gold for Jerusalem? From the outlying lands. Neither Eden nor Israel, it seems, were rich in precious stones. The Jews got the raw materials for the Tabernacle and the gems for the High Priest's ephod from Egyptian spoil (Exodus 35) and from their travels in Havilah (Arabia). Solomon's Temple was adorned with gold and gems from other lands (2 Samuel 8:11; 1 Kings 7:51; 9:28; 10:11). The message is that God's house cannot be fully built until all nations are converted and cooperate in its spiritual development. As the rivers of spiritual blessing go out from Jerusalem (the Church), so the nations return their tithes for her adornment.

It remains to note that altars were also holy mountains, ladders to heaven. We have just mentioned the contrast between Jacob's ladder and the Tower of Babel. More broadly speaking, there is a contrast between the Tower of Babel and the altars of worship set up by Abraham. Abraham's altars were probably just pillars made up of stone and earth, but what they symbolized is set out for us in an important vision in Ezekiel 43.

Ezekiel describes an altar in the form of a stepped pyramid. The top section is called "the Mountain of God," and the platform on top for the fire is called the "hearth." A literal translation of Ezekiel 43:15 is: "And the Mountain of God: four cubits (high); and from the hearth four horns extend upwards."[14]

While the altar in the Tabernacle did not have this shape, the statement in Ezekiel clearly expresses the *theology* of the altar (see Diagram 12.8). When God appeared on Mount Sinai, the top was covered with fire and smoke (Exodus 19:18). We can hardly fail to see the visual association of this with the burning sacrifices on the bronze altar, and the incense on the golden altar. Moreover, altars for sacrifice were generally built on the tops of mountains before the Tabernacle was set up (cf. Genesis 22:9), and during the interregnum between the dissolution of the Tabernacle and the building of the Temple (cf. 1 Samuel 9:12). Thus, the association of altar with holy mountain is fairly pervasive.

Diagram 12.8
The Altar of Ezekiel 43:13-17

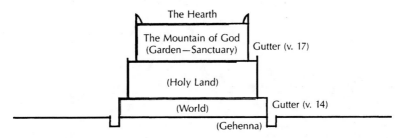

Conclusion

First, with all this information before us we can construct a symbolic picture of the original world (see Diagram 12.9). Above the earth was the firmament-heaven, a picture of the highest heaven. Below the earth was the sea, a picture of the Abyss. Rising out of the center of the earth was the Holy Mountain, from which flowed four rivers to carry Spiritual influences to the four corners of the earth. Stationed at the top of the pyramid was man, God's agent for world transformation. From this vantage point, man could look up and see the heavenly blueprint, and then come down the mountain to work with the earth, making it like heaven.

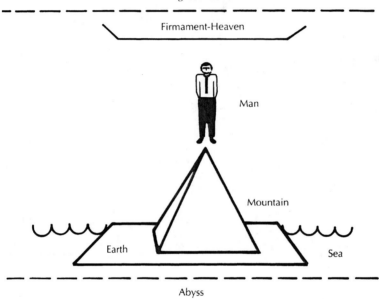

Diagram 12.9
The World in Cross Section

Highest Heaven

Firmament-Heaven

Man

Mountain

Earth

Sea

Abyss

Second, we are now to the point of summarizing the concept of a ladder to heaven. Any ladder to heaven is of necessity a model of heaven and earth, with heaven at the top, and the earthly sanctuary, the gate of heaven, lower down or at the bottom. We can also say that any heaven and earth model is also a ladder to heaven. For instance, the Tabernacle of Moses: The Israelite citizen was admitted to the forecourt or gateway of the Tabernacle courtyard, where he offered sacrifice. He was not allowed to ascend the Holy Mountain of the Bronze Altar, and thus he was not to go farther back into the courtyard than the Altar. The Altar as Holy Mountain ascended up to the firmament. The Laver of Cleansing thus signified the heavenly sea of Genesis 1:7 (and *not*, N.B., the cosmic or Gentile sea of the waters below). The Holy Place had to do with the visible or firmament-heaven, God's outer court, while the Most Holy had to do with the Highest Heaven, the very Throne of God (see Diagram 12.10). The Bible speaks of both the highest heaven and the firmament-heaven as tents or tabernacles of God (Job 36:29; Psalm 18:11; 19:4; 104:2; Isaiah 40:22). We shall, of course, look at the Tabernacle in more detail in Chapter 15; for now we only wish to see it and the Temple as models of heaven and earth, and thus as ladders to heaven.

Ladders to heaven and models of heaven and earth speak of two related things. It is relatively easy for us to see that they speak of environments. Heaven is an environment, and so is the earth. The Tabernacle and Temple, with their courtyards, were environments — physical environments. A special tree, an altar, a monument pillar, a holy mountain — these are physical environments.

Each of these, however, pictures a social or human environment. We have seen that the heavenly host has to do very often with rulers or with saints. In terms of the political arrangement of a nation, the heavens are the rulers and the earth is the ruled (Isaiah 13:13; 34:4). In terms of the spiritual polity of the world, God's people are positioned in the heavens (Philippians 3:20; Ephesians 1:20; 2:6; Hebrews 12:22-23).[15] We have seen that trees speak of people, and that an environment of trees, such as the Temple and Tabernacle, speaks of a body politic. We have seen that the Temple and Tabernacle were symbols both of the righteous individual, and thus of Jesus Christ, the True Ladder

Diagram 12.10
The Mosaic Tabernacle

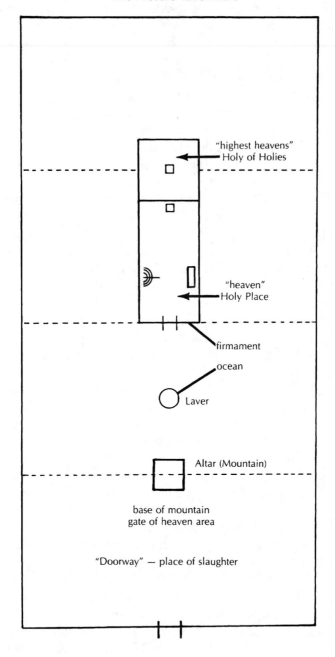

"highest heavens"
Holy of Holies

"heaven"
Holy Place

firmament

ocean

Laver

Altar (Mountain)

base of mountain
gate of heaven area

"Doorway" — place of slaughter

to Heaven, and also of the Church as a body politic. The same thing is true of mountains, which symbolize nations and people (Isaiah 41:14-16; Jeremiah 51:25, 42; Zechariah 4:7; Matthew 21:21-22).[16] God's people are His Mountain, a Mountain that grows and fills the earth (Daniel 2:35).

This imagery is absolutely fundamental to Biblical revelation. We have to consider each passage in context to see what it is saying, of course; but we need to be alert to symbolism and imagery. The Bible uses these images to express its worldview, according to each stage of history. To an examination of these stages of history we must now turn our attention, beginning with the world of Noah.

PART FOUR

THE MOVEMENT
OF HISTORY

Guide me, O Thou great Jehovah,
　Pilgrim through this barren land;
I am weak, but thou art mighty,
　Hold me with thy powerful hand;
　　Bread of heaven,
　Feed me till I want no more.

Open now the crystal fountain
　Whence the healing stream doth flow;
Let the fire and cloudy pillar
　Lead me all the journey through;
　　Strong deliverer,
　Be thou still my strength and shield.

When I tread the verge of Jordan,
　Bid my anxious fears subside;
Death of death and hell's destruction,
　Land me safe on Canaan's side;
　　Songs of praises
　I will ever give to thee.

William Williams[1]

THE WORLD OF NOAH

We have already looked at the rite of world transformation, in Chapter 10. We now begin to apply it to the world and to humanity. We shall find that Biblical history follows the following pattern.

After the fall of man, the world entered into a *decline*. This decline is always a prelude to God's first step, which is His *taking hold of the situation*. God comes to a man, a prophet, and announces judgment on the old world, and His intention to form a new world. To use the language of the Bible, God announces the destruction of the old heavens and earth, and His intention to create a new heavens and earth. For instance:

- At the Flood, the first physical heavens and earth were destroyed, and a new physical heavens and earth were set up, which will endure until the return of Christ.

- At the Cross and Resurrection of our Lord, the old Adamic heavens and earth were shaken down, and a new heavens and earth were set up, with the God-man seated on the heavenly throne. Thus, in a judicial sense, the New Heavens and Earth began at that time.

- At the end of history, the present heavens and earth will be transfigured into the fullness of the New Heavens and Earth.

- But, each time God brought judgment on His people during the Old Covenant, there was a sense in which an old heavens and earth was replaced with a new one: New rulers were set up, a new symbolic world model was built (Tabernacle, Temple), and so forth.

So, God's first step, in terms of the formula we have chosen to use to organize our material, is His laying hold on the situation, His announcement that He is going to change the world. We shall call this phase of history God's *announcement*.

Second, having grasped His people in His hand, God moves them from one place to another, from one situation to another, from one world to another. We shall call this transition an *exodus*. The exodus from Egypt is the most celebrated of these transitions, but hardly the first or the last, as we shall see. The end result of this exodus or transition is the establishment of a new world order.

Third, once the exodus has been accomplished, God gives His Word of promise and command: He distributes the new world to His people, and gives them laws and rules to obey as they exercise dominion over it. In connection with this, God sets up a symbolic world model as His sanctuary. We shall call this stage by the word *establishment*.

Fourth, once the new world order has been established, God gets history moving again. This post-establishment history is a time when God makes evaluations of His people, in terms of their faithfulness or disobedience. It is a time of the application of positive and negative sanctions, in terms of the treaty or covenant set up at the establishment. Before the Cross, this phase was always a time of decline toward judgment. After the Cross, we have a promise that it will be a time of growth. (See Chapters 18 and 19 on this.) We shall call this phase by the phrase *history and decline*.

Fifth, and finally, God comes in judgment. His judgment, however, is always simultaneously an announcement of His intention to create a new world; and so the cycle or spiral begins again. In Genesis 1, this fifth point was God's sabbath, His rest. After tasting and evaluating, we said, comes relaxing and enjoying. Because of the sin of man, however, God kept having to start up new worlds instead of relaxing in the existing one. With the coming of Jesus Christ, however, this cycle is broken. God is willing to "relax and enjoy" the Kingdom, knowing that it can never fail.

There are two observations I wish to make at this point, before we turn our attention to Noah. First, God's coming to His people to make evaluations is a sabbath phenomenon, also termed Day of the Lord or Lord's Day. The sabbath was the seventh day of God's week of creation, but the first full day of man's week. Thus, the time of sabbath, of judgment and evaluation, is simultaneously the last day of an old week and the first day of a new week.[2] It is the time of covenant-renewal, and thus of worship. The worship service, then, should be a time of leaving behind the old world of the previous week, and receiving the gift of the Kingdom, the new world, for the new week.

Second, this sequence helps us understand better the Biblical view of time. In traditional paganism, time and history are conceived of as a bondage from which you want to escape through religious activity. In Christianity, however, time is *opportunity*. The succession of moments continues to put before us new choices, and new opportunities to do better than we have done before.

The Christian view of time is also *linear* rather than cyclical. In paganism, time and history are a series of endless cycles, in which no real progress is or can ever be made. Christianity, however, sees real progress in history, as each new "world" is more glorious than the one before.[3]

The Christian view of time is, however, not linear in the modern secular sense: a succession of moments without meaning. Rather, time and history are *rhythmical*; that is, there are fundamental patterns that repeat. There are indeed historical cycles, but they are spirals, not circles. The fact that the patterns repeat, with variations, is of course related to what we have mentioned earlier, which is that the Biblical view of history is fundamentally typological.

Finally, the Christian view of time is *liturgical*. We begin in sabbath at the throne of God, move out into the world and work, and then return at the Lord's Day for His evaluation and blessing. All history proceeds from God's alpha, and develops into His never-ending omega.

Announcement

After the sin of man in the Garden of Eden, and his expulsion, we read of the sin of Cain in the Land of Eden, and his expulsion. Cain went out and built a city, a city basically built on his brother's blood. This city became a city of blood; and in the seventh generation from Adam, we find the murderer Lamech celebrating his violence in song (Genesis 4).

The seventh from Adam in the line of godly Seth was Enoch, who walked with God and was taken to heaven after living a year of years in this world (Genesis 5:23-24). It seems, though, that the godly line of Seth fell away. Three generations later, only Noah was left to find favor in God's sight. What happened? I believe that the line of Seth committed the sin of intermarriage with the line of Cain, and that this is what is meant by the statement that the "sons of God [Sethites] saw that the daughters of men [Cainites] were fair; and they took wives for themselves, whomever they chose" (Genesis 6:2). There are other views of this passage, but this is the only interpretation that provides an explanation for why the Sethites disappeared.[4] Notice that the Sethites committed the sin of Adam in the Garden. Just as the forbidden fruit was *seen* to be *fair*, so were the daughters of the Cainites (Genesis 3:6).

God made a preliminary judgment, recorded in Genesis 6:3, and gave humanity 120 years to repent. We shall find that God always gives preliminary judgments and opportunities to repent before bringing in full judgment.

Things continued to get worse, however, and eventually God determined to destroy the world. Simultaneously, He laid hold on Noah and told him that he and his family would be saved.

Exodus

Noah was told to make the Ark. During the Flood year, the only "land" that was emergent from the sea was the Ark. Thus, the Ark was the only human habitat in the world. Additionally, the Ark was a world model composed of three decks (see Diagram 13.1). Meredith G. Kline has written that the Ark was:

> a spiritual house of God, which has its symbolic external prototypes in the Creator's cosmic house of heaven and earth and later in Israel's microcosmic Tabernacle and Temple. What is now to be observed is that the design of the ark suggested that it was intended to be a representation of God's Kingdom in this cosmic house form. For the ark, however seaworthy, was fashioned like a house rather than like a sailing vessel. All the features mentioned in the description of the ark belong to the architecture of a house; the three stories, the door, the window.[5]

Diagram 13.1
Noah's Ark as
World Model

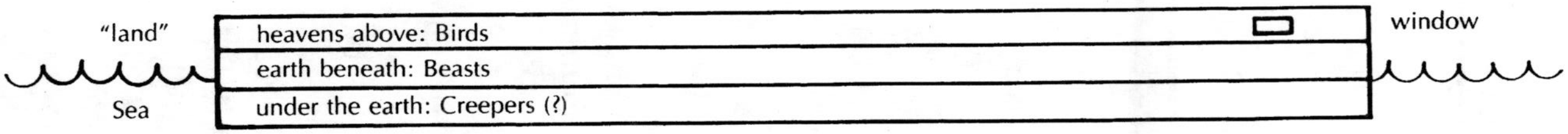

heavens above: Birds

earth beneath: Beasts

under the earth: Creepers (?)

"land"

Sea

window

Kline goes on to note that the three stories of the Ark correspond with the heavens above, the earth beneath, and the waters under the earth. The lowest deck may be associated with the crawling things, for they burrow in the earth to some extent; or it may be that the lowest deck is associated with the water "under the earth" simply because it was submerged the deepest. As we have seen, there is a rough correlation between the three land environments and the three spatial environments, so that crawling things are parallel to sea creatures (and birds to domestic animals, with wild animals parallel to land animals in general). Kline writes clearly,

> the window of the ark is the counterpart to "the window of heaven," referred to in this narrative (7:11; 8:2). Appropriately, the window area is located along the top of the ark, as part of the upper (heavenly) story. One is naturally led then to compare the door of the ark with the door that shuts up the depths of the sea, holding back its proud waves. (For this cosmological imagery see Job 38:8-11.)[6]

Even though God did not tell Noah to put the birds in the top story, beasts in the middle, and creeping things in the lowest; yet every time the animals are mentioned they are listed broken down into categories, creating an in-context conceptual parallel (Genesis 6:7, 20; 7:8, 14, 21, 23; 8:17, 19; 9:2).[7]

Another aspect of the Ark as world model is the fact that God dictated its dimensions to Noah, something only done when a world model is being set up (Exodus 25ff.; 1 Chronicles 28:16; Hebrews 9:5; Ezekiel 40ff.; Revelation 21:10ff.). Thus, the Ark was a world model, and as such has always been regarded as a type of the Church, God's new creation.[8]

Additionally, the Ark was made of wood. What else would it have been made of? God's command to make it of wood seems unnecessary and superfluous, except for the spiritual associations of wood with trees. In Chapter 7 we noted that the various periods of history are associated with various trees. The "gopher" wood of the Ark is peculiar to it. In fact, no one knows what "gopher" wood is! Like the Tabernacle and Temple, the Ark of wood was a picture of God's Edenic Grove.

This exodus was a wholly miraculous event. A few moments' meditation will show just how extraordinary it was. First, it involved a miracle for all the animals to come to Noah and enter the Ark. We should consider this parallel to the movement of God's people out of Egypt to Mount Sinai, remembering that animals are images of humanity.

Second, it involved a miracle for these animals to be at peace with one another. During the wilderness wanderings, God performed many miracles, miracles of judgment, to force the people to keep peace and to put down rebellion (cf. esp. Numbers 11:1-3; Numbers 16–17).

Third, feeding and caring for these animals involved some kind of miracle. It would not have been possible to carry on the Ark enough food to feed all these animals for a whole year. God fed Israel with manna in the wilderness, and it is easy to imagine that something similar happened here. Then again, perhaps many of the animals hibernated for the whole year.

Thus, the exodus transition was accomplished by a whole series of miracles. While Noah and his family were sustained on the Ark, the angels were busy remaking the world. They were burying animals to make oil, and plants to make coal, and in many other ways preparing a new world for humanity.

A detailed study of the Flood will reveal many re-creation motifs at work.[9] The subsiding waters revealed the land, just as in the creation week. The dove hovering over the water recalls the Spirit's hovering at creation, and the dove-Spirit hovering over our Lord at His baptismal inauguration of the New Covenant.

Establishment

With the resting of the Ark, we have a transferring of the world model to the world. We shall see this again at Mount Sinai, when the configuration of that mountain is transferred to the configuration of the Tabernacle. Here with Noah we find that the triple-decker Ark becomes the model for a new triple-decker world. The waters recede, and the world is made anew after the image of the model.

The arrival of the Ark is like the arrival of Israel in Canaan. God gave the world anew to Noah, telling him to be fruitful and multiply in the new creation (Genesis 8:16-17). God promised that this new world would be permanent, and that He would act to prevent man's sinfulness from ever again maturing from youth to full age (Genesis 8:21). With this new heaven and earth came a change in God's covenant arrangements. God allowed Noah and his descendants to eat meat, apparently for the first time, and forbade the drinking of blood. Parallel to the drinking of blood is the shedding of blood in murder; and God also bestowed on man, for the first time, the right and privilege to sit as judge and execute murderers (Genesis 9:2-7). Associated with this new privilege was a robe of authority, signifying man's new estate as judge.[10]

God gave a special sign for the new Noahic covenant: He placed His warbow in the sky as the rainbow (Genesis 9:12-17). The warbow, God's weapon, is parallel to the flaming sword of the cherubim (Genesis 3:24), this being the special sign of the Adamic covenant under judgment.

We are to the point now of summarizing the ways in which this new establishment parallels the first establishment in Genesis 1-3. First, the new triple-decker world is like the first one, except that the new one is permanent.[11]

Second, the new high ground, holy mountain, is Ararat. As we have seen, this is probably the same location as Eden originally. Humanity will proceed from Ararat as they proceeded from Eden. Also, in terms of future parallels, note that the resting of God's house, the divinely designed Ark, on the top of Ararat is parallel to the placement of the Temple on top of Mount Moriah.

Third, as there was a Garden in Eden, so Noah planted a vineyard. As Adam sinned in the Garden, so Ham sinned in the vineyard (Genesis 9:18-27).[12] As Adam seized at a symbol of the as yet forbidden prerogative of rulership, so Ham seized at Noah's robe of authority.[13]

Fourth, as God judged Adam, so Noah judged Ham. This change came about because God had committed judgment into human hands, and given Noah a robe of authority as symbol of his office. Noah was a new Adam, but a glorified Adam, an Adam who had some of God's office bestowed on him. Unlike Adam in the Garden, Noah was a prophet. Noah judged Ham the way Adam was supposed to judge the serpent. Noah judged

Ham the way God judged Adam. There are parallels, but there is also an advance in glory. History is not cyclical but spiral.

Fifth, there is a parallel, as mentioned, between the flaming sword of God's wrath and His unstrung warbow of peace. The Garden and the flaming sword were gone, though the latter would continue to play a role in the Tabernacle and Temple until the coming of the New Covenant. There has been, however, a very real and important change from wrath to grace.

Although Noah's vineyard designedly reminds us of the Garden of Eden, yet there is an important difference: Noah's vineyard was not God's garden-sanctuary. In the world immediately after the Flood, there was no garden-sanctuary, nor was there a holy land. Remember that God originally created the world, and then set apart the land of Eden, finally planting a garden-sanctuary in Eden. We find the same sequence after the Flood. Until the time of Abram there was no special land set apart. Until the time of the Tabernacle and its courtyard, there was no earthly garden-sanctuary in the world.

So, what was this "new heavens and earth" after the Flood like? Well, first, in terms of world structure we have the seventy nations of the world, given in Genesis 10. Although the number of nations in the world soon grew beyond seventy, the symbolic number of the nations remains seventy in the Bible.[14] Before the Flood, the land of Eden had been dominant over the whole earth — all the rivers came from Eden. After the fall of man, the land of Nod with its counterfeit city-sanctuary Enoch dominated the world (Genesis 4:16-24). There was a one-state world, ruled by the Nephilim, mighty men (Genesis 6:4). There were not many nations, though various lands had been listed in Genesis 2. Rather, there were simply two genealogical lines, and the line of Cain came to dominate the world. After the Flood, however, there were seventy nations, and no one-world state.

Second, in these seventy nations we have city-states ruled over by priest-kings. The preeminent Biblical example of this is Melchizedek, who was priest of "God Most High" and also king of Salem (later Jerusalem) (Genesis 14:14-22). This rule by priest-kings, or by kings and priests, "chiefs and medicine men," together, is an advancement over the situation before the Flood. Thus, the political heavens before the Flood were the mighty men who dominated the whole earth; while after the Flood, the political heavens were the priest-kings of the seventy separated · nations. Some of the priest-kings were godly, and some were ungodly; but whatever the case, we have moved into a new heavens and earth, with nations and city-states. This would continue to be the situation in the world at large until the time of Israel's exile, when we move into the world-imperial stage of history. (See Diagram 13.2.) For as long as Israel remained a nation, however, the Gentile world was also organized into nations with city-state capitals.

Diagram 13.2
Polities

	Pre-Flood World	Noahic World	Exilic World
Heavens	Mighty Cainite men who dominate:	Priest-kings who rule:	World emperors (Daniel 2, 7)
Earth	a one-world state; all people	many separate nations	many nations gathered under one ruler

Third, as just noted, the name of God in use among the nations was "God Most High." God Most High was regarded as Possessor of heaven and earth, a name of international significance. Melchizedek, priest of God Most High (Genesis 14:18), blessed Abram with these words: "Blessed be Abram of God Most High, Possessor of heaven and earth; and blessed be God Most High, who has delivered your enemies into your hand" (14:19-20). The name God gave to the Hebrew Patriarchs was "God Almighty," the God who has the ability to fulfill His promises (Genesis 17:1; 28:3; 35:11; 48:3). Melchizedek, however, used the Gentile name. Note also what Abram said to the king of Sodom: "I have sworn to the Lord, God Most High, Possessor of heaven and earth, that I will not take a thread or a sandal thong or anything that is yours" (14:22-23). Abram identified his own God, the Lord, with the one known among the Gentiles as God Most High, Possessor of heaven and earth.

In summary, the world established under the Noahic covenant had the following aspects:

Names:

God:	God Most High, Possessor of heaven and earth
People:	God-fearers (Acts 10:2, 22, 35; 13:16, 26)

Grant: The whole earth

Promise: No future Flood

Stipulations:

Sacramental:	No drinking of blood
Societal:	No murder

Polity: Priest-kings with the right to put murderers to death, ruling separate nations

Symbol: "the seventy nations of the world"

History and Decline

Adam rebelled and was cast from the Garden. Ham rebelled and was cursed from Noah's vineyard. After Adam's sin, Cain became a murderer and went out and built a city. After Ham's sin, the Hamite Nimrod became a "mighty hunter" (of men, by implication), and built a city: the Tower of Babel (Genesis 10:8-12; 11:1-9). God had put away His warbow, but man had not. The city of the Prince of Peace is made of rainbow jewels. The city of this prince of hunters was made of mud bricks.

God had promised, however, to cut off man's sin in its youth. Ham, Noah's *youngest* son (Genesis 9:24), had been prevented from seizing forbidden fruit. Now Nimrod, the new Cain, would be prevented from attaining the heights of power and the depths of depravity of Cain and Lamech of old. His city was cut down.

Nimrod was attempting at the Tower of Babel to re-create the pre-Flood world. His goal was a one-state world, with his mighty men, his neo-nephilim, in charge. By scattering the people from Babel, God created the seventy nations of the world, enforcing the post-Flood polity. Having failed at Babylon, Nimrod went out and created Nineveh and Assyria (Genesis 10:10-11). Thus, both of these two mighty hunter-conqueror cultures were created by one man, who was carefully carrying on the policy of Cain. Both Babylon and Nineveh are to be seen as extensions of Enoch, the city of Cain.

God's judgment on the Tower of Babel, however, was accompanied as always with a new announcement of salvation. All the things that man had sinfully tried to seize at Babel—land, name, priestly influence—God announced that He would bestow upon Abraham.

They had wanted land, "lest we be scattered abroad over the face of the whole earth" (Genesis 11:4). God, however, scattered them (11:8), and gave land to Abram: "Go forth from your country, and from your relatives and from your father's house, to the land which I shall show you" (Genesis 12:1).

They had wanted a name: "And let us make for ourselves a name" (Genesis 11:4b). God, however, confused their languages, so that they could not understand one another's names (11:7), and gave a great name to Abram: "And I will make you a great nation, and I will bless you, and make your name great" (Genesis 12:2).

Finally, they had wanted to be religious leaders. Their tower was to reach to heaven. They would be the points of contact between other men and "god" (Genesis 11:4). God, however, prevented their tower-building (11:8) and set up Abram and his seed as the priestly nation: "And so you shall be a blessing; and I will bless those who bless you, and the one who curses you I will curse. And in you all the families of the ground shall be blessed" (Genesis 12:2-3).[15]

This brings us to the world of the Patriarchs, which we must now consider.

The God of Abrah'm praise,
Who reigns enthroned above;
Ancient of everlasting days,
And God of Love:
JEHOVAH GREAT I AM!
By earth and heav'n confest;
I bow and bless the sacred Name,
Forever bless'd.

The God of Abrah'm praise,
At whose supreme command,
From earth I rise—and seek the joys
At his right hand;
I all on earth forsake,
Its wisdom, fame, and power;
And him my only Portion make,
My Shield and Tower.

The God of Abrah'm praise,
Whose all-sufficient grace
Shall guide me all my happy days,
In all my ways:
He calls a worm his friend!
He calls himself my God!
And he shall save me to the end
Through Jesus' blood.

He by Himself hath sworn,
I on his oath depend,
I shall, on eagle's wings up-borne,
To heaven ascend;
I shall behold his face,
I shall his power adore,
And sing the wonders of his grace
Forevermore.

—Thomas Olivers "The God of Abrah'm Praise,"
    A Christian paraphrase of the *Yigdal*[1]

THE WORLD OF
THE PATRIARCHS

We have stated that there is always a decline that partially explains the need for a new covenant. It is also true, however, that even if man had not sinned there would have been advances from glory to glory. Thus, the coming of a new covenant is not wholly to be explained by the failure of the previous one. Also involved is the fact of human maturation, so that what was once appropriate and fitting at a certain stage of childhood now must be superseded. As children grow, we have to keep getting them new shoes and new clothing, partially because the old ones are wearing out, but also because the child has outgrown them.

This explains why God never simply calls His people back to the previous covenant. The prophets come and tell the people that they have broken the covenant and remind them of their duties in terms of the old covenant; but when covenant renewal comes, it is never simply a return to the old ways. Rather, it is a renewal of the old ways in a new form, a form appropriate to the times and to the stage of growth.

As we move into the period of the patriarchs, it will be helpful to set out a rough overview of covenantal history. After the Flood, God re-created the *world* with the Noahic covenant. With the sins of Ham and then Nimrod, the world order was threatened, and God took advantage of the opportunity to set aside a new (Edenic) *land* with the Abrahamic covenant, designating one nation, the Hebrews, to be priests to the rest. That nation of priests fell into sin in Egypt, and God took the opportunity to re-create the (Garden) *sanctuary* with the Mosaic covenant, setting aside the Levites and Aaronic priests to guide the Israelite nation. Next, just as God planted a Garden in Eden and then made a man to rule it, so also, after the priests of Israel fell into sin (1 Samuel 1–3), God took the opportunity to re-create the (Adamic) *king* with the Davidic covenant. With the collapse of the Davidic covenant and the exile, God took the opportunity to inaugurate the *imperial* stage of history, and placed Israel under the protection of world emperors. With the collapse of the imperial stage of history, seen in Rome's crucifixion of the Son of God, God enthroned Jesus Christ to be the True Noahic Gentile, the True Abrahamic Hebrew, the True (Mosaic) Aaronic Priest, the True Davidic King, and the True World Emperor.

Each of these covenants is built on the previous one, by way of being added to it. Each one, however, transforms the previous one as well. Once Abram's family had been set aside as priests, it was no longer enough for the Gentiles to obey the Noahic covenant. They were also required to bless Abram. Once the Tabernacle was set up, it was no longer proper for the Hebrews to have altars in many places.[2] The only altar permitted was at the Tabernacle. Once the Temple was set up, there was no more moving around of the Tabernacle from place to place. Once the Imperial stage of history was inaugurated, God's people were required to "render to Caesar." Of course, with the coming of the New Covenant, there were radical transformations of the entire Old Covenant series.

With this as background and context, let us look at the age of the patriarchs. We have already noticed God's "laying hold" on the situation in His call of Abram out of Ur of the Chaldees. We find that in Ur, Terah had sons, but his son Haran died (Genesis 11:27–28). We find that in Ur, Abram took a wife, but his wife was barren (Genesis 11:29–30). The message was clear: If you have sons in Babylon, they will die; and if you take wives in Babylon, they will be barren. An exodus is clearly needed.[3]

Exodus

What follows is the second exodus in the Bible, the first being the Flood. The exodus is the second step in the typological pattern of history, the transition from the old world to the new. It is the act of breaking down and restructuring, as when I remove a glass from the cabinet and water from the pipe, and put them together into a new thing: a glass of water; or as when Jesus, having taking hold of bread, broke it and gave it a new name: His body. What is seen very simply and basically in such acts of restructuring is seen at large in the exodus pattern.[4]

The following are some of the most important exoduses in the Bible:

1. Noah's removal from captivity in the Old World to the New.

2. Abram's removal from death in Babylon to life in Canaan (Genesis 11:27–12:5).

3. Abram's deliverance from captivity in Egypt to life in Canaan (Genesis 12:6–13:18).

4. Lot's deliverance from Sodom (Genesis 19:1-16), God's offer of life at The Mountain (19:17-19), and Lot's death in the wilderness (19:30-38).[5]

5. Abraham's deliverance from danger in Philistia (Genesis 20).

6. Isaac's deliverance from danger in Philistia (Genesis 26).

7. Jacob's deliverance from enslavement in Mesopotamia (Genesis 31).

8. Israel's deliverance from enslavement in Egypt (Exodus 1–15).

9. The Ark of God, taken captive by Philistines, defeats their gods and is returned, laden with spoils (1 Samuel 5-6).

10. David's sojourn in the wilderness and Philistia, and then his return to the land (1 Samuel 21–2 Samuel 2).

11. Israel's return from Mesopotamia, after the exile.

12. Jesus' "exodus at Jerusalem" (Luke 9:31); His renunciation of Jerusalem and the Temple, and His crucifixion outside the walls; the new Kingdom of the Mount of Olives.

13. The removal of the Church from Jerusalem before her destruction in 70 A.D. (Matthew 24:16-18; Acts 1-28).

When we remember that the Bible regards the Philistines as a sub-group of the Egyptians (Genesis 10:13-14), we see that there are basically two avenues of exodus in the Old Testament: those from the North (Babylon, Mesopotamia) and those from the South (Egypt, Philistia). All of these find their fulfillment in Christ's abandonment of Jerusalem, and thus of the whole old world.

The sequence of events in the exodus is this:

1. *Some threat, some aspect of sin or of the curse, drives God's people from their home.* Adam was driven from paradise. Famines drove Abram to Egypt (Genesis 12:10), Isaac to Philistia (Genesis 26:1), the Hebrews to Egypt (Genesis 43:1). The disaster at Sodom drove Abraham to Philistia (Genesis 19:28; Genesis 20). Wicked oppressors drove Jacob to Mesopotamia (Genesis 27:42-43) and David to Philistia (1 Samuel 20:31). Personal sin put Lot in Sodom (Genesis 13:7-13). Conquest removed the Ark to Philistia (1 Samuel 4) and Israel to Babylon (2 Kings 24–25). Love for His people caused our Lord to leave Heaven to save us.

2. *During the sojourn in captivity, Eve is assaulted by the Serpent, who wishes to use her to raise up his own wicked seed.* There was intermarriage before the Flood (Genesis 6:2). Pharaoh and Abimelech attacked Sarah (Genesis 12:13; 20:2). Lot's daughters were corrupted (Genesis 19:30-38). Abimelech's people threatened Rebekah (Genesis 26:10). Laban disinherited Rachel and Leah (Genesis 31:14-16). Pharaoh killed the boy babies and kept the girls for his people (Exodus 1:15-22). Amalek attacked David's wives in the wilderness (1 Samuel 30:5). Esther was taken by Ahasuerus during the exile (Esther 2). Demons ravaged Israel during the ministry of our Lord. The bride of Christ was assaulted continually by the Jews in the book of Acts.

3. *The righteous use "holy deception" to trick the serpent and protect Eve.* The serpent had deceived Eve in the beginning (1 Timothy 2:14); and eye for eye, tooth for tooth, it becomes the woman's trick to deceive the serpent. Thus, Abraham called Sarah his sister on two occasions; and Isaac called Rebekeh his sister, because they knew that an honest ruler would not simply seize their women without negotiating with them.[6] (Of course, the tyrants seized them anyway.) Jacob tricked Laban to recover his wives' dowries (Genesis 30:37-43). The Hebrew midwives lied to Pharaoh and saved Israelite boys, and were blessed by God for doing so (Exodus 1:18-21). David feigned madness in Philistia, and pretended to serve the Philistines (1 Samuel 21:13; 1 Samuel 27, 29),

while actually defending Israel. Jesus protected and saved His holy bride by drawing Satan's fire to Himself.

4. *Very often, God's people are enslaved during the sojourn outside the land.* Jacob was virtually enslaved by Laban, and Laban regarded him as his slave.[7] Israel was enslaved in Egypt. Israel was virtually enslaved at the beginning of the Babylonian captivity. Jesus was dragged before Pilate and cast into prison.

5. *God brings blessings upon His people during the captivity, but plagues the tyrant, either progressively or as part of the deliverance.* Abram acquired wealth in Egypt (Genesis 12:16), but Pharaoh's house received plagues (Genesis 12:17). Despite persecution, Isaac became wealthy in Philistia (Genesis 26:12-17). God made Jacob wealthy in Mesopotamia, but gradually decapitalized Laban (Genesis 31:5-12). Israel multiplied in Egypt (Exodus 1:12), but Egypt was plagued. The Ark brought plagues on the Philistines during its captivity (1 Samuel 5:6–6:1). David gathered an army and wealth while in exile, but Saul was plagued by demons (1 Samuel 16:14; 22:2; 1 Samuel 25). The Jews prospered in Babylon; and important Jews were found at court, while Nebuchadnezzar was driven insane (Daniel 4). The work of Christ on the Cross redeemed the world, ensured our blessing, and destroyed Satan, while apostate Israel was plagued by demons during Christ's ministry and throughout the book of Acts.

6. *God miraculously intervenes, often with visions to the pagan lord, in order to save His people.* Noah's Ark and Flood were miracles, as we have seen. God's glory appeared to Abram in Ur (Acts 7:2). God appeared to Abimelech to deliver Sarah (Genesis 20:6-7). Angels came to save Lot, and worked miracles (Genesis 19:11). God appeared to Laban and ordered him to leave Jacob alone (Genesis 31:24). The miracle of Passover saved Israel from Egypt (Exodus 12). The plagues on Philistia were miraculous (1 Samuel 5-6). God appeared to Nebuchadnezzar and converted him, causing him to favor God's people more than before (Daniel 4). God sent Pilate's wife a vision (Matthew 27:19). God raised Jesus from the dead.

7. *Very often the serpent tries to shift blame and accuses the righteous man of being the cause of his difficulty.* Thus, Pharaoh blamed

Abram (Genesis 12:18), Abimelech blamed Abraham
(Genesis 20:9), Abimelech blamed Isaac (Genesis 26:10),
Laban blamed Jacob (Genesis 31:26), Pharaoh blamed
Moses (Exodus 10:28), and Saul blamed David (1 Samuel
20:31). Herod and Pilate tried to shift the blame to each
other. Pilate washed his hands, and then put a sign on the
Cross blaming God and the believers. The Jews blamed
the Christians (Acts 5:28).

8. *God humiliates the false gods of the enemy.* By implication the
false gods of Egypt and Philistia were humiliated when
Abram and Isaac were delivered. Rachel sat on Laban's
gods (Genesis 31:34), and Jacob buried them (Genesis
35:4).[8] God judged all the gods of Egypt (Exodus 12:12).
The Ark humbled Dagon of the Philistines (1 Samuel 5:3),
and then destroyed him (v. 4). Nebuchadnezzar and
Darius were converted and renounced their false gods
(Daniel 4; 6:7, 26-27). Christ defeated Satan, and the
ascended Christ destroyed the Temple, which had become
an idolatrous abomination.

9. *God's people depart with spoils.* Noah brought the true wisdom
of the old world with him (Genesis 8:20-22). Abram left
Egypt with spoils (Genesis 12:16). Lot, of course, barely
got out of Sodom alive, but Abraham received large gifts
from Abimelech (Genesis 20:16). Jacob had nothing when
he went to Mesopotamia, but came back extremely rich
(Genesis 32–33). Israel spoiled the Egyptians (Exodus
12:35-36). The Philistines sent the Ark back laden with
gold (1 Samuel 6:17-18). David inherited Saul's Kingdom.
The Jews came back from Babylon with much spoil
(Zechariah 6:10-11). Between 30 and 70 A.D., the Church
spoiled the Old Covenant. She now spoils the world,
bringing all into the kingdom.

10. *Finally, God's people are installed in the Holy Land.* This is, of
course, the goal of the exodus. Sometimes the people are
brought out of bondage, but reject the Kingdom, as in the
cases of Lot and of Israel in the wilderness. Eventually,
though, they come into the new world.

11. Installation in the new land means setting up worship,
building God's house out of some of the spoils, and setting
up a priesthood. (This "Victory-Housebuilding Pattern"[9] is
actually what we are calling the establishment phase that

comes after the exodus, but for completeness let us take note of it here.) Noah built an altar and offered sacrifice (Genesis 8:20). When Abram came out of Ur, he built altars in the land (Genesis 12:7-8). When Abram came out of Egypt, he restored the altar at Bethel (Genesis 13:4). When Abraham was delivered from Abimelech, God opened Sarah's womb and gave him a son (Genesis 21:1). Remember: the altar, the Temple, etc. are all symbols for God's people. Thus, the miraculous birth of a messianic son corresponds to the building of a house for God. This is "counterfeited" with the birth of Lot's sons after his deliverance from Sodom (Genesis 19:30-38).[10] When Isaac was delivered from Philistia, he built an altar (Genesis 26:25). When Jacob arrived back in Canaan after his captivity in Mesopotamia, he built an altar (Genesis 33:20). When Israel escaped from Egypt, she built first a golden calf out of spoil, and then the Tabernacle (Exodus 25:1-9; 32:2-4). The return of the Ark from Philistine captivity eventually led to the building of the Temple. The booty from David's Philistine wars also went to the Temple, after David's exodus and enthronement (1 Chronicles 22:14-16). The Temple was rebuilt after the return of Israel from Babylonian exile (Ezra, Haggai, Zechariah). After Jesus' exodus on the Cross, and His priestly installation in heaven, the true Temple of the people of God began to be built of living stones.

Such is the exodus pattern as we find it in the Bible. It is interesting to note a couple of other instances of the pattern. There is a counterfeit exodus in Judges 17-18. There we read of the erection of a counterfeit Tabernacle and the ordaining of a counterfeit priest. Subsequently we have a counterfeit journey by apostate Danites who had rejected the land God gave them. This issues in a counterfeit conquest and the full establishment of a counterfeit sanctuary in Dan.[11]

Another interesting exodus is that of Jeroboam. Like Abraham, Jeroboam was promised part of Canaan (1 Kings 11:29-37). Solomon drove him into Egypt (1 Kings 11:40). When Solomon died, his son Rehoboam acted foolishly. Jeroboam returned to the land, and Northern Israel made him their king (1 Kings 12:1-20). Jeroboam proceeded to apostatize, and built counterfeit sanctuaries and set up counterfeit priests (1 Kings 12:25-32).

Establishment

Now that Abram has made his exodus from Babylon and come into the land, what is the nature of the covenant established with him, and with the succeeding patriarchs Isaac, Jacob, and the sons of Israel? First, the name of God given in connection with the new covenant is, as we have mentioned, God Almighty. By this name, God assured the patriarchs that He was fully capable of performing what He promised.

Second, God gave new names to His restructured people. God changed Abram to Abraham and Jacob to Israel. Jacob means Supplanter, and pointed to his being the younger son who replaces the older. The older son is often a type of Adam, and the younger of the Second Adam. Thus, Seth replaced Cain, Shem replaced Japheth (Genesis 5:32; 9:24; 11:10), Isaac replaced Ishmael, Jacob replaced Esau, Joseph replaced the older brothers, Ephraim replaced Manasseh (Genesis 48:18), Eleazar and Ithamar replaced Nadab and Abihu (Exodus 6:23; 24:1; Leviticus 10:1-6), David replaced his older brothers, and Jesus replaced Adam. Israel, however, means God's Prince. When we get to Exodus and the Mosaic covenant, we find that the priestly nation is called "children of Israel," a race of princes and princesses. During the patriarchal period, however, they were known as Hebrews, descendants of the Shemite Eber (Genesis 11:16; 14:13; 43:32; Exodus 1:15; 2:6; 3:18; 5:3; 21:2).[12]

The grant made to Abram and his descendants was the land of Canaan (Genesis 15:18-21). The stipulations that came along with this grant were to obey all of God's law (Genesis 26:5) and in the area of sacraments, circumcision (Genesis 17).

The new world polity that came into being meant that the Hebrews were a nation of priests to evangelize and guide the Gentiles. This is what it meant for Abraham to be a "father" to other nations (Genesis 45:8; Romans 4:11). The evangelistic ministry of the patriarchs is symbolized by their altars and wells, as we shall see.

The internal polity of the people of Abraham was a simple patriarchal or clan order: The family head was also the spiritual leader. Since they were not yet a nation, and did not govern any territory, they did not exercise the sword of civil authority. Thus, "separation of church and state" was not an issue during the patriarchal period. The Hebrews were a family and a church, but not a state.

Symbolism

Six symbols stand out as especially relevant to the Abrahamic covenant and the patriarchal era. These symbols picture the nature of God's people and of their ministry. The symbols that come to play prominently in the patriarchal era are stars, dust, altars, pillars, trees, and wells. These symbols will recur in the Mosaic covenant, where they will be organized into a package, the Tabernacle. During the patriarchal era, however, the symbols were distributed "under the open sky."

God told Abram, "I will make your descendants as the dust of the earth; so that if anyone can number the dust of the earth, then your descendants can also be numbered" (Genesis 13:16; cf. 22:17; 28:14; 32:12). God also told Abram that his seed would be like the stars of the heavens in quality (Genesis 15:5; see Chapter 5) and quantity (Genesis 22:17; cf. 26:4; 37:9-10). Thus, the people of Abraham would be a new heavens and a new earth. The promise to Abraham was that a righteous people would *fill* the earth as the dust, and that a righteous people would *rule* the earth as the stars. The Kingdom of God, the spiritual people of Abraham, would someday cover the earth and rule it.[13]

Abraham was to conduct a ministry of evangelism and guidance among all the nations of the world. In this way he would be a "father" of many nations, and they would be his spiritual children. Paul picks this theme up and expands on it in Romans 4, but it is found in Genesis (cf. Genesis 45:8). Abraham began his evangelistic ministry in Haran, before he got to Canaan; and we read that many converts came with him on his exodus (Genesis 12:5).[14] He conducted this ministry by erecting altars, which were as we have seen, models of the holy mountain, ladders to heaven. At these altar sites, Abraham and his descendants led their converts in worship, and taught them the ways of God (Genesis 12:7, 8; 13:4, 18; 22:9; 26:25; 33:20; 35:1, 3, 7).

Abraham pitched his altars in connection with special trees, also ladders to heaven, as we have seen in Chapter 7 (Genesis 12:6; 13:18; 14:13; 18:4, 8; 21:33; 23:17; 35:4, 8). The association of trees with altars, holy mountains, reminds us of the Garden of

Eden. Edenic imagery is reinforced by the attention given to wells of water in connection with the patriarchal ministry (16:14; 21:19, 25, 30; 26:15, 18-32). This is no accident. Abraham's evangelistic ministry was a call to people to make a spiritual pilgrimage back to God.

In Adam's Garden there was a holy mountain, a grove of trees (cp. Genesis 23:17), a well of water, and also a woman. Significantly, it is in connection with wells that the patriarchs found their wives. Rebekah and Rachel were both found at wells (Genesis 24:11-45; 29:2-10), and Moses found Zipporah at a well (Exodus 2:15). Jesus presented Himself as the True Groom to a Samaritan divorcee and adulteress at a well (John 4:6-26).

The altars spoke of the coming sacrifice of Jesus Christ on God's holy mountain. The trees spoke of God's glory and shade, ladders to heaven. The springs spoke of spiritual nourishment, a nourishment offered by the nation of priests to the Gentiles (see especially Isaac's ministry in Philistia, Genesis 26:12-33).

The patriarchs dug wells, built altars, and planted trees (Genesis 21:33); and everything suggests that these things were done together in grove settings.[15] They created open-air sanctuary-gardens. They did not build a house for God. In our survey of the eleventh step in the "Exodus Pattern" above, we noted that in patriarchal times, after each exodus there was an altar built; while in subsequent eras, a house was built after each exodus. The contrast is important. In the house, all the various materials are organized together: laver, altar, wooden boards (trees). The house structure is an appropriate analogue for a nation. The Hebrews were not an organized nation in the age of the patriarchs, however. Thus, neither a portable house-tent nor a permanent temple would have been appropriate. Once the people progressed from glory to glory, into a full-fledged nation, then the altar-tree-spring garden would progress into the glory of Tabernacle and Temple.

The places Abraham made as his ministry headquarters were Shechem, Bethel, and Hebron (Genesis 12:6-8; 13:18). Jacob later made these the sites of his ministry also (Genesis 33:18, 20; 35:1, 6, 7, 27; 46:1). These were the key sites initially captured by Joshua when he conquered Canaan (Joshua 7:2; 8:30; 10:3). Thus, Abraham and Jacob were engaged in a "shadow conquest" of the land. More important, we see from this what true conquest is. The building of altars of evangelism preceded the cultural conquest. If we wish to build a Christian civilization in our land, we had best start with altars.

The pillar also becomes an important patriarchal symbol, though only in one instance. When Jacob had his vision of the True Tower of Babel (Babel = Gate of Heaven), he awoke and

> took the stone that he had put at his head-place and set it up as a pillar, and poured oil on its top. And he called the name of that place Bethel (House of God); however, formerly the name of the city had been Luz (Genesis 28:18-19).

This means that whenever we read of Bethel in Genesis, the people of that day called it Luz. Jacob stood outside the city and renamed it Bethel by faith, faith that someday Luz would indeed be a House of God. When Jacob came back into the land, he went again to Luz, and God again appeared to him.

> Then God went up from him in the place where He had spoken with him. And Jacob set up a pillar in the place where He had spoken with him, a pillar of stone, and he poured out a drink offering on it; he also poured oil on it and once again named the place Bethel (Genesis 35:13-15).

God's ascension from this spot is clearly to be associated with the ladder to heaven.

Thus, Jacob's stone pillars were symbols of God's holy mountain, the true ladder to heaven. In fact, Jacob explicitly called the pillar the "house of God": "And this stone, which I have set up as a pillar, will be God's house" (Genesis 28:22a). Jacob poured out wine at the pillar, just as he would have poured it out at an altar (cp. Numbers 15:1-10). He poured oil over it, just as the Mosaic House of God, the Tabernacle, would be permeated with oil (Exodus 40:9), and just as God's human house, His priest, would have oil poured on him (Leviticus 8:12). This oil represented God's cloud coming down on the mountain, filling the Tabernacle, anointing His new Adam. The Bible pulls this imagery together in Psalm 133:

Behold, how good and how pleasant it is
For brothers to dwell together in unity!
It is like the precious oil upon the head,
Coming down upon the beard, Aaron's beard,
Coming down upon the edge [mouth, top] of his robes.
It is like the dew of Hermon,
Coming down upon the mountains of Zion;
For there the Lord commanded the blessing:
Life forever!

Thus, the mist of God's cloud upon His mountain is parallel to the oil poured on Jacob's stone. It was a symbol that at the top of the holy mountain, the ladder to heaven, was the glory-cloud of God. Jacob performed this ritual, which seems so strange to our symbol-impoverished twentieth-century minds, in the sure and certain confidence that someday God's glorious cloud, His heavenly Kingdom, would come to earth. The cloud and the oil represent the Holy Spirit, the Bond of unity in the Kingdom. The descent of the cloud on the mountain, and of the oil on the pillar, find their typological fulfillment with the descent of the Spirit on our Lord at His baptism, and upon the Church at Pentecost.[16]

History and Decline

For a while, God's priestly nation was faithful to Him. They prospered despite tribulation. They had successful ministries with the Philistines, who were anxious to be led in worship by Abraham and Isaac (Genesis 21:22-34; 26:26-33). As a climax, God converted the Pharaoh of Egypt, and put Joseph in charge of the whole world.[17] When Joseph married the daughter of the priest of Heliopolis, we see a unification between the older Noahic Gentile priesthood and the new Abrahamic special priesthood.[18] During these years, the nation grew larger and larger, so that while only seventy from Jacob's immediate family went down into Egypt (Genesis 46:27), yet the number of people in the nation was so great that they had to be given the entire land of Goshen, the best of that Edenic land, to dwell in (Genesis 47:6; cf. 13:10).

After a prosperous season in Egypt, however, the people lapsed into idolatry (Joshua 24:14). God raised up a tyrant to scourge them, and thus put them into a crucible to restructure them. He tore apart the nation, reducing it to slavery, but only so that He could rebuild it again more glorious than before.

Conclusion

The patriarchal establishment was a relatively loose one. There was no national political organization, because the people existed under the government of other nations. Thus, in terms of analogical symbolism, there was no house or temple signifying them as God's people.

The patriarchs dwelt in tents. It is a myth to think of them as nomads, moving from place to place. Actually, the patriarchs lived in only a few places, and for years at a time. Abraham lived at Hebron for about twenty-five years, and at Beersheba in Gerar for about seventy-five years. If you live in a tent for such long periods of time, you obviously are not living in a teepee or a "Bedouin" tent. To get an idea of the patriarchal tent, we need look no further than the Tabernacle. Such tents had wooden boards for walls, embedded in sockets and held up with metal rods. They had wooden pillars separating various rooms. They were covered with roofs of water-tight leather. The only thing that made them "tents" was the fact that they had curtains along the walls (along with the boards), and the fact that they could, if necessary, be dismantled.

Thus, the patriarchal tent was a semi-permanent affair. The patriarchs were not constantly on the move. This means that the sanctuary-groves they set up were not meager affairs. If you live in a place for twenty-five years, it stands to reason that you will make your place of worship into something nice. The patriarchal worship-oasis was not a rude affair.

Nevertheless, even though the imagery is very Edenic, there is an important difference between the patriarchal worship-garden and the Garden of Eden. God planted the Garden of Eden. God set up that sanctuary. The patriarchal gardens were set up by men, though under divine guidance. Like Abraham's and Jacob's "shadow conquests" of the land, these sanctuary-oases were "shadow gardens." Not until Moses would God give explicit directions and take steps to plant His own garden-sanctuary in the earth.

In summary, the patriarchal establishment had the following features:

New Names:
      God: God Almighty
      People: Hebrews

Grant: Canaan (anticipated)

Promise: Your seed will possess it

Stipulations:
      Sacramental: Circumcision
      Societal: God's charge, commandments, statutes, and laws (Genesis 26:5)

Polity: Patriarchal family heads and worship leaders

Symbol: Oasis-Sanctuary

Though nature's strength decay,
And earth and hell withstand,
To Canaan's bound I urge my way,
At his command:
The wat'ry deep I pass,
With Jesus in my view:
And thro' the howling wilderness
My way pursue.

The goodly land I see,
With peace and plenty bless'd;
A land of sacred liberty,
And endless rest.
There milk and honey flow;
And oil and wine abound,
And trees of life forever grow,
With Mercy crown'd.

— Thomas Olivers
"The God of Abrah'm Praise," stanzas 5 and 6

THE WORLD OF
THE TABERNACLE

Psalm 102 tells us that the heavens and the earth eventually wear out, and have to be changed:

Of old Thou didst found the earth; and the heavens are the work of Thy hands. They themselves will perish, but Thou dost endure; and all of them will wear out like a garment; like clothing Thou wilt change them, and they will be changed (Psalm 102:25-26).

Whether the psalmist has in mind the physical heavens and earth, or the social polity of the world, is not immediately clear. Perhaps his language is designed to encompass both.[1] The principle he articulates, however, clearly applies to both; and it applies to the Abrahamic heavens and earth. They waxed old as the people grew into a nation. Eventually there were too many people to be ruled by simple clan structures. The people began to break out of the seams of the old heaven-and-earth garment.

God acted to change the garment. For one thing, once the people were reduced to slavery, the distinction between the blood line of Jacob and the multitudes of servants in the nation broke down.[2] All were servants now. When Israel came out of Egypt, we do not find an aristocracy of true-blooded Israelites dominating a plebeian class made up of the descendants of the servants, as probably would have been the case had God not put the nation through the crucible of enslavement. The result of this change was that government by patriarchs shifted into government by elders (Exodus 3:16; 4:29). Men of discernment rather than men of blood came to hold power in Israel.

Just as the social polity was forced to change, so was the symbolic polity. Living in cities during the period of slavery (Exodus 1:11), the Hebrews were not able to establish worship-oases. As a result, they began to worship at special tents set aside for the purpose. There is a clear reference to a special tent for God, a "tent of meeting," in Exodus 33:7-11. This passage cannot be referring to the Tabernacle because it had not yet been built.

These two changes in social and symbolic polity *anticipated* the new covenant that was to come, though in only a very rough way. As the Hebrews dreamed of freedom, they doubtless envisioned a return to the garden-oases of their fathers. God had something else in mind, something far more glorious, something they could not have envisioned. God would organize them as a nation around elders and judges, who at last would be able to serve as true magistrates. God would set up a symbolic polity in the form of a glorious tent of gold and precious tapestries.

Thus, God *laid hold* on the Hebrews, and *broke them down* in the fires of His refinement (Exodus 3:2,7). He then *restructured* them into a nation, giving them a new *name* (Israel instead of Hebrew), and revealing a new name for Himself (the Lord, the One who keeps the promises made to the fathers, Exodus 6:3-8).

The Mosaic Law

The Mosaic establishment, since it entailed a change in priesthood, also entailed a change in law (Hebrews 7:12). The sacramental law of the patriarchal establishment was circumcision. The center of the Mosaic sacramental law was Passover, though circumcision continued. Stemming from the Passover were all kinds of other sacramental laws.[3]

The center of the Mosaic social law was the Ten Commandments. Stemming from the Ten Commandments were all kinds of other social laws. One major change in social law instituted with Moses was an expansion of the laws of incest. Formerly, only cross-generational incest had been forbidden (Genesis 2:24; 19:30-38). Abraham had married his sister, just as Cain and Seth obviously had married theirs (Genesis 20:12). Jacob had married two sisters (Genesis 29:18-30). Now both brother-sister marriages and marrying two sisters were forbidden (Leviticus 18:6-18).

In making His people a nation, God gave them social laws as part of the Mosaic law. There is a good deal of misunderstanding about the Mosaic law in Christendom today. The three most common errors about the law are that it was harsh, was impossible to obey, and is irrelevant to us today.

Against the first misconception, that the law was harsh, we have to say that our God is a God of love. God never gave any mean, harsh, unreasonable, or cruel laws. God's laws, even those thundered from Sinai, were loving, joyous, peaceable, patient, kind, good, faith-filled, gentle, longsuffering, temperate, and spiritual. If they seem harsh to us, it is either because we have misinterpreted them, or because we are still looking at them from a secular humanistic perspective. We dare not, however, judge the Bible by our own modern standards.

Against the second misconception, that the laws were so tough, so demanding, and so stringent that nobody could ever keep them, we must say that this is not so. The Bible tells us that Zacharias and Elizabeth "were both righteous in the sight of God, walking blamelessly in all the commandments and requirements of the Lord" (Luke 1:6). Clearly, the law could be kept, and was kept by many godly people. True, they were not perfect, but they kept the law by bringing sacrifices to cover their sins.

Galatians 4:1 says that the people in the Old Covenant were like children, and Galatians 3:24 says that the law was like a tutor for children. The law, then, was a "simplified accommodation" for children. We expect more from adults than from children. Adults have greater responsibilities and are more accountable than children. Thus, the New Covenant law is actually much tougher to obey, because it makes so many demands on our inward attitudes.

Why do people think the Mosaic law was hard to keep? In general, it is because they do not know what the law really commanded, and because they have the Mosaic law confused with the rabbinical traditions of Judaism. The rabbinical traditions were a "heavy yoke" (Matthew 15:1-20; Mark 7:1-23; Acts 15:10; Matthew 23:4). Jesus called the people back to the Mosaic law, making it His own, and in doing so said that He was offering an "easy yoke" (Matthew 5:20-48; 11:29-30). We should, then, briefly look at the Mosaic law.

What about all those sacrifices, you may ask? There were the Burnt, Meal, Peace, Thank, Votive, Sin, Reparation, "Heave," and "Wave" Offerings, for starters. Some used salt, and some did not. Some used oil, and some did not. Some required a lamb; others, oxen; others, birds. Leavened bread was used with some, unleavened with others. Some parts of the animal were burned up, others given to the priests, and others were eaten by laymen. These things differed for each sacrifice. It was an awful lot of detail to master. The Israelite citizen, however, never offered any sacrifices himself. Only the priests were allowed to do the sacrifices, and they did them every day. They soon became familiar with all these details.

Compare the details of the complicated sacrificial system with the details of auto repair, and it suddenly becomes clear just how simple the priest's job was. How many different kinds of cars are there? Add on the fact that they change from year to year. Now consider all the different parts and aspects that can go wrong. Next time you take your car in, look at all the volumes of "Chilton" auto repair manuals that your mechanic keeps on hand, and compare their size and detail with the book of Leviticus. If your mechanic can learn to fix cars, and enjoy it, obviously the priests of Israel had no trouble managing the sacrificial system.

What about the sabbath? Wasn't that a burden? No, it was a time of rest. But weren't they forbidden to cook on the sabbath? No, they kept the sabbath as a feast. But weren't they forbidden recreation on the sabbath? No, the Bible nowhere says this. Well then, what did they do? They went to church to worship God at the synagogue (Leviticus 23:3), and relaxed the rest of the day. The sabbath was not an "impossible burden."[4]

What about all those cleansing rules in Leviticus 11–15? Well, in the first place, becoming unclean only meant one thing: You were not permitted to go into the forecourt of the Tabernacle and bring a sacrifice. Since most forms of uncleanness only lasted a day or a week, it was no real burden to be unclean. Second, if you were seriously unclean, you could make other people unclean for a few hours (until sundown) if you touched them; but again, that was only a matter of concern if the other person were on his way to offer a sacrifice. At the most, being unclean was an inconvenience. Of course, if you were unclean for months on end, and could not attend festivals, it became a more serious matter.

The laws of uncleanness were not hard to keep. You were to wash out a pot if a lizard fell into it and died. We would do the same today. You were not supposed to marry your sister, aunt, or child. Few of us would be tempted to. You were not supposed to eat dog-burgers or salted roast roaches. Most of us wouldn't either. That is because these are our customs, and we don't find them burdensome. If we were used to eating dog meat, as some cultures do, then the restriction would be temporarily burdensome until we got used to it. The Jews were not to eat pork either, but that was not hard for them. They were no more tempted to eat pork than we are to eat roaches.

So, the Mosaic law was not horribly complicated or impossible to keep. Of course, in the New Covenant we are not under the Mosaic law. The sacrifice of Jesus Christ replaces all the sacrifices of Moses. Christ has cleansed the world once and for all in His Resurrection, and so the laws of uncleanness no longer apply to us. That is, they no longer apply as laws. In terms of their symbolism, they still provide wisdom.

That does not mean that the law is irrelevant, however, which is the third common misconception. The Mosaic law has been ignored by the Church for a couple of centuries. In reaction against this, some have taken up the Mosaic social laws as a virtual blueprint for modern society.[5] The proper middle ground is to understand the typological nature of the Mosaic economy. The Old Covenant is a type of the New, and the Mosaic establishment, like the other establishments we are looking at, is a type of the Kingdom of Christ. As a type, it is filled with wisdom for us.[6]

A proper approach to the Mosaic law asks four questions. First, it asks what this law meant in the Old Covenant. Second, it asks how this law was fulfilled in Jesus Christ. Third, it asks how this law is to be fulfilled in the Church, which is in union with Christ. And fourth, it asks what relevance this law may have in shaping wider society outside the Church. If we keep such a procedure in mind, the Mosaic laws can be of great value to us; and we can avoid the dangers of legalism on the one side, and antinomianism on the other.

Remember that a *type* is something that makes an *imprint*. If we allow the Mosaic law to imprint itself on our hearts, meditating on its Old and New Covenant significance, we will acquire inner wisdom; and this inner wisdom will enable us to apply God's fundamental principles creatively to modern problems, many of which are not explicitly dealt with in the law (for instance, pornography).

The Mosaic Polity

We turn now to the social "heavens and earth" of Israel under the Mosaic establishment. There was a clear separation of "church" and "state" in the Mosaic covenant. Only the family of Aaron could serve as priests in the Tabernacle, and only the tribe of Levi could assist them. This meant that no officer of the state could be an officer of the church, and separated the two institutions definitively (cf. 2 Chronicles 26:16-19). The law distinguished between civil punishments on the one hand, and ecclesiastical ones, such as "cutting off from the people," or excommunication, on the other.[7]

The civil polity of Israel had been anticipated during the Egyptian sojourn, and consisted of elders who served as judges. When Israel came out of Egypt, she had never before been a nation in the sense of having a civil order. Her elders had simply been "leading men." Now, however, a system of courts was needed. God brought Jethro to help them set it up (Exodus 18). Jethro was a Noahic priest-king (Exodus 2:16; 18:12), head of the Kenite branch of the Midianite nation (Genesis 25:2; Exodus 2:16; Judges 1:16; contrast Numbers 22:4; Numbers 25; 31). Jethro was Moses' father-in-law, and for forty years Moses had observed Jethro managing a nation (Acts 7:30). Thus, Moses had been trained in civil government. Under Jethro's God-inspired advice, Moses set up a series of judges and appeals courts in Israel: elders over tens, fifties, hundreds, and thousands, with himself as Supreme Judge.

Moses' successor was Joshua, and after him came other judges, some who oversaw the entire nation, and others who judged in more localized areas. None of these judges was a king, and those who aspired to be were thwarted.[8] None had a standing army or "praetorian guard." Rather, in time of military distress they had to depend exclusively on the Israelite voluntary militia.[9] The last of these judges was Samuel, who presided over the dissolution of the Mosaic establishment, and who laid the foundation for the new Davidic establishment that replaced it.

In the patriarchal establishment, as we have seen, there were many garden-oasis sanctuaries set up by men. These were places of routine worship and sacrifice. In the Mosaic establishment, the patriarchal-oasis church was divided into two institutions: Tabernacle and synagogue. The synagogue continued the patriarchal tradition of being set up in many places at the determination and design of men. The Tabernacle continued the patriarchal-sanctuary in that in the Tabernacle architecture, the altars, trees, and wells of the patriarchs were woven into an organized structure. The Tabernacle, however, was expressly designed by God, and was located at His command, the new location being indicated by the movement of the glory-cloud.

The sacrificial worship, focused at the three annual festivals, was centralized at the Tabernacle. Only the priests might approach the altar and the Tent to offer sacrifice and to maintain the Tent. The Levites were set apart as guards and helpers of the Tabernacle area. By way of contrast, the worship of preaching and prayers was decentralized into local synagogues, pastored by Levites who lived in the towns (Deuteronomy 14:27, 29; Judges 17:7; 19:1).

For the most part, scholars use the term "synagogue" to refer to the highly structured institution that had developed by the time of our Lord, and that continues in Judaism today. According to Jewish tradition, this synagogue structure was established by Ezra, but it is more likely that it developed later than Ezra's time. Unfortunately, focusing on the New Testament synagogue has often blinded Bible students to the clear statements of the Old Testament to the effect that there were centers of worship (not of sacrifice) throughout Israel. Such houses of prayer were places of "holy convocation," which was required every sabbath (Leviticus 23:3). Worship services were also held on the new moons (2 Kings 4:23). During the Mosaic period, the Levites were the pastors of these local churches. I don't know what we should call them unless we call them "synagogues," and so that is what I shall call them in this book.

The synagogue was the place of sabbath day worship, and came into existence with the Mosaic Exodus. It is unclear whether or how the Hebrews kept the sabbath day before Sinai. God rested on the seventh day, after completing the world. There is a sense in which the new world, begun at the Flood, was not completed until Moses, since there was no new garden-sanctuary until that time. Perhaps God did not reinstitute the sabbath in its fullness until then. Given the hebdomadal (seven-day) patterns in Genesis, it is reasonable to infer that the Patriarchs worshipped on the sabbath (e.g., Genesis 7:10, 12). There is little evidence to suggest that the sabbath, at least in its Mosaic form, was binding on the Noahic nations.[10]

It is surely doubtful, however, that the Hebrews were able to observe the sabbath during the Egyptian bondage. Thus, the sabbath as a day of rest, festivity, and worship became a distinct and wonderful blessing of the Mosaic exodus. The book of Exodus is organized in terms of a passage from slavery to sabbath. The Book of the Covenant, Exodus 21–23, starts and ends with sabbath laws.[11] Deuteronomy 5:15 says that the reason for keeping the sabbath was to memorialize not only the creation, but also the exodus. Thus, the creation of the synagogue parallels the establishment of the weekly sabbath.

The Symbolic Polity

In the wilderness, God had his holy army, the militia, camp around Him in a special symbolic array. It is important for us to consider this, because it correlates to certain features of the design of the Tabernacle, the symbol of the body politic. The Book of Numbers shows Israel as God's host, His army (Numbers 1:2-3). When Israel encamped, the Aaronic priests were positioned on the east side of the Tabernacle, as guardians of the door (which was on the east). Around the Tabernacle on the other three sides were the three groups of Levites. As an outer ring of warrior guards were the twelve tribes, carefully positioned on the four sides (see Numbers 2, 3; also see Diagram 15.1). In this way, the army clearly formed a human tabernacle for God's dwelling (cp. Exodus 23:17; 34:23; Deuteronomy 16:16).

Diagram 15.1
The Israelite Camp

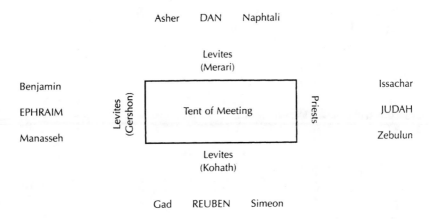

Asher   DAN   Naphtali

Levites
(Merari)

Benjamin   Levites (Gershon)   Tent of Meeting   Priests   Issachar

EPHRAIM   JUDAH

Manasseh   Zebulun

Levites
(Kohath)

Gad   REUBEN   Simeon

Meredith G. Kline has written that God's "house-building, as depicted in Exodus, is of two kinds. There is first the structuring of the people themselves into a formally organized house of Israel."[12] This took place in Exodus 18–24, with Jethro's reorganization of the nation, the giving of the Ten Commandments, and the giving of the social laws of the Book of the Covenant. Then,

> having narrated the building of this living house of God's habitation, the Book of Exodus continues with an account of the building of the other, more literal house of Yahweh, the tabernacle. . . . Though a more literal house than the living house of Israel, the tabernacle-house was designed to function as symbolical of the other; the kingdom-people-house was the true residence of God (a concept more fully explored and spiritualized in the New Testament). The Book of Exodus closes by bringing together these two covenant-built houses in a summary statement concerning Yahweh's abiding in the glory-cloud in his tabernacle-house "in the sight of all the house of Israel" (40:34-38).[13]

This brings us to a consideration of the Tabernacle as the symbol for the Mosaic establishment. There are five aspects of the Tabernacle we wish to consider. First, the Tabernacle was a house for God. Second, since the universe of heaven and earth is God's house, the Tabernacle symbolized the heavens and the earth. Third, the Tabernacle was a holy mountain, specifically reproducing the configuration of Mount Sinai. Fourth, since God's house is His people, the Tabernacle symbolized the body politic of Israel at this stage of history. And fifth, since the people-house started out "in Adam" and eventually came to be "in Christ," and since Christ is the True Israel, the Tabernacle also symbolized the righteous individual person, and as such was a type of Christ.[14]

The Tabernacle as God's House

First of all, the Tabernacle was a place for God to dwell. The innermost chamber, the Most Holy, was His throne-room. God sat enthroned upon the wings of the cherubim, with His feet resting on the mercy seat.[15] Into this room only one man, the High Priest, could go, and only once a year, to clean the foot-stool (Leviticus 16:14-15). This was basically to prevent God from becoming displeased, lest He remove His feet from the foot-stool and depart from Israel, thus withdrawing His protection.

The outer room, the Holy Place, was the living area of the tent. In it were three pieces of furniture. There was a lamp to give light. There was a dinner table with bread on it. And there was an incense platform. We today use potpourri and scent-sprays to make our homes smell nice. In the ancient world, be-fore flush toilets were developed and when animals lived very close at hand, the noisome smells were stronger, and people burned incense regularly to make their homes smell nice.

Outside the tent was the kitchen area. Before the days of gas and electric ovens, people who could afford it put their kitchens in rooms off to the side, or even in a separate building. Just so, the kitchen was outside the Tabernacle. Here the animals were slaughtered, gutted, and skinned. They were washed in the sink (the laver) and cooked on the altar.

Such was God's tent, His house. God did not want His house to become dirty, of course. It had to be kept clean, because if the people let it get too run down and filthy, God would leave. Now, while doubtless physical dirt was wiped off of the Tabernacle fur-niture, it was mainly moral filth and ceremonial "uncleanness" that defiled His house. (After all, the soil under the Tabernacle was "holy ground" and thus was cleansed from the curse of Genesis 3.) The purpose of the purification offerings of Leviticus 4 and 5 was to cleanse the house of these defilements. Blood was put on those parts of the house that had become unclean, blood being the sacrificial "detergent." The Tabernacle curtains, for instance, if defiled with ceremonial dirt, had to be washed (sprinkled) with blood.

The Tabernacle as Cosmic House

The Bible tells us that the Tabernacle and its courtyard symbolized the heavens and the earth, God's dwelling places.[16] Heaven was God's throne, and the earth His footstool (Isaiah 66:1; Matthew 5:35; Acts 7:49). This was set out in two ways in the Tabernacle. In the Most Holy Place, the heavenly throne was pictured by the winged cherubim. God sat enthroned on the outspread wings of the cherubim, with His feet on the mercy seat that covered the Ark of the Covenant. Thus, the Ark of the Covenant with its mercy seat lid had to do with the earth and humanity as God's footstool.

Second, the whole Tabernacle proper was a model of heaven (Hebrews 8:5; 9:23-25). The Most Holy Place itself was a model of the highest heavens, with the firmament or earthly heavens pictured in the Holy Place, and the earth pictured in the courtyard. (See Diagrams 15.2 and 15.3.) The courtyard altar was the holy mountain that reached toward the sky, pictured in the Holy Place behind the first veil, a veil of sky blue. Associated with the holy mountain was the laver of cleansing, which means that the laver is to be connected with the waters of Eden (Genesis 2:10-14). As we pass through the firmament-heavens of the Holy Place, we come to a second altar, which is as it were a second ladder stretching from the firmament-heavens to the highest heavens. Beyond the cherubic second veil, behind this golden altar was the Most Holy Place, the Highest Heavens.

The courtyard thus represented the earthly garden-sanctuary. Adam had been cast from this sanctuary; and it was only under very tight restrictions, codified in the laws of cleanness, that anyone might be admitted to it in the Mosaic system. Even so, the layman might only come into the forecourt. He

Diagram 15.2
The Tabernacle Complex

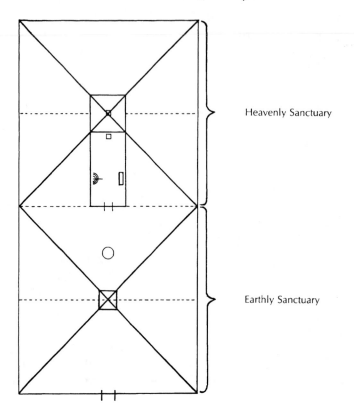

Heavenly Sanctuary

Earthly Sanctuary

The Bible nowhere explicitly says that the Ark of the Covenant is to be positioned in the center of the heaven half, and the altar in the center of the earthly half of the Tabernacle complex. Doubtless, depending on the terrain of a given encampment, these things might have been positioned differently. At the same time, however, the dimensions of everything connected with the Tabernacle tend to come in squares or double-squares, and so the configuration illustrated above is symbolically the most appropriate. After all, if you had a chance to set it up in a flat place, would you do it any other way? Notice how this arrangement brings out the correspondence between altar and Ark. The altar or holy mountain is the center of the earth, and the Throne of God is the center of heaven.

Diagram 15.3
Environments

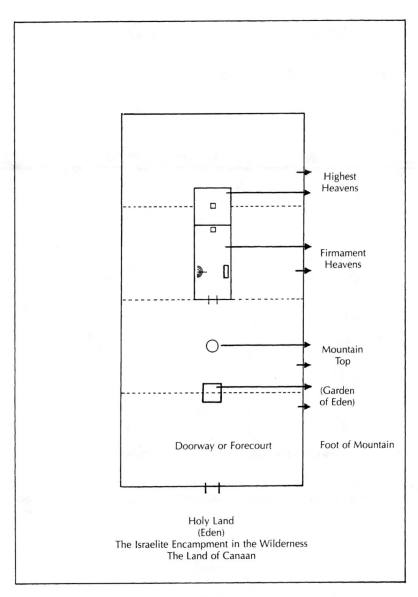

Highest
Heavens

Firmament
Heavens

Mountain
Top

(Garden
of Eden)

Doorway or Forecourt   Foot of Mountain

Holy Land
(Eden)
The Israelite Encampment in the Wilderness
The Land of Canaan

World

Diagram 15.4
Environments

Place	Symbol	Occupant	Guardian	Furniture	Tabernacle Garment	Boundary Shield
Highest Heavens	Most Holy	God	Cherubim (High Priest)	Ark Mercy Seat	1/2 Tabernacle Curtain	Inner Veil
Firma-ment Heavens	Holy Place	God	Priests (High Priest) (Cherubim)	Altar Lamp Table	1/2 Tabernacle Curtain	Outer Veil
Garden	Court-yard	(Priests)[1]	Levites (Priests)	Laver Altar	Tent Curtain	Court Curtain
Eden	Canaan	Israel	Israel Army	Dwellings (Lev. 11)[2]	Red Ramskin	River & Boundary[3]
World	World	Gentiles	Gentiles	Dwellings	Dolphin	Four Corners of the Earth

Notes:
[1]Adam and Eve were living in the garden, but were kicked out. The temporary and partial privilege of the priests to dwell there pictured man's eventual return to that estate.

[2]The dwellings of the Israelites had to be clean. Dead animals defiled them. Leprosy defiled them. They had to be cleansed annually of all old leaven before Passover.

[3]The importance of these boundaries is highlighted by the huge attention given them in Joshua 15-22. Note also the symbolic boundaries in Ezekiel 48.

This information is taken from James B. Jordan, "From Glory to Glory: Degrees of Value in the Sanctuary," and summarizes the material presented there.

was forbidden on pain of death to approach the holy mountain of the altar.

The area outside the courtyard was the camp of Israel, and later the Holy Land. This corresponds to the land of Eden, the homeland of the priests. Canaan also had very carefully set boundaries, and these boundaries were also guarded (Joshua 13–21). In this case, the guards were the Israelites themselves, a nation of priests. The land of Israel could never be owned permanently by anyone except Israelites, for it reverted to its Israelite owners every fifty years (Leviticus 25). Thus, except for the cities, no one but an Israelite was allowed to dwell in the land. Finally, outside the land was the world — the world of the Gentiles, converted and unconverted. The converted Gentile did not need to be circumcised and become an Israelite, but could remain a Noahic believer. Such Gentiles were welcome at the Feast of Tabernacles, but they could not live in the holy land.

Thus, we have five environments: highest heavens, firmament-heavens, garden-sanctuary, holy land, and world (see Diagram 15.4). A full study of this would reveal the following degrees of holiness:[17]

Highest Heaven/the Most Holy Place:
   God
   Cherubim and angels

Firmament-Heavens/the Holy Place:
   High Priest
   Priests

Garden of Eden/Sanctuary Courtyard:
   Tabernacle Courtyard/War Camp/Nazirites
   Levitical Cities/Wilderness War Camp

Eden/Homeland:
   Cities/Wilderness Camp
   The Land of Israel

World:
   Converted Nations
   Apostate Nations

The Holy Place, or firmament-heavens, is of particular interest. The seven lamps of the lampstand can readily be associated with stars, as Revelation 1:20 makes explicit. It can be suggested, though not proved, that the seven stars are to be associated with the seven planets of the ancient world. The planets were the "stars" that moved, and the Tabernacle was portable. Another suggestion is to associate the seven lamps with the seven sisters of the Pleiades (Job 9:9; 38:31; Amos 5:8).[18]

The twelve loaves of showbread on the table of showbread should be correlated to the manna that rained upon Israel from heaven during the wilderness sojourn (Nehemiah 9:15; John 6:31). As the people ate this heavenly bread, they were symbolically transformed into a heavenly people. They became the "stars" of the Abrahamic promise.

Finally, the cloud of smoke arising from the altar of incense is to be associated with God's glory-cloud, as it appeared in the firmament-heavens (Exodus 19:18). Incense has to do with prayer, and the glory-cloud environment is an environment of ceaseless angelic prayer (Isaiah 6:3-4; Revelation 5:8).

It is very interesting to note that synagogue buildings dating from the early Christian era very often have three sections of mosaics on their floors, stretching from the door to the front. The first mosaic is generally nondescript; but the one at the Beth Alpha synagogue is a picture of the sacrifice of Isaac, clearly a courtyard, holy-mountain theme. The second mosaic, occupying the center of the hall, is almost invariably a zodiac. The third mosaic, at the front, is a "sacred portal," filled with imagery of the highest heavens. Obviously the zodiac has to do with the firmament-heavens, in this sequence derived from the Tabernacle and Temple. Similar zodiacs are found in early Christian churches.[19]

The Tabernacle as Holy Mountain

While the altar in the Tabernacle complex was a holy mountain, leading toward heaven, in a wider sense the entire Tabernacle complex was a holy mountain, or extended ladder to heaven. What makes this clear is the connection between the Tabernacle and Mount Sinai. We have already noted that the three-storied Ark of Noah was a world model, a model that transferred itself to the three-storied configuration of the world after the Flood. We see the same thing here: Mount Sinai was a world model that transferred itself to the Tabernacle. When the people left Mount Sinai, they took the Mountain with them.[20]

God's cloud covered the top of the mountain, thus establishing it as a Most Holy Place. Moses and Moses alone was allowed to enter this place, just as later on only the High Priest would be allowed to enter the Most Holy of the Tabernacle (Exodus 19:19-24). At the top of the mountain God gave the Ten Commandments, which were later put in the Most Holy Place of the Tabernacle.

Midway down the mountain was the Holy Place. Only the elders of Israel were allowed to go into this area, and there they ate a meal with God. These elders were the "sun, moon, and stars" of the nation, and correlate with the lampstand. The meal they ate correlates with the table of shewbread. The elders themselves correlate with the Aaronic priests, who alone might enter the Tabernacle Holy Place. While the elders ate, "they saw the God of Israel; and under His feet there appeared to be a pavement of sapphire, as clear as the sky itself" (Exodus 24:10). The blue sapphire pavement is equivalent to the veil that separated the Holy Place from the Most Holy.

The courtyard of the mountain was marked off with a boundary, and anyone who trespassed was put to death (Exodus 19:12). Inside this boundary was placed an altar, and only certain select young men might approach it (Exodus 24:4, 5; cp. 19:22, 24). The priests at this point were the firstborn sons, who had been saved by God at Passover. When they fell into sin at the golden calf, they were replaced by the Levites and the sons of Aaron, who thereafter took care of the sacrifices at the altar (Exodus 32:28-29; Numbers 8:14-18). The boundary around the mountain correlates to the boundary inside the courtyard that kept the people from approaching the altar.[21]

In this way, then, the Tabernacle (and later the Temple) were models of the ladder to heaven, of the holy mountain. Israel did not need to go back to Mount Sinai, or regard it as anything special, after the Tabernacle was built. The Tabernacle was God's portable mountain.

The Tabernacle as Symbol of the Body Politic

More than this, however, the Tabernacle symbolized humanity as God's true environment. The Tabernacle was a symbol of the Israelite body politic (1 Corinthians 3:16). For this reason, when the citizens of Israel sinned or became symbolically unclean, corresponding invisible marks "appeared" in the Tabernacle. The more unclean the people became, the more unclean the Tabernacle, its furniture, vessels, curtains, pillars, etc. became. To cleanse the Tabernacle, then, symbolized cleansing the people (cp. Exodus 24:4, 8). Only a cleansed people could draw near to God, and God would remain dwelling only in the midst of a cleansed people. Only a cleansed people could form a throne for God, so that He would be willing to sit enthroned on the praises of Israel, His feet resting on them (Psalm 22:3).

Ultimately, then, the entire tent was symbolic. The veils signified ranks of guardians around the Throne, places where God's "feet" would rest. The veils of cloth became defiled when the people they represented became defiled. To cleanse the people, blood was put on the veils, and on the altars and mercy seat. [22]

The ranks of guardians stood to keep people away from God, lest God either become angry and destroy them, or become even angrier and pack up and move out, leaving His House desolate and abominated, and leaving His people to their doom (Ezekiel 8-11). Thus, these ranks of guardians were *shoes* between God and the cursed soil of humanity. Accordingly, the veils were also *shoes*. The outermost veil was significantly made of the same stuff as fine shoes: dolphin leather, and this correlation is made plain in the allegory of Ezekiel 16:10, "I clothed you with embroidered cloth, and put sandals of dolphin leather on your feet; and I wrapped you with fine linen and covered you with silk." Except for the silk, this is a description of the Tabernacle and its veils.

The only kind of people God would permit to draw near to Him were people who properly imaged Him (Genesis 1:26). Such people also needed to be shod. Of course, since the Tabernacle was set up on holy ground, they did not have to wear shoes there, but they had to wear shoes everywhere else.

As we have seen in Chapter 8, the animals that symbolized God's holy people were all animals who wore shoes or who were particular about where they set their feet. If a man ate an unshod animal, he became symbolically unshod himself, and could not enter the sanctuary precincts to offer sacrifice.

The three zones of the Tabernacle complex symbolized three groups of people. If the High Priest sinned, blood had to be sprinkled on the Ark in the Most Holy Place (Leviticus 16:11-14). If a regular priest sinned, blood was sprinkled on the veil and on the golden altar in the Holy Place. Thus, the Holy Place furniture was closely associated with the priests as the "heavens" of Israel. If the congregation as a whole sinned, this also defiled the Holy Place, which meant that the congregation as a whole was a "heavenly people" to the nations of the world (Leviticus 4:1-21). If a citizen sinned, blood was put on the courtyard altar, and this was also the case if a civil leader sinned (Leviticus 4:22-35). Now, all of the above were for "unintentional" sins. Once a year, atonement was made for the "high-handed" sins of the congregation; and on this occasion, blood was put on the Ark in the Most Holy Place (Leviticus 16:15-16).

What emerges from this is a series of associations, a societal worldview. The congregation is associated with the highest heavens, with the firmament-heavens, and with the courtyard. They are both stars and dust, both heavens and earth, both cherubic veil and altar of earth. The High Priest, as supreme spiritual ruler, is associated with the Most Holy; the lesser priests, with the Holy Place; and civil leaders, with the courtyard. The priests rule in "heavenly things" and the leaders rule in "earthly things."

Once we understand that the Tabernacle was a symbol of Israelite society, there are all kinds of correlations that can be made. The Inner Veil of the Most Holy has to do with God's angelic guardians. The Outer Veil of the Holy Place has to do with the priestly guardians. The goat's hair tent curtain over the Tabernacle has to do with the courtyard and the Levites. The red ramskin cover that was on top of the goat's hair tent curtain is to be associated with Passover, and thus with all Israel, who were claimed at Passover. The dolphin leather cover has to do with the Gentiles — dolphin being a *sea* creature.[23] Interesting as it would be to go on with this, looking at the gold and bronze utensils and other features of the Tabernacle complex, we must move on. We shall consider the altar as a symbol of the body politic in more detail in Chapter 16. The point that has been established and illustrated is that the Tabernacle complex symbolized

Israelite society. When the Tabernacle complex is torn apart, in 1 Samuel, it symbolizes the rending of Israelite society.

The Tabernacle as Human Person

Finally, the Tabernacle symbolized the righteous man, the heavenly man, the man made in God's own heavenly image (John 1:14; 2:21; 1 Corinthians 6:19).[24] We ought not to think of this as a visual symbol, so that the Most Holy Place is the head and the altar the feet. Rather, the Tabernacle symbolized the person in a more holistic fashion. The Most Holy Place symbolized the innermost parts of the man, both head and heart. The Holy Place had to do with the senses, while the courtyard had to do with the outer man, the skin.

Jesus said that "the lamp of the body is the eye; if therefore your eye is clear, your whole body will be full of light; but if your eye is bad, your whole body will be full of darkness" (Matthew 6:22-23a). There is a kind of inverted metaphor here. Lamps shine forth light, but eyes take light in. The rest of Jesus' statement is forcefully symbolic also: If our eye is good, the light fills our body with light. This can immediately be related to the lampstand in the Tabernacle, which filled the house with light. The righteous man lets the light of God's glory fill his body, his life.

But what is true of the eye is also true of the other organs, also. If the lamp of the body is the eye, then the incense of the body is the nose. If our nose is unstopped, our body will be filled with incense. Similarly, the food of the body is the mouth. If our taste is good, our body will be filled with God's heavenly manna and showbread. Let us also recall that the high priest always wore bells when he entered the Holy Place (Exodus 28:34-35). The bell of the body is the ear. If our ear is clear, our body will be filled with God's glorious voice.

All these things relate to God's glory-cloud. The cloud made a wonderful sound, replicated in the bells. It was a cloud, replicated by the sweet cloud of incense. It shone with light, copied by the lamp. And it rained manna, copied by the table of bread. As Kline has shown, the cloud signified the Spirit of God.[25] So then, the righteous man is filled with God's cloud, His presence, His Spirit. The Holy Place symbolizes the sensory avenues by which God's life comes to His righteous man. The man filled with light is wise. The man filled with music is permeated by the voice of God's Word. The man filled with incense is a man of prayer. The man filled with manna is filled with life.

The Ark in the inner room symbolized the heart and mind. It contained the law, as the law was to be written on the heart. It also contained a pot of manna, showing God's life within the heart. Finally, Aaron's rod that blossomed, a picture of prayer, was found within the heart. God's throne of glory was over the Ark, showing that the righteous man has God enthroned on his heart. As head or mind, the Ark pictured leadership, the self-control of the righteous man.[26]

The righteous man's outer life was symbolized by the Courtyard. The laver showed that the righteous man lives a clean and moral public life; and the altar showed that the righteous man is a man who worships in public, not just in his heart.

Conclusion

A worldview is a complex thing. It is as broad and complex as the world itself. The Tabernacle complex, the description of which covers over a thousand verses, was a world model, and thus was very rich. We have only scratched the surface of the marvels to be found there. Even so, we may have become somewhat lost in the details, so let us summarize the nature of the Mosaic establishment.

New Names:	
God:	The Lord (Yahweh or Jehovah), the God who keeps the promises made to the fathers.
People:	Israel comes to replace Hebrews as the prevailing term.
Grant:	The land of Canaan.
Promise:	God will be with them, in their midst.
Stipulations:	
Sacramental:	Passover, and the whole sacrificial, uncleanness, and festival system.

Societal:	The Ten Commandments, and the Mosaic Law as a whole, both as it symbolized society (Tabernacle and sacrifice) and as it legislated for society (the "case laws" of Exodus and Deuteronomy).
Polity:	Separation of Church and state.
Church:	Priests at Tabernacle, Levites at synagogues.
State:	Local elders, with judges at the top.
Symbol:	The Tabernacle complex.

There dwells the Lord our King,
THE LORD OUR RIGHTEOUSNESS
(Triumphant o'er the world and sin),
The Prince of Peace;
On Zion's sacred height,
His Kingdom still maintains;
And glorious with his saints in light,
Forever reigns.

—Thomas Olivers
"The God of Abrah'm Praise," stanza 7

THE WORLD OF
THE TEMPLE

After Israel had been settled in the land for a while, the Mosaic heavens and earth began to wear thin. Once again, the nation began to break out of the seams of the covenantal garment, and a new covenant began to be anticipated.

The History and Decline of the Mosaic Establishment

In terms of social polity, Israel was governed by elders over tens, fifties, hundreds, and thousands, with one or more Supreme Judge as final court of appeal. These judges also led the people in war when the nation was attacked. As the nation developed, however, and the population increased, there was more and more of a national spirit developing. Actually, a two-nation spirit developed, with a Northern Israel ethos centered in Ephraim, and a Southern Israel ethos centered in Judah. God had said that eventually a king would come out of Judah, but only when He was ready (Genesis 49:10). For a long time, most of Judah was disqualified to hold public office, because they were descendants of bastards (Genesis 38), and bastards were excluded from public office until the tenth generation (Deuteronomy 23:2). Accordingly, none of the judges in the book of Judges was from Judah. The genealogy at the end of Ruth is designed to show that there were ten generations between Perez and David, so that David was a legitimate Judahite King.[1] Still, Israel failed to see the Lord as their true King, and lusted after human kings (Judges 8:22-23; 9:6; 11:9; 17:6; 18:1; 19:1; 21:25).[2] Their desire for a human king was thus both an anticipation of the next covenant, and also a symptom of moral decline.

In terms of symbolic polity, we see the Tabernacle turning into a Temple. The Hebrew word for *temple* also means *palace*, and God's Temple was simply His earthly Palace. Such a Palace-Temple is associated, however, with the time of Israel's kings, for they too dwelt in palaces. The Tent of God corresponded to Israel's dwelling in tents. Once Israel settled in the land, and built houses, it was natural for the Tabernacle to become more houselike, and less tentlike. Since the Tabernacle stayed in one place for a long time, it was natural for other buildings to be built around it for storage, to house Levitical assistants, to house the increasingly extended family of Aaronic priests, and for other purposes. Thus, the Tabernacle at Shiloh grew into a temple complex, and the area was called "the temple of the Lord" (1 Samuel 1:9; 3:3). Of course, the Tabernacle itself continued to be what it had always been: a tent of curtains and boards set in sockets on the ground. The outlying buildings, however, created a palace complex.

What was to come could not be envisioned, of course. Israelite political philosophers doubtless meditated on the king to come, but had no idea that he would sustain as close a relationship with the Lord as came to pass. They may not have realized that the king would have a small professional permanent army.[3] Certainly they would not have guessed that the country would be divided up into administrative tax districts that were different from the tribal divisions (1 Kings 4:7-19). Just so, Israelite liturgists may have speculated on a fuller temple to come; but they would have had no idea that the laver would turn into a huge bronze ocean riding on the backs of twelve bulls, or that there would be ten golden lampstands in the Holy Place, with silver lampstands in the courtyard, or that there would be ten water "chariots" in the courtyard, or that there would be two huge pillars on either side of the door (1 Kings 6-7; 1 Chronicles 28:11-19; 2 Chronicles 3-4). These new features were not simple extrapolations of Tabernacle symbolism, but were radical transformations of it.

The Breakdown of the Mosaic Cosmos

After the glory days of Joshua, the nation of Israel entered into a long period of slow decline. There were times of apostasy and times of revival, but basically the course was that of decline.

These were the preliminary judgments. The depth of the decline came when Israel was defeated by Philistia and the Ark was taken into captivity. God also slew the High Priest and his sons (1 Samuel 4). This was the full judgment on the Mosaic establishment.

The final judgment on the Old Covenant is always simultaneously an announcement of a new one, as we have seen. It was at this juncture of history that God intervened to raise up messiahs to restore the nation. Two men were miraculously born of barren wombs, both of whom would be Nazirites, special warrior priests, all their lives. These two men were Samson and Samuel.[4] Both men entered into their ministries at about the age of twenty, the age of citizenship and military service (Numbers 1:3).

As we have already seen in Chapter 14, the Ark plagued the Egyptians and made an Exodus out of Philistia with spoils (1 Samuel 5-6). This was the initial defeat of Philistia, but it took twenty years for Samson and Samuel to rebuild the nation to the point where they could inflict a major military defeat on the Philistines. For twenty years Samson caused the Philistines to appear ridiculous by making sport of them, while Samuel toured the country teaching the Bible and raising up a new, righteous generation.[5] At the end of his career, Samson killed all five princes of the Philistines, and most of the Philistine priesthood and nobility (Judges 16:23, 27). With their leadership destroyed, the Philistines were easily defeated by Israel at the battle of Mizpah (1 Samuel 7:9-11).

The crucible of enslavement to Philistia (and remember, Philistines were Egyptians, Genesis 10:13-14) had the effect of rending the fabric of the Mosaic establishment. The Israelite judge, Samson, had to spend most of his time in hiding, while Samuel had to lay low. As a result, the system of judgeship in Israel tended to break down. Also, during the captivity, the Philistines removed all the weapons of the Israelite militia. The battle of Mizpah was won only by a miracle (1 Samuel 7:10). Even after this victory, Israel was still dominated by Philistia, though not enslaved; and she still had no weapons (1 Samuel 13:19-22).

As a result of this situation, the people demanded a king. Their fabricated pretext was that Samuel's sons were not performing very well as judges. We notice, however, that these young men were judging in Beersheba, on the border of Israel,

about as far away from the center of national life as you could
get. Moreover, their offense was bribe-taking, which was nowhere near as serious as the offense of Eli's sons a generation earlier (1 Samuel 2:12-17, 22-25). In addition, all the elders of Israel
needed to do was ask that the men be removed from office. Instead they demanded a king (1 Samuel 8).

They wanted a king like the kings of the other nations, "that
we also may be like all the nations" (1 Samuel 8:20). This was
not the kind of king God had in mind for them. God's king
would be a shepherd, like David. He would rule by service, as
the servant of the people. The kind of king they wanted, though,
would rule through fear and domination, and would tax the people to death. Jesus summed up the difference this way:

> You know that those who are recognized as rulers of the Gentiles
> lord it over them; and their great men exercise authority over
> them. But it is not so among you, but whoever wishes to become
> great among you shall be your servant; and whoever wishes to
> be first among you shall be slave of all (Mark 10:42-43).

The crucible of Philistine enslavement also tore up the symbolic polity of Israel. When the Ark returned to the land, it was
not placed back in the Tabernacle, but was enshrined at Kiriath-
jearim. We are not told why this was, but Samuel was the leader
in Israel at this point, and it must have been under his guidance
that it was done. Not until the Temple was built, a century later,
was the Ark restored to a House of God. During this century,
when there was no central sanctuary, the people were permitted
to offer sacrifices at "high places," local "holy mountains" analogous to the oasis-sanctuaries of the Patriarchs (1 Kings 3:2; and
cf. 1 Samuel 6:15; 7:16-17; 9:12-13; 10:5, 8, 13; 11:14-15; 16:3-5;
20:6, 29; 2 Samuel 15:12). Later, when the Temple was set up,
this kind of high place worship was no longer acceptable (Deuteronomy 12:13-14; 1 Kings 15:14; 22:43; 2 Kings 12:3; etc.). For
now, however, the nation was clearly torn apart, with no center.

I believe that the rending of the Tabernacle should be associated with the rending of the animal in the sacrificial system. It is
a picture of death, and the building of the Temple is a picture of
resurrection. Nereparampil has shown that in John's Gospel,
Jesus is pictured as "tabernacling" with His people before His

death, and as a "temple" in His resurrection.[6] Thus, what Israel experienced under God's judgment was a kind of death, and under His grace, a kind of resurrection. The Temple would be a glorified Tabernacle, a resurrection body if you will.

The Building of the Kingdom

The empty Tabernacle was moved to Nob (1 Samuel 21:1) and later to Gibeon (1 Chronicles 16:39-40). The priests maintained it as a vacant house for God. Once Saul became king, perhaps God would have moved back into a tent. But Saul fell from grace almost as soon as he was crowned, and the Philistines continued to oppress Israel.[7] This corresponds to the wilderness period of Israel after she rejected God's offer to conquer Canaan, and David's wilderness wanderings illustrate this.[8] After David defeated the Philistines, and Israel could settle down once again, God moved back into a tent; but even when David moved the Ark to Jerusalem, he set up a separate tent for it, and did not move the Tabernacle there (1 Chronicles 16:1, 37-38).

God also smote the priesthood. Because of their sins, the High Priest, Eli, and his two sons were killed the day the Ark was captured (1 Samuel 4:11-18 — In spite of his sins, righteous Eli was more upset over the capture of the Ark than at the death of his sons). God swore that the line of Eli, the line of Aaron's son Ithamar, would no longer serve as High Priests (1 Samuel 3:14).[9] Saul in his demonic fury slew all the priests at Nob, including Eli's grandson Ahimelech (1 Samuel 22:11-19). The son of Ahimelech, Abiathar, escaped to David, and wandered with him in the wilderness until he came to the throne (1 Samuel 22:20). During David's reign there were two High Priests, Abiathar of Ithamar's line, and Zadok of Eleazar's line (1 Chronicles 24:3).[10] Abiathar conspired against Solomon, and Solomon deposed him from being High Priest (1 Kings 2:26-27). This left Zadok as sole High Priest, and finalized the transfer of the High Priesthood.

Now, when there is a change of priesthood, there is of necessity a change of law (Hebrews 7:12). The gradual changes in the priesthood during the century between the Ark's removal from the Tabernacle and its re-enthronement in the Temple were accompanied by gradual changes in the law. It is easiest to look first of all at the big picture, however. We have shifted from

Ithamar to Eleazar. We have also shifted from Tabernacle to Temple. In social polity, we have shifted from judges and seers to kings and prophets (as discussed in Chapter 11). In the kingdom we now have a small professional army that protects the king and that serves as a buffer against attack while the militia is called up. To support the legitimate needs of the palace and the king, we have a system of taxation; and the nation is divided into tax districts that do not correspond to tribal boundaries (1 Kings 4:7-19).

All of this gradually came into place. To summarize the transition: During Samuel's judgeship, the Ark was at Kiriath-jearim and the Tabernacle and High Priest were at Shiloh. During Saul's kingship, the Ark was at Kiriath-jearim, the Tabernacle at Nob, and the High Priest in the wilderness with David. During David's reign, the Ark was in Jerusalem with Abiathar, and the Tabernacle was at Gibeon with Zadok.[11] Under Solomon, the Ark was re-enthroned in the Temple with Zadok as High Priest. Putting all this together indicates that God refused to put the Ark back into a House until the line of Eli was out of the way, and the transition to the new priesthood was completed.

As we saw in the previous chapter, God sets up His new social polity, the human house, before setting up His new symbolic polity, the physical house. Thus, when Samuel made Saul king, he wrote a new constitution: "Then Samuel told the people the ordinances of the kingdom, and wrote them in the book and placed it before the LORD" (1 Samuel 10:25). It would be interesting to have a copy of this constitution, this new law which was placed before the Lord, that is, in the Most Holy Place along with the Mosaic Law. We do not have it, however.

To me this is most significant. Samuel's new constitution was a transformation of the Mosaic Law for the New Covenant. God has left us the Mosaic Law, but has also shown us that it must be *applied* by transformation to new covenantal situations. Such an application must be made by *wisdom*, and thus wisdom literature comes into focus during the Davidic establishment. The books of Proverbs, Psalms, Ecclesiastes, and Song of Solomon were written either largely or exclusively by Solomon and David; and Job was probably added to the canon at this time. This fact strikes a blow against any simplistic and legalistic attempt to impose the

Mosaic legislation in the New Covenant, but it also reminds us that the foundation of our social wisdom must be a careful consideration of that Mosaic Law.

From reading Samuel and Kings, and from a close study of 1 Chronicles 11–27, we can see many features of the new constitution. A full study of this goes beyond the limitations of the present book, but we have already mentioned some of the changes: a small professional army, a system of taxation, a palace complex for the king. The most important feature of the new polity, however, was that the king must always submit to the word of the prophet, for the prophet is the ambassador of the King of kings (1 Samuel 10:8; 13:8-14).[12] It was precisely this that Saul refused to do, and for his rebellion he lost his throne. Throughout the books of Samuel and Kings, we find the interaction of the prophets with the kings. Good kings hearkened to the prophets, while bad ones rebelled.

David defeated the Philistines once and for all. He also captured and secured Melchizedek's ancient capital, Jerusalem. For the first time, the entire land was subdued. Now at last God could move into His capital city and build a permanent sanctuary. David wanted to build a physical house of cedar for God (2 Samuel 7:7), but God told him that it was more important that God have a human tree-house (v. 10). David's own house, said God, would be His new human cedar house (cf. Ezekiel 17), His new messianic community gathered around Him. Only when that human house had been set up would God permit David's son to build Him a physical house (vv. 12-16).

The New Heavens and Earth

When a new heavens and earth is set up, first of all the world is rebuilt. The nations of the world are "restructured," which meant in this case that the oppressive nations had to be defeated. In terms of the wider world, the New Covenant meant that Israel now took her place among the nations as a kingdom, and was no longer immature in this sense. After the world is reconstructed, the land of Eden is recreated. As we mentioned above, it was David's task to reorganize the kingdom in this social polity sense. David had to deal with internal rebellions and thereby quieten the land. At the beginning of Solomon's reign, there were succession wars. The new land of Israel, unlike the old, had a capital city: Jerusalem. The new federal government in Jerusalem set up administrative districts for federal purposes, while the tribal governments continued to handle the affairs of the tribal republics.[13]

At last the land was at peace, and God was ready to plant a new Garden in the new Eden. The new Garden embraced the Temple and Palace complex on Mount Moriah in Jerusalem. This is a significant change from the Mosaic establishment. There was now an Adam in the Land, a King. The High Priest was the Supreme Adam in the Garden-Sanctuary, and had been since Moses' day. Now there is a Supreme Adam in the Land. The Kingdom of God is moving outward from Garden to Land. The King's Palace adjoined and was connected to the Temple or Palace of God (1 Kings 7:1-12; 14:28). The King was the son of David. David himself never lived in this Palace; it was built at the same time as the Temple. Remarkably, God refused to move into His Palace until the Palace of His vice-regent had been built (1 Kings 6:38; 7:1; 9:10). God and Solomon moved into their Palaces at the same time.[14]

Diagram 16.1 shows the progress in glory from the time of Noah to the Davidic or Solomonic establishment.

The Symbolic Polity

Let us first consider Mount Zion as a world model. Zion figures heavily in the Psalms as God's new mountain, because the Temple was set on one of her hills. Zion replicates the three-story universe. At her Northern extreme is the Temple, a model of heaven. To the south of the Temple, on Zion proper, is the city of Jerusalem, a citified Eden. The undeveloped mountain below represents the world. Below the mountain to the South, in a deep crevasse, is Gehenna, the pit, symbol of hell or the Abyss.[15] Thus, Zion reproduces the North-South imagery of creation, as well as the vertical imagery of the three-decker world[16] (see Diagram 16.2).

A second expansion of symbolic polity is seen in the Song of Solomon, also called Canticles. We have mentioned that with the Davidic covenant we have not only the world, land, and garden reestablished; but also a premier Adam put into the land.

Diagram 16.1
Maturation of the Cosmos

	Creation	Noah	Patriarchs	Mosaic		Davidic
				Wilderness	Settlement	
Garden				Tabernacle	Fixed Tabernacle	Palace/Temple Complex
Land of Eden			Land of Promise	Tents	Towns	City (Jerusalem)
World		70 Nations	Canaanites rule the Land	Israel interacts with other nations inside the land: Canaanites, Philistines; or near cousins: Ammon, Moab		Israel interacts with nations outside the Land: Sheba, Syria, Egypt, Assyria, Babylon

Diagram 16.2
Zion as a World Model

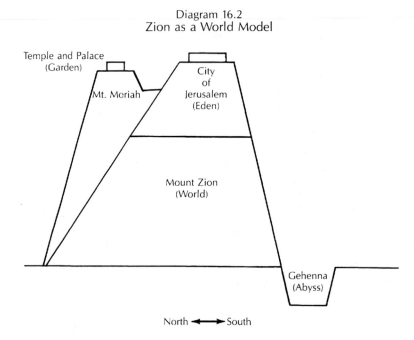

This is the meaning of the King, and of the King's palace being associated with the Temple on Mount Moriah (between the Temple and the Edenic city on Mount Zion). There is a parallel between the king's palace-garden and bride, and God's Temple-garden and bride (Israel). The Song of Solomon shows us Adam and Eve restored to the garden. The book abounds in garden or paradise imagery. We see the bride tempted to unfaithfulness. We see much talk of trees and fruit, and the husband feeding the bride. Also, there is a great deal of architectural imagery in Canticles, comparing the human body to God's Temple.[17] Thus, Christian expositors have usually seen Canticles as a parable of Christ and the Church, though it is also a celebration of the restoration of marital love.[18]

The Temple, of course, is the major symbolic polity change. As the Tabernacle symbolized the political cosmos of Israel in the Mosaic era, so the Temple symbolized the political cosmos during the Davidic era. The Temple proper consisted only of the two rooms, the Most Holy and the Holy Place. The dimensions of the Most Holy were doubled, which made it eight times as large; while the Holy Place was twelve times as large.[19] The Temple itself was shaped as a stepped pyramid, its walls becoming thicker stage by stage as one approached the ground (1 Kings 6:6; Ezekiel 41:7). (See Diagram 16.3.) Leaning on these stages were three stories of outlying rooms. The floor of the Temple was no longer made of dirt but of gold (1 Kings 6:30). The walls of the Temple were engraved with cherubim and palm trees, symbolizing God's two hosts of angels and men (1 Kings 6:29). In the Most Holy, there were now four cherubim guarding God's throne. He "sat" on the wings of two, and the wings of the other two overshadowed the throne. This new arrangement was called God's Chariot, and in Ezekiel we see the four cherubim repositioned as the four wheels of the Chariot (1 Chronicles 28:18; 1 Kings 6:23-28).

In the Holy Place there were ten new golden lampstands in addition to the tree-lampstand from the Tabernacle. There were also ten tables for the utensils of the new lampstands (2 Chronicles 4:7-8).

Outside the Temple was an open porch flanked by two huge freestanding pillars named Jachin and Boaz (1 Kings 7:15-22). Jachin represented the High Priest, and Boaz the King, as the two servant-guardians of God's Kingdom. The design of these pillars symbolized ladders to heaven, with the bronze shaft associated with the Courtyard, the arboraceous collar representing the Holy Place, and the cubic Lily at the top representing the Most Holy[20] (see Diagram 16.4).

Also in the courtyard was a huge bronze sea (1 Kings 7:23-26; 2 Chronicles 4:2-5). This replaced the small laver of cleansing of the Tabernacle. The bronze sea also replicated the Temple, with its bronze bowl associated with the Courtyard, the row of bulls representing the Holy Place, and the Lily design at the top signifying the Most Holy. The twelve bulls under the bronze ocean were positioned in the same configuration as Israel's encampment in Numbers 2, and thus represented Israel and the land.

Diagram 16.3
The Temple of Solomon

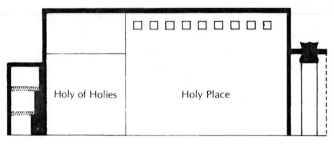

Holy of Holies

Holy Place

Cross section, side view

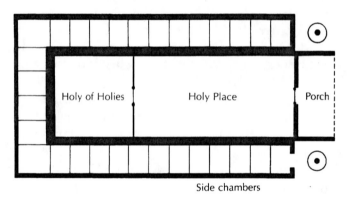

Holy of Holies

Holy Place

Porch

Side chambers

Cross section, top view

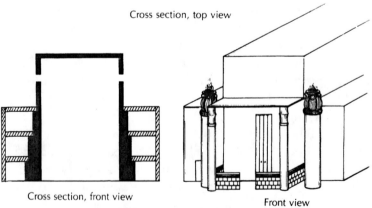

Cross section, front view

Front view

All diagrams assume walls one cubit thick.

Diagram 16.4
Temple Pillar

—4 cubit lily (Holy of Holies; head)

—1 cubit collar (Holy Place; neck)

—18 cubit pillar (courtyard; trunk)

There were ten huge fixed stands in the courtyard that held water, and that, though immovable, were made in the design of chariots (1 Kings 7:27-39). There were also silver lampstands in the courtyard to give light at night (1 Chronicles 28:15).

The altar was greatly increased in size (2 Chronicles 4:1), and was separated from the laity by a low wall, creating two courts and institutionalizing the separation of the layman from the altar that had been in effect in the Tabernacle (1 Kings 6:36).

All of this shows a tremendous increase in glory and in revelation. Although the people still could not get into the Temple and see the inner furniture, they could see equivalent symbolism on the pillars and bronze ocean. The pillars, of course, were brand new, not extensions of anything found in the Tabernacle. As mentioned, they had to do with the institution of Kingship, which was the definitive change in the Davidic covenant.

The change from Tabernacle to Temple forced some changes in law. For instance, the jealousy inspection of Numbers 5 could no longer be performed according to the Mosaic rules, since the water of jealousy had mixed with it the holy dirt of the Tabernacle floor (Numbers 5:17); and the Temple floor was made of gold. Some kind of adjustment had to be made. Also, since the Levites no longer had the duty of carrying the Tabernacle, they were given new tasks by David under Divine inspiration (1 Chronicles 24:25 – 26:32).

History and Decline

No sooner had the Kingdom been established than Solomon wrecked it through sin. Samuel had portrayed a tyrant king in 1 Samuel 8, and both Saul and David at various times had filled the description, though David unlike Saul repented of it. Now Solomon became a tyrant.

The people had been taxed and enlisted to help build the Temple and Palace. This was fitting for two reasons. First, they had demanded a king, so it was fitting that they build his palace. Also, however, the people had made contributions to build the Tabernacle (after all, in part it symbolized them); so it was fitting that the people contribute to building the Temple. Sadly, after these works were finished, Solomon continued to lay heavy burdens on the people.

In Deuteronomy 17:16-17 Moses provided the people with three laws of kingship. The king was not to multiply horses or gold, or take more than one wife. In 1 Kings 10:14 — 11:8 we find Solomon breaking all three of these laws. First, Solomon took in 666 talents of gold per year (1 Kings 10:14).[21] According to the *Open Bible*, a talent of gold in 1985 money would be worth U.S. $5.76 million.[22] This means that Solomon was taking in over $3.84 billion each year. This was hefty revenue for a country the size of New Jersey. Second, Solomon multiplied horses and chariots (1 Kings 10:26). *Adding* a few horses and chariots for the small professional army would not have been wrong, but Solomon went overboard. Finally, of course, Solomon committed polygamy, and his wives turned his heart away from God (1 Kings 11:1-8).

This disruption in the spiritual environment of the covenant manifested itself right away in a rending of the social polity, as the ten northern tribes, with God's blessing, seceded from the nation (1 Kings 12). An equivalent disruption in the symbolic cosmos occurred when Pharaoh removed the gold from the Temple and Palace, and these were replaced with bronze (1 Kings 14:25-27).

These were only preliminary judgments, however. There were good times as well as bad times during the Kingdom establishment. Good kings listened to God's ambassadors, the prophets, and being blessed by God, were able to restore much of the gold to the Temple.

The kingdom of (Northern) Israel was separated from the Temple in Jerusalem. The people were supposed to go into Judah and worship God at the Temple, but then return to their homes in the separate kingdom of Israel. Of course, the apostate kings of Israel resisted this, and sometimes even closed the borders to prevent the people from leaving the country to worship (2 Chronicles 16:1). Thus, for much of their history the people in Israel were left only with synagogue worship.

On one occasion God provided them with proper sacrificial worship. When Elijah challenged the prophets of Baal on Mount Carmel—Carmel means "fruitful place"—he built an altar and God honored it. God would not accept such non-Temple altars, because He would not accept strange fire, fire that He Himself had not lit (Leviticus 9:24; 10:1-2; 2 Chronicles 7:1). On this occasion, however, God sent His own fire from heaven to consume Elijah's sacrifices (1 Kings 18:38).

Elijah's altar was a model of God's kingdom. First of all, it was a symbol of the religious body politic of Israel, both north and south:

> And Elijah took twelve stones according to the number of the tribes of the sons of Jacob, to whom the word of the Lord had come, saying "Israel shall be your name." So with the stones he built an altar in the name of the Lord (1 Kings 18:31-32a).

As a cosmic model, the altar had a trench around it (for Gehenna, or the Abyss). Wood was put at the top, to be burned for the sacrifice of course, but also as a sign of God's arboraceous garden (vv. 32-33). The burnt offering on the wood reminds us of the animals in the Garden.

Then Elijah poured water all over the burnt offering and wood. Why? Not just to make it harder for God to light the sacrifice. Remember, Elijah offered this sacrifice after three years of drought (1 Kings 17:1; 18:1). The water pouring over the altar was a sign of rain pouring over the holy mountain of Israel, which of course was what happened that very day (vv. 41-45). The water washed over the altar and filled the Gehenna-trench. Just so, as it rained the brook Kishon filled with water and flushed the dead bodies of the prophets of Baal out of the holy land and into the sea, cleansing the land (v. 40).

Elijah's altar speaks clearly of the cosmic significance of the altar. The four elements found in the Garden of Eden—trees, animals, water, and priest—are all present here. The destruction of the altar by God's fire substituted for the destruction of the world represented by the altar: "Then the fire of the Lord fell, and consumed the burnt offering and the wood and the stones and the dust, and licked up the water that was in the trench." When we remember that the stones represented Israel, and that man is made of dust, we see that the destruction of this altar and its components signified the destruction of the world. The altar received the wrath that Israel deserved. The water on the altar was dried up, so that water could once again come to the land. Thus Israel was spared the judgment of God.

The Northern Kingdom, however, slid downhill very fast, and was taken captive by Assyria. The Southern Kingdom endured longer, but God eventually judged it as well. The last preliminary judgment is recorded in 2 Kings 24. Nebuchadnezzar conquered Jerusalem and carried off the nobility, including such persons as Daniel and Ezekiel. He also carried off the gold of the Temple, which was symbolically equivalent to these leading men.

Israel refused to repent, however, and so Nebuchadnezzar returned. This time he blinded the king, burned the city, burned the Temple, and carried off all the people. After being told of the deportation of the people, we are told that he broke up the bronze pillars and took away all the bronze "service" utensils of the Temple (2 Kings 25:11-17). These small bronze vessels were the symbolic equivalent of the ordinary people, while the breakup of the pillars, to which special attention is called, is to be associated with the destruction of the king.[23]

Summary
The Kingdom establishment can be set out as follows:

New Names:

God:	No new name is really highlighted, but in David's prayer of 2 Samuel 7, when the Davidic Covenant was made, the name used is Lord God, which in Hebrew is "the Master, the Lord." Since the condition of the Kingdom was that the human King recognize the Lord as Supreme King, this phrase "Master, Lord" seems eminently appropriate.
People:	The House of David is a new name here. Also, the name Israel comes to be associated with Northern Israel, and thus with apostasy; while the name Judah comes to signify the relatively more faithful Southern Kingdom. Yet another name that comes into play is "Remnant," denoting the faithful in times of apostasy.

Grant:	The city of Jerusalem, as capital of the Kingdom.
Promise:	God will not forsake the House of David.
Stipulations:	
Sacramental:	Slight changes in the worship system reflecting the change from Tabernacle to Temple. Also, certain sacrifices were paid for by the King, acting as Chief Layman (e.g., 2 Chronicles 35:7).
Societal:	The new constitution of the Kingdom, in particular the rule that the King hearken to the prophet.
Polity:	
Church:	Priests at Temple, prophets and Levites at synagogues.
State:	Elders and judges, with King at the top.
Symbol:	The Palace/Temple complex.

He keeps his own secure,
He guards them by his side,
Arrays in garments, white and pure,
His spotless bride:
With streams of sacred bliss,
With groves of living joys—
With all the fruits of Paradise
He still supplies.

—Thomas Olivers
"The God of Abrah'm Praise," stanza 8

SEVENTEEN

THE WORLDS OF EXILE
AND RESTORATION

The Davidic heavens and earth had hardly gotten under way before it fell into sin. The Kingdom was split, and the Temple was raided. Thus, both social and symbolic polities were changed. In time, the fabric of the Davidic covenant began to wear thin. It was no good trying to put a patch on it; a new garment was needed.[1]

The new garment consisted of a World Imperial order, with Israel under the protection of (or at the mercy of) a world emperor. Within Israel the synagogues, which had previously had Levites as local pastors, were now run by laymen. The Restoration Temple, the symbolic polity, was nowhere near as glorious as Solomon's, but what it symbolized was a far more glorious and powerful Spiritual presence.

All of this had been anticipated in the centuries before the new covenant came into being. First, in terms of symbolic polity, the loss of Temple-glory matched the loss of the Davidic house when the Kingdom split. This anticipated the relatively less glorious Restoration Temple.

Second, in terms of local "holy convocations," while Levites continued as local pastors in Judah, in Northern Israel there were very few Levites. Most of them moved to Judah as a result of persecution (2 Chronicles 11:13-14). Thus, God raised up prophets; and these prophets set up theological seminaries, the "schools of the prophets," to train local pastors.[2] The synagogues of the faithful (the "remnant") continued to meet on sabbaths and new moons (2 Kings 4:23), but their pastors were laymen trained and ordained by the prophets. Thus, while the Levites

241

continued to have Temple duties, there was a shift away from
them at the synagogue level.

Third, in terms of social polity, both Judah and Northern
Israel were repeatedly conquered and vassaled by powers to the
North and South. This anticipated the world imperial system
that would come in with the Restoration Covenant. Once the
people went into Babylonian captivity, God completely broke
down the Davidic establishment. There was no king, and the
people were directly under the imperial government. There was
no Temple, and the people had to get used to the idea of a
Spiritual Temple. There was no regular synagogal structure,
and the people had to make do without Levitical leadership.

The new polity was thus anticipated, but the full nature of it
could never have been envisioned by the people living during
Israel's decline. In exile they still envisioned that a renewed covenant would be much like the old Davidic covenant. The New
Covenant, however, was far more glorious than the previous one.

First, God wanted the World Imperial era because it facili-
tated evangelism. The Jews (their new name) had been told to
settle in Babylon and work for the good of their new cities (Jeremiah 29:4-7). As a result, the faith was spread throughout that
land. In the Restoration Covenant, God's Spirit would be given
in greater measure, and the Jews would travel land and sea,
making Gentile converts.

Second, God wanted non-Levitical synagogues, because
these brought out the spiritual gifts of laymen, and anticipated
the New Covenant Church.

Third, God wanted a smaller Temple. With the Restoration
Temple we have great shift in meaning. Moses had seen the pattern on Mount Sinai, and had built it below. The Mosaic Tabernacle symbolized both the nature and the glory of the Mosaic establishment. Similarly, David had been given the directions for
the Temple. The Solomonic Temple symbolized both the nature
and the glory of the Davidic covenant. This time Ezekiel was
given a vision and blueprint for the post-exilic Temple, but it
was a temple so vast and huge that it could never be built. Ezekiel's visionary Temple symbolized both the nature and the glory
of the restoration establishment, but the Temple actually built
by Ezra was a small affair. Ezra's Temple symbolized the nature,
but not the glory, of the new restoration covenant.

The New Heavens and Earth in Prophecy

God announced His intention to bring judgment on His wayward people, and on the nations, repeatedly through His prophets. One famous passage in Jeremiah uses the cosmic language of "heaven and earth" to describe the fall of Judah's body politic:

> I looked on the earth, and behold!
>   formless and void;
> And to the heavens, and they had no light.
> I looked on the mountains,
>   and behold, they were quaking,
> And all the hills moved to and fro.
> I looked, and behold, there was no man,
> And all the birds of the heavens had fled.
> I looked, and behold, the fruitful land
>   was a wilderness,
>   and all its cities were pulled down
> Before the Lord,
> Before His fierce anger.
>
> For thus says the Lord,
> "The whole land shall be a desolation,
> "Yet I will not execute a complete destruction.
> "For this the earth shall mourn,
> "And the heavens above be dark,
> "Because I have spoken,
> "I have purposed,
> "And I will not change My mind,
> "Nor will I turn from it" (Jeremiah 4:23-28).

These announcements of judgment were always accompanied by announcements of a restoration, a new covenant, a new heavens and earth to come. The new covenant and the new heavens and earth ultimately point to the coming of Christ, but their first fulfillment is to be found in the restoration of Israel from exile.[3] That restoration was a downpayment, a pledge of God's faithfulness. After all, each new covenant, being a resurrection in more glorious form of the previous one, pointed to *the* New Covenant.

It is often overlooked that the restoration establishment was indeed a new covenant, and an advance in glory beyond the Davidic establishment. Whether we call the post-exilic establishment a new covenant or simply a "covenant renewal," the fact is that there were very great changes involved in the new cosmos, changes equivalent to the changes involved in previous new covenants. Also, the point of Zechariah 3 is that the Davidic covenant had become so defiled that it could not be renewed, and thus what is shown in Zechariah 3 is the establishment of a New Covenant. We shall return to this when we consider Zechariah's night visions later in this chapter.

The book of Ezekiel is a useful place to see the Restoration heavens and earth portrayed in prophecy. The message of Ezekiel to the first group of exiles was that even though the Temple was going to be torn down, the true Temple was in heaven and was with them wherever they went. As Solomon had made clear, God Himself did not dwell in the Temple, only His "name" (1 Kings 8:27-29).

In the first chapter of Ezekiel, the prophet is given a vision of the Cherubic Chariot that had been symbolized by the four cherubim in the Most Holy Place. Only High Priests ever entered the Most Holy, and this alerts us to the possibility that Ezekiel will be the High Priest of Israel during the exile. The fact that Ezekiel is addressed as "son of man," that is, as a second Adam, highlights this. Daniel, Ezekiel's friend and co-worker in Babylon, saw the Messiah as the Son of Man. Ezekiel, as High Priest, typified the true Second Adam to come.[4]

In Chapter 1, Ezekiel sees the Chariot in Babylon. This meant that God was with His people in exile. He had not abandoned them, though He was chastising them. In Chapters 8-11, Ezekiel sees the Chariot of Glory get up and move out of the Temple, and fly away. The Temple, now abandoned and "desolate," has become an "abomination," and God will destroy this "abomination of desolation." After the destruction of the Temple comes the exile of the prince, the king of Israel (Ezekiel 12), but a twig of the Davidic house will be preserved (Ezekiel 17:22).

In Ezekiel 24:16-27, God told Ezekiel that He was going to take away his wife. The death of Ezekiel's wife was a symbol of God's judgment against Israel, His own bride. From the time of her death until word reached the exiles of the destruction of Jerusalem, Ezekiel would be dumb, unable to speak. When the first of the new refugees arrived, Ezekiel would once again be able to prophesy (Ezekiel 33:1-22). The intervening chapters of Ezekiel are taken up with prophecies against the nations of the world. It seems that during his period of muteness, Ezekiel wrote these prophecies. The fact that they are bracketed by the destruction of Jerusalem means that the judgment on Jerusalem entails judgment on the whole world. Tyre, once allied with Jerusalem when her king helped build the Temple, would be destroyed. All the nations would be brought into the new World Imperial system, and be subjected to Nebuchadnezzar: Ammon, Moab, Edom, Philistia (Ezekiel 25), Tyre (Ezekiel 26–28), Egypt, Ethiopia, Put, Lud, Arabia, Libya (Ezekiel 29–32), Assyria, Elam, Meshech-Tubal, and Sidon (Ezekiel 32). God was laying hold on the world and tearing it apart, so that He could rebuild it as a new heavens and earth.

After the judgment on the sanctuary, on Eden, and on the world, Ezekiel sets out the nature of the restored world. Ezekiel focuses on the renewal of the land, which he even calls Eden (Ezekiel 36:35). After discussing the coming Restoration and peace (Ezekiel 34–37), he tells them that there will come a time of severe trouble (Ezekiel 38–39). An army made up of people from many nations, under the leadership of a prince named Gog, will invade the land, but will be defeated. The immediate fulfillment of this prophecy was the invasion of Palestine by Antiochus Epiphanes during the inter-testamental period. According to Revelation 20, however, this war provides a picture of the Church's conflict in all eras. Ezekiel uses symbolic and exaggerated descriptions to highlight the fact that not only literal battles but also spiritual warfare was to be involved in this conflict. For that reason, Christian expositors have always seen the battle of Gog and Magog as having spiritual relevance.[5]

Housebuilding follows an exodus from captivity and the destruction of an enemy. The destruction of one nation, Egypt, led to the building of the Tabernacle. The destruction of several enemies in Canaan and Philistia led to the building of Solomon's bigger Temple. Now Israel defeats all the nations of the world, organized by Prince Gog. Thus, in Ezekiel 40–48 we have a description in highly symbolic terms of a vast, huge restored Temple and land.

This is not a picture first and foremost of the New Testament, but of the spiritual realities present in the Restoration. This is indicated by the context of the prophecy, but there are also clear indications in the text, especially the fact that the river in Chapter 47 only flows in one direction, not four, and only to the edge of the Holy Land, not into the wider world.[6]

The prophecy begins with Ezekiel's being taken to a very high mountain north of a city (Ezekiel 40:2). The city obviously is visionary Jerusalem, and the mountain is visionary Moriah, north of Zion. We notice that the mountain is growing higher and higher with each new heavens and earth. In Chapter 40, the Temple is described with a tremendous stress on doorways and guard chambers. The new Restoration establishment will be a time of greater openness for the Gospel than ever before (doors), and also a time of greater holiness (guards). (See Diagram 17.1).

In Chapter 43, Ezekiel sees the glory-chariot return to reinhabit the Temple. This is a promise to those who would rebuild the Temple, that God would come back to it. In Chapter 44 the prince is restored, and the priests and Levites are reestablished in their places. Also, Ezekiel shows that the sacrificial system will be restored.[7] Ezekiel describes a new huge Jerusalem that has tremendous suburban areas (Ezekiel 45:1-8). There would be no more Levitical cities in the Restoration, and so the Levites would need a place to live. In reality, they would live among the people in the land, but Ezekiel shows the spiritual reality, that they would live around the Temple (see Diagram 17.2). Ezekiel also describes the tribal boundaries in the new establishment, boundaries that are wholly geometric and symbolic in character, but which did assure the exiles that their children would return to the land (Ezekiel 48). (See Diagram 17.3).

The things Ezekiel describes in these chapters could never have been built. The Temple, City, and Land are entirely visionary and symbolic. The Kingdom of God in the Restoration was going to be so powerful and glorious that it simply could not be pictured in any architectural model that could be built. Only a vision would do.

Diagram 17.1
Ezekiel's Temple Complex

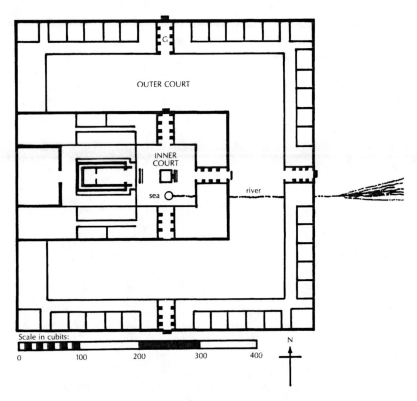

OUTER COURT

G

INNER
COURT

sea

river

Scale in cubits:

0   100   200   300   400

N

Diagram 17.2
The Center of the Land

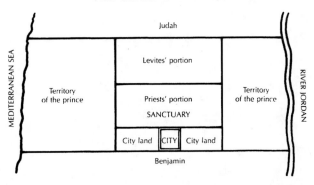

MEDITERRANEAN SEA

RIVER JORDAN

Judah

Levites' portion

Territory
of the prince

Priests' portion

SANCTUARY

Territory
of the prince

City land   CITY   City land

Benjamin

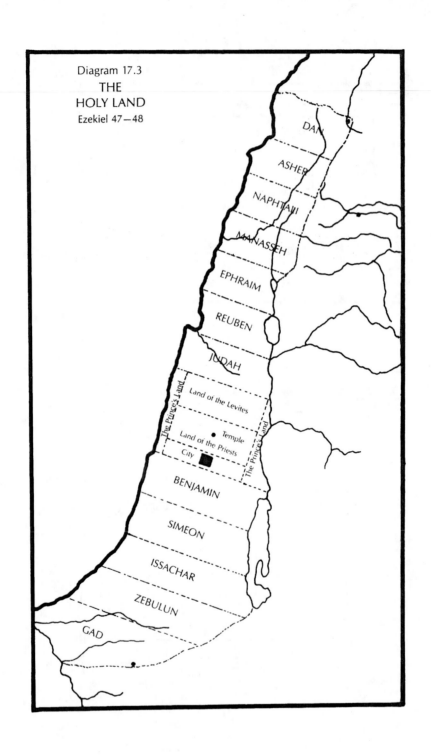

Diagram 17.3
THE HOLY LAND
Ezekiel 47—48

DAN

ASHER

NAPHTALI

MANASSEH

EPHRAIM

REUBEN

JUDAH

The Prince's Land

Land of the Levites

● Temple

Land of the Priests

City

The Prince's Land

BENJAMIN

SIMEON

ISSACHAR

ZEBULUN

GAD

The most interesting aspect of Ezekiel's Temple is its river. In Chapter 47, Ezekiel sees a river flowing out of the Temple. As it flows it becomes deeper and wider, until finally it comes to the Dead Sea and restores the sea to life. This is, of course, a picture of the cleansing of the land and of renewed life, since water has to do with cleansing and life. It is a picture of the greatly increased spiritual power of the Restoration covenant. Let us briefly trace this river. We first met it in Eden, where it flowed out as four rivers to water the whole earth. After the fall of man, the river was cut off. Man's sin cut him off from cleansing and life, and eventually the world was destroyed in the Flood. After the Flood, God called the patriarchs to minister to the world. The patriarchs dug wells in the ground and set up oasis-sanctuaries. For them, the water was down in the ground and had to be brought up. They labored to provide it for their converts.

In the Mosaic heavens and earth we find a laver of cleansing in the Tabernacle. There is still no outflow, but at least the water is no longer underground. In the Temple of Solomon, we come closer to a river. We have a huge bronze ocean, much higher and fuller than the earlier laver, and we also have ten water chariots. These chariots are fixed and do not flow out; but at least there is much more water, much more spiritual power, in the Kingdom.

During the periods of the patriarchs, of the Tabernacle, and of the Temple, God had His people placed at the center of the world. Caravans from Europe and Asia to Africa had to go through Palestine. God put His people at the center so that they could be His evangelists. He brought the nations to them, as the Queen of Sheba came to Solomon. The water stayed in the land, in the Tabernacle, and in the Temple, and the nations came to it.

In the world of the Restoration, however, the bronze ocean is tipped over. There is no laver or ocean in Ezekiel's Temple. It has finally become a river, flowing out. True, it only flows in one direction, and not to the ends of the earth, but it still flows out. For the first time, the Jews would begin to move out from Palestine as missionaries, so that by New Testament times there would be synagogues and Gentile converts in all the world.

We should conclude our survey by taking note of Revelation 22:1. Here the mountain has become so high that it pokes through the firmament, with God's throne at the apex of the pyramid. The Edenic waters thus are finally coalesced with the heavenly waters of Genesis 1. Since the city is a pyramid, it stands to reason that the waters flow down all four sides. Thus, Ezekiel's river is transcended in the New Covenant.

The New Heavens and Earth as Built

Let us now look at the Restoration as it actually came to pass in fulfillment of Ezekiel's prophecies. First, we find in the book of Daniel the fact that God's new world order involved world empires that dominated the nations. These empires would gather into themselves "the sovereignty, the dominion, and the greatness of all the kingdoms under the whole heaven"; but in the plan of God, this was only so that they could all be turned over to the Son of Man (Daniel 7:27). The Christ to come would be the final World Emperor, and His non-political Church would be the true world empire, embracing and transforming every nation without dominating or destroying any of them.[8] Daniel prophesies the course of empire in detail from its establishment under Nebuchadnezzar until the time of Christ.[9]

In this new world order, God's witnesses are to try and influence the world imperial centers. Thus, Daniel and his friends become strong at Nebuchadnezzar's court, and eventually Nebuchadnezzar is converted. The same thing happens with the Persian court later on. Thus, in the world of the Restoration, while Jerusalem may be the world's spiritual capital, the political capital of interest to the Jews will be the capital of the world empire. This theme continues in the New Testament as Paul yearns to get to Rome and go to work on Caesar's household.

Something new comes into focus at this stage of history: the importance of witness-bearing. This becomes an important theme in the books of Daniel and Esther, and points to the New Testament. Daniel must serve Nebuchadnezzar faithfully and well, but at the same time must bear witness for God Most High, the Lord of Israel, without compromise. This is the theme of Daniel 1, the test of food, of Daniel 3, the three youths in the fiery furnace, and of Daniel 6, where Daniel is forbidden to pray. Daniel is the exemplary witness; he never compromises, but also never rebels.

A more complex case is presented in Esther. At the beginning of the story, Mordecai wants to have influence at court, but shows a needless rebellious streak in refusing to bow to Haman (Esther 3:2; cf. Genesis 23:12; 33:3; 42:6; 43:26; Ruth 2:10; Esther 8:3); and Mordecai also tells Esther to conceal her identity, cloaking her witness (Esther 2:9-10; cp. Daniel 1:8). When as a result of Mordecai's proto-Pharisaical and proto-Zealot behavior the Jews are put in danger, Esther is compelled to reveal her heritage and bear witness. The result is the salvation of the Jews and the elevation of their leaders into positions of influence. The compromised Mordecai, whose name means "Worshipper of Marduk," received honor when he assisted the king (Esther 6); but he received a permanent position when he stopped concealing his witness (Esther 10).

The books of Ezra and Haggai describe the return of the people to the land and the rebuilding of the Temple. As the people began to rebuild the Temple, God gave a series of visions to Zechariah, contained in Zechariah 1-6, that explained the nature of the Temple. To be sure, to the outward eye the new Temple was not very glorious (Ezra 3:12; Haggai 2:3); but the spiritual reality of the Restoration was such that the entire heavens and earth were going to be shaken (Haggai 2:4-9). Thus, if we are going to understand the *true* nature of the Restoration establishment, we must move back into the realm of vision.

As we have seen, the Temple courtyard is the equivalent of a garden-sanctuary, leading to heaven. The altar was a holy mountain and ladder to heaven, but so were the bronze pillars Jachin and Boaz. The bronze shaft was equivalent to the bronze altar, and the capital to the heavenly temple.

This is alluded to in Zechariah 6:1,

> Now I lifted up my eyes again and looked, and behold, four chariots were coming forth from between the two mountains; and the mountains were bronze mountains.

The meaning of this verse and its allusions have been widely debated, but I believe that the clue lies in the nature of the visions themselves. Zechariah is identified as one of the twenty-four chief priests of the Temple (Zechariah 1:1 with 1 Chronicles 24:4-19; Nehemiah 12:1, 4, 16).[10] He had access to the Holy

Place, and must be compared with Ezekiel, who as acting High Priest had access to the Most Holy. Ezekiel saw the cherubic chariot of the Most Holy. Zechariah sees the lesser horse chariots of the Holy Place (the chariot-like water stands). Ezekiel saw water flow out from the restored Temple. Zechariah sees the (water) chariots ride out.

Zechariah prophesied simultaneously with Haggai. Both were exhorting the people to rebuild the Temple. Zechariah's Night Visions, like Ezekiel's earlier (Ezekiel 40–48), were designed to show the spiritual truths that the rebuilt post-exilic Temple would embody and manifest. There are eight Night Visions, and they run from sundown to sunrise, with the important transition, the new Passover, at midnight.[11]

Vision 1 (1:1-17). The first vision states that the people must lay a moral and spiritual foundation, not merely an architectural one, and then the Temple will be rebuilt. The context of the first vision is a ravine, where God's myrtle people are quietly fed by hidden waters associated with the ground water of Eden, the oases of the patriarchs, and the laver and sea in the Tabernacle and Temple.

Vision 2 (1:18-22). The second vision states that apostate worship at the horns of an idolatrous altar was the real cause of Israel's distress, but that the rebuilding of Temple and altar—the return to true worship—would be her restoration.

Vision 3 (2:1-13). The third vision states that God's glory, which Ezekiel had seen depart, would return and God would again dwell in His Temple. Just as the Tabernacle had been built after the Egyptian exodus, so the people are enjoined to make a new exodus from Babylon in order to build the Temple. Just as God had been a wall of fire between Israel and Pharaoh's army, so He would be a wall of fire to them. According to 2:8, after God's glory had taken its seat, the nations would be dealt with.

Vision 4 (3:1-10). The fourth vision concerns the investiture of the High Priest. Satan argues that because the priesthood is defiled, the Temple cannot be rebuilt. There is no way to cleanse the High Priest without Temple ceremony. Thus, we are in a "Catch-22."[12] But God sets up Zechariah as a new Moses. Moses as prophet had initiated the Tabernacle system and consecrated Aaron, based on information provided by revelation from God.

Just so, Zechariah as prophet sees that in heaven God has passed judgment, and on that basis Zechariah can tell the people that Joshua has been cleansed. The system can be set back up. This meta-liturgical vision is the pivot of the series, which runs from sunset to sunrise. It comes at midnight and points to Passover. Thus, it has more the marks of a "new covenant" than of just a covenant renewal. Joshua is given the festal robes (garments of glory and beauty) and the turban (the golden plate for his forehead), and thus the High Priest is restored.

The next morning, after these Night Visions, Zechariah would tell all this to the people. They would realize that Heaven had cleansed Joshua, and thus that Joshua could now cleanse the Temple site and rebuild the Temple.

Vision 5 (4:1-14). The fifth vision concerns the lampstand and the ministry of God's anointed king. This complicated vision shows us a new lampstand, now with forty-nine instead of a mere seven lamps. This is a symbol of God's Spirit and power, which now will run throughout the whole earth, bringing the light of the Gospel to the nations. The mountains of the world will become plains before the sons of David. Just as Pentecost came after the Crucifixion and Resurrection of Christ, so this great outflow of the Spirit came after restoration of Joshua the High Priest.

Vision 6 (5:1-4). The sixth vision concerns the cleansing of Israel. The rebuilding of the Temple and of the Holy Place (whose Tabernacle dimensions are here alluded to, v. 2), will result in the return of God's specific judgment of leprosy for hidden sin. Israel will be purged.

Vision 7 (5:5-11). The seventh vision is a parody of the Ark of the Covenant. Instead of cherubim we have unclean storks. Instead of a holy box, we have a round ephah containing wickedness. Instead of a trip to the Holy Land and an establishment in the Temple, we have a trip out of the Holy Land and an establishment in the land of Nimrod. The point is that God's presence will not coexist with evil; and when God returns to the Temple, evil will be driven out.

Vision 8 (6:1-9). And so we come to the eighth, or sunrise vision. The symbolism of the vision draws from the Temple in that there were ten water chariots in the Temple courtyard. We should associate them with the four horse-drawn chariots seen in the vision. Also, though, the four chariots are the four winds of heaven, which have already been identified as God's holy people in 2:6. That being the case, the bronze mountains, the pillars Jachin and Boaz, should also be people, and who else can they be in context but Joshua the High Priest and Zerubbabel the Prince? The chariots run out to cleanse and convert the world.

The sequence of renewal in Zechariah's Night Visions is as follows:

1. The people must repent of moral wickedness and set aside all known sin.

2. Then, the people must tear down false worship (altars) and rebuild the worship of God. (To reverse #1 and 2 is liturgical pharisaism.)

3. When this happens, God will be a wall of fire for His people; and the numbers of the righteous will increase.

4. Then God will pass judgment on their behalf, and will glorify His Church. David's wilderness camp will move to Jerusalem. Humble Bible-believing churches will meet in cathedrals.

5. As this happens, God will give them a God-fearing king, a Zerubbabel.

6. The effect of such a renewal will be that God will also expose hidden degeneracy. A more thorough cleansing will come.

7. When the impenitent see this, they will depart, and thus wickedness will be further removed from the land.

8. Finally, God will enable the Gospel to go forth with power to shake up and convert the world.

Conclusion

The Restoration is the least familiar and least studied phase of Old Covenant history. It is often assumed that the Kingdom of God went into the doldrums during this period, and that the people simply suffered until the coming of Messiah. Such an understanding of the post-exilic era utterly fails to do justice to the case. The Restoration was actually a far more glorious time than ever before, in terms of spiritual power, though not in terms of outward glory and splendor.

The Restoration establishment can be set out as follows:

New Names:

God: Lord of Hosts. God had been called this before, but a glance at a concordance will show that this name comes into tremendous prominence in the post-exilic books, especially Zechariah. It stands to reason. After the exile, the Jews no longer had an army, and had to depend on God's army for their protection. By giving them this name as their peculiar treasure, God assured them that He would indeed be a wall of fire around them.

People: Jew. This comes from Judahite, and is exclusively post-exilic. All the children of Israel come to be considered as part of these "Judahites," even those of the already-exiled northern tribes who joined back up with Judah during the Babylonian exile.[13]

Grant: Jerusalem and the Holy Land, but with influence throughout the empire. In a sense, the Jews became a "world people," as the Christians would later be. The grant began to be expanded.

Promise: The visions of Ezekiel, Haggai, and Zechariah showed them that God was with them.

Stipulations:

Sacramental: Slight changes in the worship system reflecting the new Temple, the loss of many Levitical genealogical records, the loss of Levitical cities, the full establishment of the non-Levitical synagogue.

Societal:
The Kingdom constitution was nullified, since there was no longer an independent kingdom and army. The Mosaic establishment also no longer applied in many respects, since the Jews were under overarching imperial laws. Note that God left them to apply the *wisdom* of these systems to constantly changing circumstances. They were maturing, becoming more "adult," and thus were left to make their own applications. Also, witness-bearing becomes an important new duty.

Polity:

Church:
Priests and Levites at Temple, lay-leaders at synagogues.

State:
World emperor who protected God's people, or who chastised them. Imperial overseers, such as Nehemiah, and local Jewish prince, such as Zerubbabel, over the land.

Symbol:
The Temple in Jerusalem, but only as a rude representation of the visionary Temples of Ezekiel and Zechariah.

Before the great THREE-ONE
They all exulting stand;
And tell the wonders he hath done
Thro' all their land:
The list'ning spheres attend
And swell the growing fame;
And sing the songs which never end,
The wondrous NAME.

The God who reigns on high,
The great archangels sing,
And "Holy, holy, holy," cry,
"ALMIGHTY KING!
"Who Was, and Is, the same;
"And evermore shall be;
"JEHOVAH — FATHER — GREAT I AM!
"We worship Thee."

Before the SAVIOUR's face
The ransom'd nations bow;
O'erwhelmed at his Almighty grace,
For ever new:
He shows his prints of Love —
They kindle — to a flame!
And sound through all the world above,
The slaughtered LAMB.

The whole triumphant host,
Give thanks to God on high;
"Hail, FATHER, SON, and HOLY-GHOST,"
They ever cry:
Hail, Abrah'm's GOD — and *mine!*
(I join the heav'nly lays,)
All Might and Majesty are Thine
And endless Praise.

—Thomas Olivers
"The God of Abrah'm Praise," stanzas 9-12

THE NEW WORLD

The coming of the New Covenant is a story that does not need rehearsing in full here. There was a decline in the centuries before Christ, as the Jews gradually lost a true understanding of the Old Covenant, and developed a corrupting tradition. The announcement of the Kingdom by John the Forerunner was simultaneously a condemnation of the corruptions of Judaism (Matthew 3:7-12). John's announcement was the preliminary judgment, and Jesus' announcement was the full judgment (Matthew 23-24). The Exodus was made by our Lord on the Cross, on behalf of His people (Luke 9:31). After this transition, there was a new world established, with a new name for God (Father, Son, and Holy Spirit; Jesus Christ) and a new name for the people (Christians; Acts 11:26). The new grant given God's people was the Kingdom in its fullness, including the whole world. There was a new law (John 13:34), new sacraments (baptism and holy communion), and a new visionary symbol (the New Jerusalem).

The Summation of the Old Covenant

From the perspective of the New Covenant, the Old Covenant in its entirety, from Adam to John the Baptist, was inadequate and imperfect. It was a system "under law" in the sense that it could only condemn men, not save them. The entire Old Covenant stood in Adam, and Adamic humanity existed under the condemnation of the first covenant: Having seized the forbidden fruit, they were exiled from God and destined for death.[1] Although each of the new covenants before Christ provided a more glorious kingdom establishment for God's people; yet before the coming of the Messiah, the world was still "in Adam." Thus, the glories of the Old Covenant could never be anything other than provisional and anticipatory.

In order for a wholly new covenant to come, someone had to fulfill all the righteousness of the law, something Adam had failed to do. There had to be a new Adam and thus a new creation. And so we read that "when the fullness of time came, God sent forth His Son, born of a woman, born under law" (Galatians 4:4). Jesus took unto Himself the law, God's perfect standard of holiness as expressed in terms matching human nature at that stage of history, and fulfilled its terms. In the death of Jesus Christ, the law, indeed the Old Adamic Covenant in its entirety, died. In the resurrection and transfiguration of Jesus Christ into glory, the law and the Old Covenant were resurrected as the New Covenant.

We have mentioned that during the Old Testament period, the prophets would call the people back to the standards of the earlier covenants; though when the revival came, the new form of the covenant would always transform and transcend the terms of the previous one. Just so, Jesus began His ministry by calling men back to the Old Covenant law. His prophetic words are found in Matthew 5:17-20:

> Do not think that I came to abolish the Law or the Prophets; I did not come to abolish, but to fulfill (v. 17).

The word "fulfill" here does not mean simply "cause to stand," but implies transformation into a newness of power.[2] It means to bring something into its fullness, a fullness not previously seen. Thus, it is a good term to use to refer to the transformation of the old into the new. The New Covenant is not going to replace the Old with something different in kind, but only different in glory.

> For truly I say to you, until heaven and earth pass away, not one jot or one tittle shall pass away from the Law, until all is accomplished (v. 18).

As we have seen throughout this book, the passing away of the heavens and earth does not need to refer to the physical world. It often refers to a covenantal establishment. Here that is clearly what is in view. After the Cross, the Church certainly does not keep every jot and tittle of the Old Covenant law. Once

Jesus had accomplished His work, the law was changed, for "when the priesthood is changed, of necessity there takes place a change of law also" (Hebrews 7:12). The old heavens and earth passed away in the first century A.D.; and at that time, many of the jots and tittles also passed away, their purpose fulfilled at last.[3]

> Whoever then annuls one of the least of these commandments, and so teaches others, shall be called least in the kingdom of heaven; but whoever does them and teaches them, he shall be called great in the kingdom of heaven (v. 19).

The idea here is this: Anyone who presently ignores the Old Testament Law will find disgrace and condemnation in the new kingdom that will come; but anyone who scrupulously keeps all the Old Testament Law at the present time, will be great in the kingdom when it comes.

The Pharisees in their teaching were setting aside the commandment of God in order to keep their traditions (Mark 7:9). Such men were annulling some of the commandments, and they would find condemnation. Thus, Jesus concludes by saying:

> For I say to you, that unless your righteousness surpasses that of the scribes and Pharisees, you shall not enter the kingdom of heaven (v. 20).

We are used to thinking of the scribes and Pharisees as meticulous men who carefully observed the jots and tittles. This is not the portrait found in the Gospels. The scribes and Pharisees that Jesus encountered were grossly, obviously, and flagrantly breaking the Mosaic law, while keeping all kinds of man-made traditions. Jesus' condemnation of them in Matthew 23 certainly makes this clear, as does a famous story in John 8. There we read that the scribes and Pharisees brought to Jesus a woman taken "in the very act" of adultery (John 8:1-11). How did they know where to find her? Where was the man who was caught with her? Apparently he was one of their cronies. Also, when Jesus asked for anyone "without sin" (that is, not guilty of the same crime) to cast the first stone, they all went away, because they were all adulterers.

Remember the point we made in Chapter 15: The Mosaic Law was an easy yoke. It was not hard to keep. The parents of John the Baptist kept it perfectly (Luke 1:6). They obeyed the law; and when they fell into sin, they did what the law said to do about it. Thus, when Jesus called the people back to the law and warned them to do a better job than the Pharisees, He was not laying some heavy burden on them. Actually, He was lightening their load.

Each time the covenant changed in the Old Testament there was a change in law. In one sense, each time the change was total in that the *form* of the law changed and the *historic circumstances* of its phrasing and application changed. Yet, since the law reveals God's character, its fundamental *content* can never change. At the same time, God only reveals His law to man in specific forms and circumstances. Even the form of the Ten Commandments changed between Exodus 20 and Deuteronomy 5. It is because the fundamental content of the law never changes that the prophets called men back to the older law each time; but it is because the circumstances of history change and mature that the new covenant, when it comes, is always different in form. The changes in law during the Old Testament were relatively minor compared to the change from the Old Adamic Covenant to the New Covenant, as we shall see.

Law, Wisdom, and Paradox

In calling the people back to the Old Covenant Law and Prophets, Jesus simultaneously advanced the standards of the kingdom a step further. We have seen that God gave the people a written law for the Mosaic establishment, but that in the Davidic establishment, the focus is on wisdom based on the law. The people were to take the principles of the Mosaic Law and apply them to new and changing circumstances. In the Restoration establishment, wisdom was taxed further since under imperial rule the Jews were unable to keep much of the law in its original form. Jesus takes us one step further, from law and wisdom to what I shall call *paradox*. A paradox is an apparent contradiction that forces us to meditate on deeper meanings.[4]

There is a great deal of paradox in Jesus' teaching and in the teaching of the New Testament as a whole. In the Sermon on the

Mount itself, Jesus said concerning adultery that if your eye offends you, pluck it out; and if your hand offends you, cut it off (Matthew 5:27-30). Concerning justice, Jesus said not to resist him who is evil, and to give to him who asks of you (Matthew 5:38-42). Those who wish to become pacifists and take Jesus "literally" on the subject of not resisting evil, must also take Him literally on chopping off hands and ripping out eyes. Of course, no one does the latter, and the Church has always recognized the wisdom-paradox nature of Jesus' teachings here.

A second realm of paradox is seen in the parables, which were both clear and deliberately obscure. Jesus made it plain that He used parables in order to instruct the righteous and to confuse the wicked (Matthew 13:10-17). This conception of truth and teaching is utterly opposed to the Greek rationalistic tradition in Western thought, which assumes that unaided "reason" is able to apprehend truth. Jesus says the opposite, maintaining that the truth is only finally reasonable to the elect, while the wicked can ultimately never regard it as reasonable. This applies not only to the parables, but also to the whole of truth. It is a fundamental aspect of Christian epistemology.

A third realm of paradox lies in the area of reward. Speaking to the children of Israel, God (Leviticus 26) and Moses (Deuteronomy 28) held out rewards for faithfulness and punishments for disobedience. In general, the rewards had to do with prosperity and the punishments with affliction. By the time of Solomon, wisdom had begun to perceive a more mature view of reward and punishments. In Job, the wise man found that the righteous sometimes suffer for no cause of their own. In Ecclesiastes, the wise man found that simply looking at rewards and punishments gets you nowhere in evaluating the world.

In the New Testament, however, we find highlighted such thoughts as these:

> My son, do not regard lightly the discipline of the Lord, nor faint when you are reproved by Him; for those whom the Lord loves He disciplines, and He scourges every son whom He receives. It is for discipline that you endure; God deals with you as with sons; for what son is there whom his father does not discipline? But if you are without discipline, of which all have become partakers, then you are illegitimate children and not sons (Hebrews 12:5-8).

The first part of this statement is from Proverbs 3:11-12, but it is a truth that comes to sharper focus in the New Covenant. Why? Because in dealing with "children" (Galatians 4:1-3), we must express reward and punishment in terms of pleasure and pain; but in dealing with adults, we can invite the wise man to consider that chastisement is itself a reward, and a sign of sonship. To be sure, the rewards and punishments expressed in Deuteronomy 28 are not abolished in the New Covenant, but with them also comes a paradoxical and wisdom-inducing reward of suffering.

The Order of the Kingdom

In the New Covenant a different kind of polity was established, though it had been anticipated earlier. The synagogue as it developed moved gradually away from the Levites and prophets into the hands of gifted laymen. In the New Covenant the sacramental aspects of worship were transferred from the Temple to the synagogue, and the Church was born.

The Church is the first, but not the only form of the kingdom. When the kingdom comes to a new locality, it does not come first by force of arms and the establishment of a Christian civil order. It comes first by persuasion and charity and the establishment of worship. Worship is man's first duty. When the Church as a sacramental, instructional, and governmental body has become established in a locality, kingdom influences flow out into society, and a new Jerusalem is built around the new sanctuary.

The transition from the Mosaic establishment to the New Covenant entailed a gradual shift from civil to ecclesiastical punishments. The Mosaic law prescribed death for a variety of crimes. During the later years of the Davidic establishment, when bad kings were on the throne, the Mosaic penalties were ignored. It was necessary for the synagogues to enforce the law through excommunication. This became even more important during the Restoration, when the Jews were frequently under imperial law and could not exercise civil punishments (John 18:31).

With the opening of heaven and the restoration of the keys to man—the flaming sword given by the cherubim back to Peter and the apostles—the central form of discipline in the kingdom became excommunication (Matthew 16:19). The wielding of these keys, which must always be in terms of Biblical standards,[5] is a far more powerful social force than mere capital punishment, according to the spiritual insight of the New Covenant.[6] Of course, when the Church influences society, then Godly punishments are set up in society as well. All the same, the most important fulfillment of the Old Testament penalties lies in the sanctions exercised by the elders of the Church.

The Restoration of Type and Symbol

The Jews of this period had almost completely perverted the law. As we have seen, they were not keeping the moral requirements of the law. Neither did they understand the symbolic aspects. When Jesus told the Jews that if they destroyed the Temple He would raise it up in three days, referring to His body, they were utterly confused (John 2:19-21). Similarly, when Jesus talked with Nicodemus and referred to the water-cleansing rites of the Old Covenant as a means of resurrection and new birth, Nicodemus was confused. Jesus expressed amazement: "Are you the teacher of Israel, and do not understand these things?" (John 3:10).

In the first century, the Jews had rejected Biblical symbolism and typology, and were divided into two groups. The Pharisees had turned symbolism into moralism, and were keeping the law as a means of salvation. The Alexandrian Jews had replaced Biblical typology with allegories grounded in Greek philosophy. As a result, neither group was able to recognize Christ when He came to them.

It was the task of Jesus and the writers of the New Testament to restore true Biblical symbolism and typology, and to show how the Old Testament revealed Christ. It is for that reason, among others, that John writes his Gospel as a "tour through the Tabernacle"; that Paul explains that the Tabernacle and Temple were symbols both of the individual believer and of the corporate church (1 Corinthians 3:16; 6:19); that the author of Hebrews expresses shock that his hearers do not understand the Old Testament symbolism and typology (Hebrews 5:12); and that Jesus had to explain the typology of the Old Testament to the two men on the road to Emmaus (Luke 24:27).

Thus, when Jesus came to be the true Prophet, He first of all had to restore the Old Covenant, both in its moral and in its symbolic dimensions. An interesting example of this, alluded to above, is found throughout the Gospel of John. In John's Gospel, Jesus is presented as the fulfillment of the Tabernacle.

Before looking at this, let us consider the relevance of it. If Jesus Christ is God's true Tabernacle, then we who are *in Christ* are in that true "body politic" house of God. Moreover, since the cosmic heavens and earth are also imaged in the Tabernacle, if Christ is the true Tabernacle, then all the cosmic heavens and earth must also come to be *in Christ*, so that "in Him all things hold together" (Colossians 1:17). By presenting Christ as the true Tabernacle, John is not simply giving us snapshots of redemption in the narrow sense; he is also presenting us with a worldview, a new universe. As Paul puts it in Colossians 1, the Second Person of the Trinity was the center of the first universe, and the God-man Christ Jesus is the center of the new universe (Colossians 1:15-20):

1. Creation:
   a. And He is the *image* of the invisible God,
   b. The *firstborn* [i.e., captain] of all creation.
   c. For in Him all things were *created*,
      (1) in the heavens and on earth,
      (2) visible and invisible,
      (3) whether thrones or dominions or rulers or authorities,
   d. all things have been created through Him and for Him.

2. Restoration:
   a. He is also the *head* of the body, the Church:
   b. And He is the beginning, the *firstborn* [i.e., captain] from the dead, so that He Himself might come to have first place in everything.
   c. For all the fullness was pleased to dwell in Him and through Him to *reconcile* all things to Himself, having made peace through the blood of His Cross;
   d. through Him, whether things on earth or things in the heavens.

Accordingly, the Tabernacle-commentary aspect of John's Gospel is not merely a curiosity. It is, rather, a profound statement of the nature of Biblical worldview. In Christ, the entire social order and the entire cosmic order are renewed.

One other point that should be made is this: John's Gospel is not *only* a commentary on the Tabernacle. John also comments on the various feasts of the Old Testament, and on other matters as well. The Tabernacle is only one dimension, one layer, of his Gospel. With this in mind, let us briefly tour the Tabernacle.

John begins in John 1:14 by saying that "the Word became flesh, and tabernacled among us, and we beheld His glory, glory as of the only begotten from the Father, full of grace and truth." The reference to glory is to the glory-cloud that filled the Tabernacle and was enthroned in it.

John begins where the priest would begin, with the laver of cleansing. Here the priest would wash himself and also the sacrifice before offering it. Jesus is both priest and sacrifice, and also the one who washes His living sacrifices, the Church.[7] Thus, John 1:18-34 concerns the baptism of John the Forerunner. In John 2:1-11, at a wedding Jesus takes water out of "six stone waterpots set there for the Jewish custom of purification" (2:6) and turns it into wine. In John 2:13-25, Jesus cleanses the Temple. In John 3:1-21, Nicodemus engages Jesus in a discussion of the new birth, of water and the Spirit. In John 3:22-36, John's baptism leads to an argument over purification, and a discussion of Jesus as the Bridegroom. In John 4:1-42, Jesus presents Himself as Bridegroom to a Samaritan woman at a well. In John 4:46-54, Jesus restores a dying boy to life at "Cana of Galilee, where He had made the water wine" (4:46). In John 5:1-47, Jesus heals a man at the pool of Bethesda, and then gets into a discussion with the Jews about resurrection. This concludes John's section on the laver, which has revolved around water, purification, baptism, resurrection, and Christ as Bridegroom.

John then turns to the Table of Showbread. In John 6, Jesus feeds the five thousand, calls Himself the bread of life, and tells the people that they must eat His flesh and drink His blood (v. 53). In John 7, Jesus presents Himself as the drink of life (v. 37), recalling the libations that went with the showbread and meal offerings.

The Lampstand comes next. Jesus presents Himself as the light of the world in John 8. In John 9, Jesus heals a blind man. In John 10, Jesus presents Himself as the Good Shepherd. The connection of this to the Lampstand lies in the fact that David was the Good Shepherd of the Old Covenant, and the Bible repeatedly speaks of David as a lamp (2 Samuel 21:17; 1 Kings 11:36; 15:4; 2 Kings 8:19; 2 Chronicles 21:7). There is a conceptual parallel between a lamp shining in a dark place and the voice of the shepherd heard by the sheep. In John 11, Jesus raises Lazarus, explaining that it is a matter of awakening him from darkness and sleep to light and day (vv. 9-11). In John 12, Jesus comments that those who had not believed in him were blind, but that those who did believe would become sons of light (vv. 35-41).

Starting in John 13, we move through these items of furniture a second time. Jesus washes the disciples' feet in 13:1-20. He breaks bread with them in 13:21-30. Then He moves into a discussion of the Holy Spirit, the ultimate archetype of the seven lamps in the Tabernacle (John 14–16). After this, Jesus prays His high priestly prayer at the altar of incense (John 17).

The Crucifixion and Death of Jesus involved a double motion, in terms of the Tabernacle. The sacrifice was made outside the Tabernacle in the courtyard on the altar. Then, on the day of atonement the High Priest took the blood into the Most Holy and presented it before the Throne of God (Leviticus 16:15). Just so, we see the Lamb of God sacrificed outside the gate, and then He presents His Death before the Father's throne (Hebrews 9:7, 23-26). Under the law, when the High Priest came back out from the Most Holy, still alive, it was a sign that God had accepted the sacrifice. The Resurrection of Jesus fulfills that type. Also, when the High Priest offered the sacrifice on the Day of Atonement, he put aside his garments of glory and beauty and wore a simple linen garment. Agreeably, when Peter entered the tomb, "he beheld the linen wrappings lying there" (John 20:6), because Jesus had put back on His garments of glory and beauty (Leviticus 16:4, 23-24).

When Mary Magdalene looked into the tomb, "she beheld two angels in white sitting, one at the head, and one at the feet, where the body of Jesus had been lying" (John 20:12). Arthur Pink comments,

Who can doubt that the Holy Spirit would have us link up this verse with Exodus 25:17-19 — "And thou shalt make a mercy-seat of pure gold . . . and thou shalt make *two* cherubims of gold, of beaten work shalt thou make them, *in the two ends* of the mercy-seat."[8]

The tomb enclosed by the great stone formed but one more Most Holy Place, all the more so because here the incarnate Word was placed.[9] Outside this tomb was a garden (John 19:41), a reminder of the garden-sanctuary of the Tabernacle. When Mary Magdalene saw Jesus, she rightly recognized Him as the new Gardener, the new Adam (John 20:15). The Magdalene, restored from her seven demons (Mark 16:9), symbolizes the Church, the new Eve.

John is not finished with his Edenic motifs. As God breathed life into Adam in Genesis 2:7, so Jesus breathes life into His Apostles in John 20:22. As naked Adam hid in the garden, so naked Peter hid in the sea until Jesus restored him (John 21:7). As Adam named the animals, so Peter and the rest of the disciples are told to guard and feed Christ's sheep (21:15-17).

Thus our Lord wrapped Himself in the garment of the old creation, and in His Death and Resurrection created it anew. But what is this new creation like?

The New Heavens and Earth

According to Revelation 21:1, the work of Christ brought about a new heavens and earth, "for the first heaven and the first earth passed away." This is explained a few verses later as the New Jerusalem, coming from *heaven*, overlaying a high mountain, which is the *earth*. Thus, the New Jerusalem-mountain complex is a picture of the new heavens and earth.

This is often nowadays taken to refer to the final eternal estate, but I believe the older commentaries are right in referring it first of all to the Gospel Age. After all, in the New Jerusalem the leaves of the trees are for the healing of the nations (Revelation 22:2), something that will not be needed after the last judgment. Also, people are invited to wash their robes and enter the gates (22:14), and the Spirit and bride summon outsiders to come in (22:17). Clearly, such evangelism will not take place

after the last judgment. So, while the fullness of the New Jerusalem and the New Heavens and Earth will not come until after
the last judgment, yet they are spiritual realities now. Thus,
Hebrews 12:22 says that we have already come to the heavenly Jerusalem.

Both the literal heavens and the governmental heavens have
been changed. The literal heavens were changed when a man,
Jesus Christ, ascended into them for the first time, and sat down
next to God the Father (Hebrews 9:24; Revelation 4-5). This
had never been the case before, because Adam and his posterity
had been barred from the garden and from heaven. Now that
Jesus has taken His throne, there is no longer any room for Satan
in heaven; and at last, Satan is cast out (Revelation 12:9).[10]

The change in the literal heavens necessitated a change in
the governmental heavens. The saints are seated in heaven with
Christ (Ephesians 2:6), and thus are stars (Philippians 2:15).
The total Church is pictured as seven lampstands, with her elders as seven stars (Revelation 1:20). Thus, the Church as a whole
and her leaders in particular constitute the new heavens. The
old heavens are cast down. In the Old Covenant, there were two
political heavens: the sun, moon, and stars of Israel, and the
suns, moons, and stars of the nations. The heavens of Israel
were destroyed in A.D. 70, and this is pictured in Revelation 6:11
as the fall of her sun, moon, and stars. The heavens of the nations began to be shaken down immediately after the destruction
of Jerusalem, according to Matthew 24:29. (See our discussion
of these passages in Chapter 5 above.)

As regards the earth, we find the same dual change. The
literal earth was changed at Pentecost by the descent of the
Spirit. Until the ascension there had never been a man in
heaven, and until Pentecost the fullness of the Spirit had never
been poured out on the earth. The coming of the Spirit literally
changed the earth.

This literal and cosmic change on the earth resulted in governmental changes as well. Previously, the priests had possessed
a status different from that of the lay Israelite. Only priests were
permitted to draw near into the Holy Place. Now, however, all
believers are *in Christ*, and in Christ there can be no distinction
of access. Christ is at the right hand of the Father, and in Him all

believers have fuller access than anyone had in the Old Covenant. Also, formerly Jew and Gentile had been separated, with the Jews as priests to the nations, and only Jews allowed to draw near into the courtyard and eat Passover. Now, however, all believers are *in Christ*, and in Christ there can no longer be such distinctions. Thus, the Jew-Gentile distinction was obliterated (Ephesians 2:11-22).

As a result of the elimination of these distinctions, the distinction between priestly Garden and lay-Israelite land is broken down. Also, the distinction between an Edenic land and other lands is eliminated. In fact, since the Gentile lands are often pictured as the sea, "there is no longer any sea" (Revelation 21:1).[11] Moreover, with the outpouring of the Spirit, and immediate access to heaven anywhere, there can no longer be any central sanctuary on the earth (Hebrews 9:8; 10:19-22; 12:18-24; Matthew 18:20).[12] The central sanctuary is in heaven, where Christ is.

These fundamental reorganizations mean that the kind of cosmic model found in the Old Testament will no longer do. We no longer have five environments with five different degrees of access to God (Heaven, Firmament-Heaven, Sanctuary, Land, World).[13] Now all believers have the same access, and all unbelievers are outside. There are only two environments.

The concept of the "world" changes in the New Covenant. Formerly, the "world" included converted and unconverted Gentiles, all those outside the Land. Now, however, "world" implies the realm outside the Kingdom altogether. The New Testament speaks of "worldliness" and of the "world, flesh, and devil" in a way not found in the Old Testament.

Practically speaking, the distinction between places of worship (sanctuaries), places of family life (homes), and places of work (world) is still valid. The distinction no longer has anything to do with nearness to God, however. There are no more *holy* places on earth, only *designated* places.

The radical character of this change is pointed to by Jesus in His curse upon old Jerusalem:

> that upon you may fall the guilt of all the righteous blood shed on earth, from the blood of righteous Abel to the blood of Zechariah, the son of Berechiah, whom you murdered between

the Temple and the altar. Truly I say to you, all these things
shall come upon this generation (Matthew 23:35-36).

Since the Temple in view, being rebuilt by Herod, had only
come into existence with Ezra, we might expect its destruction to
include all the martyrs from then on; but that is not what Jesus
said. Since Jerusalem had been built by David, we might expect
her destruction to include all the martyrs from then on; but that
is not what Jesus said. Since the Old Covenant received a definitive proclamation by Moses, we might expect its destruction to
include all the martyrs from then on; but that is not what Jesus
said. Since the "present heavens and earth" (2 Peter 3:7) had
been set up after the Flood, we might expect its destruction to include all the martyrs from then on; but that is not what Jesus
said. No, Jesus went all the way back to the original order of creation, to the first martyr. The whole order of the first creation,
with its Heavens-Sanctuary-Eden-World divisions, was going to
be wiped out. A new creation had come.

Thus, the cosmic model presented in Revelation 21–22 is
different from anything found in the Old Testament. There are
only two environments: inside the New Jerusalem and outside
the New Jerusalem. New Jerusalem is a hollow pyramid, a shell
of gems that comes out of heaven and is laid over a high mountain (Revelation 21:10). It symbolizes the body politic of the
Church (21:12, 14).[14] It is sanctuary and land rolled together, and
set up "on earth as in heaven," so that it is four-square in shape
like the heavenly Most Holy (21:16). It has no temple, because it
is so tall that it pokes through the firmament—except that there
is no longer any firmament—to the very throne of God (22:1).
(See Diagram 18.1.) Unlike Tabernacle and Temple, which were
enclosed and thus dark except for the lamps, New Jerusalem is
open and always daytime (21:23, 25).

In summary, the symbol of the New Covenant gives us only
two environments. There is the holy combined heaven, sanctuary, and land of the New Jerusalem; and there is the defiled
combined hell and "world" of those outside her walls. The ministry of the church is to persuade men to flee through her gates
and be saved.

Diagram 18.1
The New Jerusalem

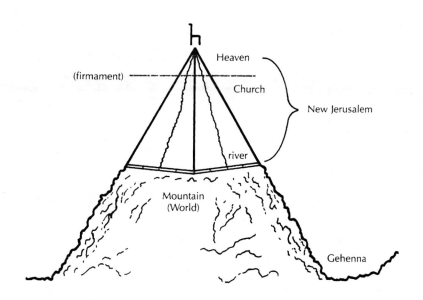

History

The coming of the new creation was in three phases. The first phase was in Jesus Christ alone. During the years of His earthly ministry, He was the Kingdom. His Disciples followed Him, and experienced a foretaste of His Kingdom; but before Pentecost, the Kingdom did not come to them. Only then were they clothed with power from on high.

The new Kingdom could not be envisioned by the Disciples. They and the rest of the Jews believed that Jesus would simply restore the glories of the Davidic monarchy in an imperial form. This was a logical vision for them to hold, in terms of the development of history, but it was an error. Just as the Hebrews in Egypt could not have envisioned the Tabernacle, and just as the Israelites of Samuel's day could not have envisioned the Temple, so the Jews of Jesus' day could not have envisioned the New

Covenant. Before Pentecost, the Disciples were still so confused as to ask when Jesus was going to restore the kingdom to Israel (Acts 1:6). After Pentecost, the believers continued to be somewhat confused over the relationship of Jew and Greek, so that it took miracles, confrontations, and a Church council to establish the new nature of the New Covenant (Acts 10-11; Galatians 2:11-21; Acts 15).

The second phase lasted from Pentecost in A.D. 30 to Holocaust in A.D. 70. This phase is known in the New Testament as the "last days," a phrase that unfortunately has been often misapplied to the time just before Christ's second coming.[15] During this phase, Ishmael and Isaac were together in the house, competing for possession of the kingdom. Finally, Ishmael was cast out, and Isaac stood forth as sole heir (Galatians 4:22-31). Also, during this forty-year period the Church despoiled the Old Covenant of its treasures, as Israel spoiled Egypt and as David spoiled the Philistines. These treasures built the new temple of God, His Church. Thus, during this period the old heavens and earth coexisted with the new.

What came down upon the disciples at Pentecost was God's glory-cloud. When we remember that the Tabernacle and Temple were Old Covenant architectural models of the glory-cloud, it is apparent that the New Jerusalem descended from heaven at Pentecost. What John sees in Revelation 21 is but a picture of what happened in Acts 2. It was on Pentecost that God gave the law from Mount Sinai.[16] As the cloud covered Mount Sinai with wind and fire and thunder, so "there came *from heaven* a noise like a violent, rushing wind" (Acts 2:2). The cloud was also filled with fire, which was distributed to the disciples (Acts 2:3). As the cloud filled the Tabernacle and Temple, so the cloud "filled the whole house where they were sitting" (Acts 2:2). In the Old Covenant, when the cloud filled the house, the priests had to flee; but in the New Covenant the Church is *in Christ*, and thus is not driven away from the Throne (cf. Exodus 40:35; 2 Chronicles 5:14). The heavenly cloud-pattern typologically imprinted itself on the house, creating a new world, and also upon the individuals in the house, filling them with the Spirit (Acts 2:4) and creating a new humanity.

The often controversial gift of other tongues was bestowed at Pentecost. According to the New Testament (1 Corinthians 14:20-22), one of the primary meanings of this gift, if not the only one, was as a sign of judgment upon Israel. The Gospel was going to the Gentiles and would be preached in new languages. If Israel was to hear it, they would have to hear it in other tongues. Indeed, the New Testament would be written not in Hebrew but in Greek! Such languages would sound like drunken speech (Isaiah 28:7-10; Acts 2:13-15), but would actually communicate judgment. Throughout the book of Acts, the Gospel went to the Jew first and then to the Gentile. Finally, in Acts 28:28, Paul declared to the Jews that full judgment was coming upon them, and that the Kingdom had been taken from them.[17]

Finally, after the elimination of the competition in A.D. 70, the new kingdom stood forth in glory. The former heavens and earth were done away, and the new had fully come.

Yet, while the initial coming of the Kingdom was in three stages, there is yet a fourth and final stage to come. After A.D. 70, God made it clear who the true heirs of the Old Covenant really were. All the same, the Church still exists in conflict in this world; and no matter how glorious the kingdom may become, she will still experience difficulty and death, and will still coexist with unbelievers. Only with the Second Coming of Christ will the Kingdom be finally come in all its fullness.

Typology

It remains only to note that all the different heavens and earth, all the different establishments of the Old Covenant are typological of the New. There is instruction for the Church in every aspect of the Old Testament. The book of Revelation, which deals largely with the destruction of old Jerusalem, begins with letters to seven churches. The message to these churches is this: You are the true heirs of the Old Covenant, but watch out. If you commit the same sins as Jerusalem, you will be punished as Jerusalem is about to be punished. So take heed!

Each of these seven churches was a true and separate church existing in Asia Minor. In the providence of God, however, each church was in a different spiritual state. These seven states correspond to seven stages of Old Covenant history. (We have only ex-

Diagram 18.2
Types of the Church in the Letters to the Seven Churches of Asia

Ephesus: Eden and the Fall

2:1	the Lord walking among tree-like lampstands (Ex.37:19-21)	the Lord walking in Eden (Gen. 3:8)
2:4-5	falling from the first love	Adam's fall

Reward:

2:7	tree of life; paradise of God	Genesis 2:9

Smyrna: The Patriarchs, especially Joseph

2:8	death and resurrection	Rom. 4:19; Gen. 25:21; 29:31; Gen. 22:1-14; Heb. 11:17-19
2:9	poverty and riches	Heb. 11:9
2:9	counterfeit Jews	counterfeit Isaac, Gen. 21:9; Gal. 4:22-31

Reward:

2:10	prison & elevation to the crown	Gen. 39, 41

Pergamum: The Exodus and Wilderness

2:13	Satan's environment	wilderness, Matt. 4:1; 12:43
2:14	Balaam	Num. 22-24; 31:16
2:14	Balak	Num. 25:1-3
2:16	sword against fornicators	Phineas, Num. 22:31; 25:7-8; 31:8

Reward:

2:17	hidden manna	Heb. 9:4 (manna hidden in ark)
2:17	white stone	Ex. 28:9-12; Zech. 3:5-9*

Thyatira: The Davidic Monarchy

2:18	bronze legs	Jachin & Boaz, 1 Kings 7:15-22
2:20	Jezebel	1 Kings 16, 21
2:22	great tribulation	1 Kings 17; Rev. 12:6; 13:5
2:23	God searches the heart	Psalms of David, esp. Ps. 51, 139

Reward:

2:26f.	Kingly rule	the Davidic Son, Psalm 2
2:28	the morning star	Root of David, Rev. 22:16

Sardis: Jeremiah and the Later Prophetic Period

3:1	almost dead	judgment and exile
3:3	invasion like a thief	sack of Jerusalem by Nebuchadnezzar (cp. Luke 12:39; Rev. 16:15; the sack of Jerusalem by Titus)
3:4	soiled garments	the garments of Joshua, Zech. 3

Reward:

3:5	white garments, Christ defending us against Satan before the Father	Zech. 3*

Philadelphia: The Return from Exile

3:7	restored David	Zerubbabel, Zech. 4*
3:8	little power	the post-exilic community (Ezra, Nehemiah)
3:8	open door	world influence (Esther)
3:9	false Jews	Ezra 4; Neh. 4, 6, 13

3:10	hour of testing	the invasion of Antiochus Epiphanes, Dan. 11

Reward:

3:12	rebuilt Temple	Haggai, Zechariah, Ezekiel 40-48
3:12	inscribed Name	Zech. 3:5, 9; 14:20*

Laodicea: The Period of Christ and the Apostles

3:15f.	lukewarm	Jews of Jesus' day
3:16	spew out of His mouth	Lev. 18:24-28; Luke 21:24
3:20	the Lord's Supper	New Covenant sacrament

Reward:

3:21	enthronement	Rev. 20:4-6

---

*On the symbolism in Zechariah, especially the identification of the white stone as the golden plate on the high priest's forehead, see James B. Jordan, "Zechariah's Night Visions," thirteen tapes available from Geneva Ministries, P.O. Box 131300, Tyler, Texas 75713.

plored six of them in this book.)[18] The imagery used to describe
each church is drawn from the stage of history appropriate to it.
This is outlined in Diagram 18.2.[19] What we learn from this is
that we can draw parallels between our present churches and
civilization to specific times in the Old Covenant, analogies that
will help us understand our present predicament. I shall make
an attempt to do just that in Chapter 19.

Conclusion

The New Covenant establishment can be set out as follows:

New Names:

God:	Father, Son, and Holy Spirit; Jesus Christ
People:	Christians

Grant:

The New Jerusalem, which is the Church and the kingdom; and the world as the place New Jerusalem is to permeate.

Promise:

I will be with you, even until the end of the world.

Stipulations:

Sacramental:	Water baptism and holy communion.
Societal:	The entire Biblical law, transformed through wisdom and paradox into the New Covenant, as illustrated but not exhausted in the Epistles.

Polity:

Church:	Temple sacraments and synagogue preaching are rolled together. There is no longer any blood line of priests. The Church is the first form of the Kingdom, around which a new culture develops.
State:	Romans 13 says that the civil magistrate is set up by God to be an avenger of blood. Under Christian influence, the magistrate is per-

suaded to avenge blood according to the standards of the Bible. Christ is world emperor before whom every local prince is to be persuaded to bow the knee. But note: we have moved beyond priest-kings, judges, kings, or emperors. Depending on times and places — the typological principle expressed above — any of these kinds of government can be appropriate, provided it is Christian.

Symbol: The New Jerusalem.

The Church's one Foundation
Is Jesus Christ her Lord:
She is His new creation
By water and the word:
From heaven He came and sought her
To be His Holy Bride.
With His own blood He bought her
And for her life He died.

Elect from every nation,
Yet one o'er all the earth,
Her charter of salvation,
One Lord, one Faith, one Birth;
One Holy Name she blesses,
Partakes one holy Food,
And to one hope she presses
With every grace endued.

The Church shall never perish!
Her dear Lord, to defend,
To guide, sustain, and cherish,
Is with her to the end;
Though there be those that hate her,
And false sons in her pale,
Against or foe or traitor
She ever shall prevail.

Though with a scornful wonder
Men see her sore opprest,
By schisms rent asunder,
By heresies distrest;
Yet saints their watch are keeping,
Their cry goes up, "How long?"
And soon the night of weeping
Shall be the morn of song.

'Mid toil and tribulation,
And tumult of her war,
She waits the consummation
Of peace for evermore;
Till with the vision glorious
Her longing eyes are blest,
And the great Church victorious
Shall be the Church at rest.

So, Lord, she stands before Thee,
For evermore thine own;
No merit is her glory,
Her boasting this alone:
Then she who did not choose Thee
Came, chosen, at Thy call,
Never to leave or lose Thee,
Or from Thy favour fall.

For Thy true word remaineth;
No creature far or nigh,
No fiend of ill who reigneth
In hell or haunted sky;
No doubting world's derision
That holds her in despite,
Shall hide her from Thy vision,
Shall lure her from Thy light.

Thine, Thine! in bliss or sorrow,
As well in shade as shine:
Of old, to-day, to-morrow,
To all the ages, Thine!
Thine in her great commission,
Baptized into Thy Name,
And in her last fruition
Of all her hope and aim.

As she on earth hath union
With God, the Three in One,
So hath she sweet communion
With those whose rest is won;
With all her sons and daughters,
Who by the Master's hand
Led through the deathly waters,
Repose in Eden-land.

O happy ones and holy!
Lord, give us grace that we
Like them, the meek and lowly,
On high may dwell with Thee;
There past the border mountains,
Where, in sweet vales, the Bride
With Thee, by living fountains,
Forever shall abide.

—S. J. Stone (1885)[1]

THE COURSE
OF HISTORY

As we come to the end of this study, let us step back and take a larger view of history (illustrated in Diagram 19.1). One thing that stands out is that each stage of history is more glorious than the previous one. There is definite growth and maturation in history; and though the wicked also grow and mature, their development is in the direction of degradation, not of glorification. The Bible clearly shows a progression for the righteous, and only a retrogression for the wicked.

The Growth of the Kingdom in the Bible

Before the Flood the whole world was corrupt, and there were only eight righteous souls to enter Noah's Ark. In the Patriarchal era, the Kingdom only existed by way of anticipation, since the Patriarchs did not possess the land. They dug their water out of the ground. In the Mosaic era, the Kingdom did hold the land, though with difficulty. A laver of water was positioned above ground in the Tabernacle, and the land drank its rain from heaven (Deuteronomy 11:11). In the Davidic era, the internal enemies of Israel were subdued permanently, and the Kingdom became much more glorious. A huge sea of water stood in the Temple Courtyard. In the Restoration, Israel began to bear witness to all the nations of the earth, and the Kingdom began invisibly to spread and influence the world. A river flowed out of the Temple. Finally, in the New Covenant, the Kingdom was fully internationalized, and the four-fold river of Eden was restored, only this time flowing out of heaven itself.

Such a vision of the growth and gradual influence of God's Kingdom was once the common coin of Christendom, though in

Diagram 19.1
A History of the Cosmos

	Prominent Symbols of the Cosmic Order	The Literal Heavens	Characteristic Political Heavens over the World	Political Heavens over the Land (Eden)	Spiritual Heavens
1st—Pre-Fall	Eden & Garden	Angels	Adam	Adam	Adam as Priest
Post Fall	Eden & Garden	Satan included	Strong Men	Seth's Line	Seth's Line
2nd—Noah 2 Peter 3:5-6	(The Ark) Rainbow, Altars	Satan included	Priest-Kings	No land	Godly Priest-Kings
3rd—Patriarchs Genesis 15:5	Oasis Sanctuaries	Satan included	Developing nations	Patriarchs (Genesis 14)	Abrahamic line
4th—Mosaic Isaiah 51:15-16	Tabernacle	Satan included	Developing nations	Judges	Aaronic priests, and seers
5th—Davidic Jer. 4:23-31	Temple	Satan included	Nations	Kings	Priests, reorganized by David, and Prophets
6th—Restoration Jer. 4:23-31	Ezekiel's Visionary Temple, and the physical Temples of Ezra and Herod	Satan included	Empires	Imperial Appointees and Jewish leaders	Priests and Synagogue leaders
7th—New Rev. 21:1	John's Visionary New Jerusalem	Man included; Satan cast out	Political Rulers		Church and Elders

the past century or so it has become more common to expect evil to triumph.[2] To be sure, the Bible does say that right before our Lord's return, the wicked will mount an assault on the holy city (Revelation 20:7-10). This attack, however, is evidence of a decline; and so we ask, a decline from what? Obviously, a decline from an earlier period of Kingdom prosperity.

In numerous places the Bible indicates the continued growth of Christ's Kingdom at the expense of Satan's. For instance, in Nebuchadnezzar's dream of the course of empire, the Kingdom of God strikes the statue of humanism. As Daniel explains to Nebuchadnezzar:

> You continued looking until a stone was cut out without hands, and it struck the statue on its feet of iron and clay, and crushed them. Then the iron, the clay, the bronze, the silver and the gold were crushed all at the same time, and became like chaff from the summer threshing floors; and the wind carried them away so that not a trace of them was found. But the stone that struck the statue became a great mountain and filled the whole earth (Daniel 2:34-35).

I believe on the basis of Exodus 20:25 that the stone cut without hands is a reference to the altar. Remember, the altar is a holy mountain, and we have seen the altar grow and become bigger throughout Old Testament history. The altar speaks of Jesus Christ, of course, but also of true worship. It is true worship that will undermine and destroy the kingdoms of this world.

Notice though, that the stone (or altar) grows until it fills the whole earth. It does not say that the altar simply coexists with the wicked world. Nor does it say that the altar jumps instantly to fill the world. No, it says that the altar (or stone) *gradually* grows to fill the world.

Along similar lines we can consider the river of Ezekiel 47. We remember that the first application of this passage is to the Restoration establishment, but since the Restoration covenant, like all covenants, is a *type* of the New Covenant, we can legitimately make applications to the New Testament era as well. Notice, then, that after the river begins trickling out of the Temple, it grows deeper and wider as it goes.

When the man went out toward the east with a line in his hand,
he measured a thousand cubits, and he led me through the
water, water reaching the ankles. Again he measured a thousand and led me through the water, water reaching the knees.
Again he measured a thousand and led me through the water,
water reaching the loins. Again he measured a thousand; and it
was a river that I could not ford, for the water had risen,
enough water to swim in, a river that could not be forded (Ezekiel 47:3-5).

Again, this is not a picture of instant Kingdom, but of gradual
growth and development.

Jesus said the same in His parables. Let us consider the
Kingdom parables of Matthew 13. In the Parable of the Wheat
and the Tares, Jesus makes it clear that the wicked will always
coexist with the righteous in this world (Matthew 13:24-30), but
this parable does not say that they remain at equal strength. No,
rather Jesus immediately tells the Parable of the Mustard Seed,
which says that the Kingdom starts small but gradually grows to
become the largest of all garden trees, so that the birds, the nations of the world, rest supported by its branches (Matthew
13:31-32). Jesus follows this up by comparing the Kingdom of
God to leaven, which gradually leavens a lump of dough (v. 33).[3]

Thus, the Bible pictures the continuing growth of the Kingdom after its establishment by Jesus Christ. Of course, theologians have debated how far this will go — whether or not there will
be a one-thousand year golden age, and the like.[4] It is not my
purpose here to get into this question, but simply to make the
point that the Kingdom is growing from glory to glory.

The Growth of the Kingdom in Church History

Since we live in an age of setback, it is not always apparent
to us that the Kingdom has, in fact, grown. But, if we take a
look at the Kingdom in the year 300, we find it suffering in pre-
Constantinian tribulation. A few centuries later, the Church was
wrestling the tribes of Northern Europe into the Kingdom; while
in the East, Christianity experienced a real golden age, and what
we call "Nestorian" Christians had influence throughout India
and China. A few centuries later, after the high "Middle" ages
and the Protestant Reformation, Christianity greatly discipled

the European countries, spread to the Americas, and gave birth to the printing press, university education, technology, and many other benefits. During the last century, Christianity extended all over the globe as a result of the missionary movement and almost eradicated slavery (though slavery still exists in some Islamic countries, and behind the iron curtain).[5]

The history of the Church is not a history of smooth advances, however. From what we have seen of Biblical history, we should expect periods of setback. We should expect that an old establishment wears thin, and declines into stultification and error, only to be replaced by a new establishment that does fuller justice to the faith. Each new establishment takes up the strengths of the previous one, but transforms it into something new and more powerful, more glorious.[6]

For instance, after a couple of centuries of tribulation, God gave Constantine to the Church. Constantine is much criticized by ignorant persons today; but there can be no doubt that his conversion was a welcome change for the thousands of maimed, crippled, and raped Christians of his day. The Constantinian Establishment may not measure up by today's standards, but it was glorious in its time. It gave peace to the Kingdom, and enabled Christianity to blossom in the East, bringing the Gospel to many peoples and bringing about tremendous blessings.

In the West, the Constantinian Establishment did not last. It was, after all, imperfect. After several centuries of strife and disorder, God brought to pass the Papal Establishment in the West. Protestants like me find it easy to find fault with the Papacy, but we should remember that the firm hand of strong godly Popes helped bring the unruly tribes of Europe into the Kingdom. Just because the Popes of Luther's day were bad does not mean they always had been. In their day, the tribes of Europe were in a state of continual warfare. By outlawing war during Lent, on Sunday, and at such times as the Peace of God and the Truce of God, the Papacy eventually brought about a condition of continual peace. Wars were declared, fought, and ended. Peace was normal. The Popes and godly emperors brought this about, using the rod of excommunication.

The Papal Establishment, however, was imperfect. It led to abuses, and the Christians of Northern Europe did not like being dominated by Italians. So, God gave the Reformation. The Reformation functioned differently in various countries, but it did bring a new and better "covenant." The Reformation brought freedom of the press, literacy, university education, and technology. But the Reformation Establishments were imperfect also. They were too closely tied to the various nations, and in the United States to separate denominations. The sense of true catholicity in Christendom was lost.

The Growth of the Kingdom in the Future

So, what is next? From our study of the Bible, we can say that when God is pleased to give us a New Establishment, it will take up the best of all the previous ones; but it will transform them into something new. The future cannot be envisioned. For me, the period of Samuel is a close analogy to our present situation. In Samuel's day, the Ark was located at Kiriath-jearim, the Tabernacle at Nob, and the High Priest out in the field with David. An evil, demonized king was on the throne.[7] I imagine that the priests at Kiriath-jearim insisted that the Ark was the most important thing. I imagine that the priests at Nob emphasized the Tabernacle and its importance. I imagine David's troops felt that the dynamic presence of the High Priest and his ephod was the most important thing. Theologians of the day doubtless speculated on how to get all this back together, but they had no idea of what was really going to happen. The New Establishment was something they could never have imagined.

Compare our situation today. We have the discipleship wing of the charismatic movement, which is composed of devout, God-fearing people who pray and work for reform. Many of them think that the best thing would be if we all joined up with them. We also have the revival in Eastern Orthodoxy, signaled by the writings of Alexander Schmemann. Of course, Orthodox theologians believe that we all need to pack up and join Orthodoxy! Then there is the strong revival in Reformational churches, centered on the profound thought of Cornelius Van Til. Many of these people go by the name "Christian Reconstruction," and wish that everyone else would join the Reconstructionist movement. As we continue our survey, we find the neo-Puritan movement in Presbyterian and Baptist churches.

These earnest people call us back to the best of our forefathers, but all too often think that this is all we need.

Now, I don't want to leave anyone out, but I'm sure I will. Time will fail me if I tell of the revival of evangelical belief in Roman Catholicism, the renewal of Psalm-singing in mainline churches, the deepening theological endeavors of various parachurch organizations, and the like. I have been involved with many of these, and in each case, those with the Ark think it is most important; those with the Tabernacle think it is most important; and those with the ephod think it is most important. Christendom today is scattered.

The future, though, cannot be envisioned. It is no good if we all join the neo-Puritans, or the Reconstructionists, or the renewed Orthodox, or the discipleship Charismatics. God has taken hold of Christendom and He has torn it apart. He intends to put it back together again in a new Kingdom Establishment. We cannot advance His timetable, or presume upon His designs.

What then? Our present duties remain the same as ever. The Christian is not called to play God and manipulate history, but to serve God in his calling. And this pulls us back to basics: Bible study, prayer, the sacraments, godly home life, public worship, faithful work on the job.

For the pastor, it means that whatever camp we are in, our duties remain the same. Let worship be a true covenant renewal, with the rite of covenant renewal restored (see Chapter 10). Let us return to God's hymnal, the Psalter, as the foundation of our hymns (not excluding the other great hymns of the Church). Let Bible study and Biblical exposition be foremost in our teaching and preaching. In this way, we lay a foundation, we build up the saints, we prepare the way for the New Establishment to come. Who knows just how wonderful it will be?

END NOTES

Introduction

1. Vincent Rossi, "Understanding History from a Christian Perspective," *Tree of Life* 4:1 (1986), p. 14.

Chapter 1—Interpreting the World Design

1. A translation of Basil's *Hexameron* is found in *The Nicene and Post-Nicene Fathers*, series 2, vol. 8 (Grand Rapids: Eerdmans, n.d.). A translation of Augustine's work by John H. Taylor is published as vols. 41 & 42 of the Ancient Christian Writers series (New York: Newman Press, 1982).
2. On Biblical chronology, see James B. Jordan, "The Biblical Chronology Question: An Analysis," *Creation Social Sciences and Humanities Quarterly* II:2 (Winter 1979):9-15, II:3 (Spring, 1980):17-26. A copy of this essay can be obtained from Biblical Horizons, P.O. Box 132011, Tyler, TX 75713.
3. On the shifting sands of science, see Thomas S. Kuhn, *The Structure of Scientific Revolutions*, 2d ed. (Chicago: University of Chicago Press, 1970); and Stanley L. Jaki, *The Road of Science and the Ways to God* (Chicago: University of Chicago Press, 1978). These two works are complementary. In my opinion, Kuhn sees too much discontinuity, but Jaki sees too much continuity.
4. On the scale of being, see Arthur O. Lovejoy, *The Great Chain of Being* (Cambridge: Harvard University Press, 1936); and Rousas J. Rushdoony, *The One and the Many* (Tyler, TX: Thoburn Press, [1971] 1978).
5. Those who wish to read further in the area of six-day creationism should consult the following studies: Gary North, *The Dominion Covenant: Genesis*, 2d ed. (Tyler, TX: Institute for Christian Economics, 1987); Gary North, ed., *The Journal of Christian Reconstruction* I:1, "Symposium on Creation" (1974); Edward J. Young, *Studies in Genesis One* (Phillipsburg, NJ: Presbyterian and Reformed Pub. Co., 1964); John C. Whitcomb, *The Early Earth* (Grand Rapids: Baker, 1972); and R. J. Rushdoony, *The Mythology of Science* (Nutley, NJ: Craig Press, 1967).
6. See James B. Jordan, *Revelation Made Practical* (tape set with syllabus available from Biblical Horizons, P.O. Box 132011, Tyler, TX 75713).
7. George E. Mendenhall, *The Tenth Generation: The Origins of the Biblical Tradition* (Baltimore: Johns Hopkins Press, 1973), p. 39.
8. The recent trend in "liberal" scholarship is to grant a bit more intelligence to the "final redactor." Of course, Divine authorship continues to be denied.

291

9. For a full discussion, see Jordan, "Saul: A Study in Original Sin," *The Geneva Papers* 2:11 (July, 1988; Tyler, Texas: Geneva Ministries).

10. Roderick Campbell, *Israel and the New Covenant* (Tyler, TX: Geneva Ministries, [1954] 1983), p. 60. Also see Othmar Keel, *The Symbolism of the Biblical World: Ancient Near Eastern Iconography and the Book of Psalms*, trans. Timothy J. Hallett (New York: Seabury Press, 1978).

11. David Chilton, *The Days of Vengeance: An Exposition of the Book of Revelation* (Fort Worth: Dominion Press, 1987), p. 33.

12. Ibid., pp. 344ff.

13. Ben C. Ollenburger, *Zion, City of the Great King: A Theological Symbol of the Jerusalem Cult* (Sheffield, England: Sheffield Academic Press, 1987), pp. 19-20.

14. In the course of this book I shall have occasion to note several such studies. I wish to advise the reader that my endorsement of such works is highly selective.

15. The most useful discussion of the difference between Biblical typology and Greek allegory in the Church Fathers is Jean Daniélou, *From Shadows to Reality: Studies in the Biblical Typology of the Fathers*, trans. Wulstan Hibberd (Westminster, MD: Newman Press, 1960). On the history of typology, see Richard M. Davidson, *Typology in Scripture: A Study of Hermeneutical TYPOS Structures* (Berrien Springs, MI: Andrews University Press, 1981).

Chapter 2 — The Purpose of the World

1. Note written by Luther inside a book of Pliny. Martin E. Marty, *Health and Medicine in the Lutheran Tradition* (New York: Crossroad Pub., 1983), p. 27.

2. The best discussion of the philosophy of "Being" versus Christianity is Rousas J. Rushdoony, *The One and the Many* (Tyler, TX: Thoburn Press, [1971] 1978).

3. Herman Bavinck, *The Doctrine of God*, trans. William Hendriksen (Edinburgh: The Banner of Truth Trust, [1918] 1977), p. 91.

4. Ibid., p. 88.

5. Quoted in ibid.

6. The finest single essay on this subject is Cornelius Van Til, "Nature and Scripture," in Paul Woolley, ed., *The Infallible Word*, 3d ed. (Phillipsburg, NJ: Presbyterian and Reformed Pub. Co., 1967). Van Til shows that natural revelation is necessary, authoritative, sufficient, and clear. From an different theological tradition, see the remarks of Alexander Schmemann, *For the Life of the World* (Crestwood, NY: St. Vladimir's Seminary Press, 1973), pp. 117-134.

7. John M. Frame, *The Doctrine of the Knowledge of God* (Phillipsburg, NJ: Presbyterian and Reformed Pub. Co., 1987), p. 230.

8. Bavinck, p. 88.

9. Ibid., p. 89.

10. Van Til, in Woolley, p. 273.

11. Bavinck, pp. 86-7. Bavinck continues, "Further, human actions are ascribed to God, as, knowing, Genesis 18:21; trying, Psalm 7:9; thinking, Genesis 50:20. . . ." He fills half a page with these.

12. Ibid., p. 87.

13. Ibid., p. 97.

Chapter 3 — Symbolism and Worldview

1. While any survey of the history of philosophy can be consulted for more information on this, for our purposes the best introduction is Rousas J. Rushdoony, *The One and the Many* (Tyler, TX: Thoburn Press, [1971] 1978). On the subject

of symbolism, all modern religious anthropological studies are written from the standpoint that religio-symbolic worldview structures are man-made, either by particular men and traditions, or arising out of a human collective unconscious of one sort or another.

2. On the equal importance of both approaches, see the remarks of John M. Frame, *The Doctrine of the Knowledge of God* (Phillipsburg, NJ: Presbyterian and Reformed Pub. Co., 1987), especially pp. 207-212.

3. See the useful discussion in Louis Berkhof, *Systematic Theology*, 4th ed. (Grand Rapids: Eerdmans, 1949), p. 89.

4. Herman Bavinck, *The Doctrine of God*, trans. William Hendriksen (Edinburgh: The Banner of Truth Trust, [1918] 1977), p. 94.

5. See Bavinck's discussion of this, p. 92.

6. My own discussion is in Jordan, *The Sociology of the Church* (Tyler, TX: Geneva Ministries, 1986), pp. 33-49.

7. Fascinating studies in the power of dress and symbol can be found in the works of Tom Wolfe, especially *The Kandy-Kolored Tangerine-Flake Streamline Baby* (1965), *The Pump House Gang* (1968), *Radical Chic and Mau-Mauing the Flak Catchers* (1970), and *In Our Time* (1980).

8. In a way what has happened with the U.S. Constitution, and with the Westminster Confession, is that their value as symbols has changed. Originally it was the *content* of these documents that was their primary value. The power of their contents has diminished over time, however. At the same time, with age they have become symbols in another sense, functioning like flags or banners, or security blankets. To put it another way, they have moved from being primarily verbal symbols to being to a considerable extent non-verbal symbols. People are loyal to the Constitution, but most have little idea what it says.

9. Further thoughts along these lines can be found in James B. Jordan, "Church Music in Chaos," in Jordan, ed., *The Reconstruction of the Church*. Christianity & Civilization No. 4 (Tyler, TX: Geneva Ministries, 1985), pp. 241-265.

Chapter 4 — The World as God's House

1. The word "heaven" only occurs in the dual in Hebrew, and so there is no implication in Genesis 1:1 of more than one heaven at this point. In other words, "the heavens" is the same as "heaven."

2. Meredith G. Kline, *Images of the Spirit* (Grand Rapids: Baker, 1980), p. 17. Kline's entire book deals with this matter, one way or another.

3. Ibid., especially chap. 2.

4. See James B. Jordan, *The Sociology of the Church* (Tyler, TX: Geneva Ministries, 1986), pp. 32, 279f.; and David Chilton, *Days of Vengeance: An Exposition of the Book of Revelation* (Fort Worth, TX: Dominion Press, 1987).

5. Kline, pp. 13-26.

6. Ibid., p. 20.

7. Meredith G. Kline, *Kingdom Prologue*, 3 vols. (by the author, 1981; available from Gordon-Conwell Theological Seminary, South Hamilton, MA) 1:49. For extended discussion, see Kline, *Images*, chap. 1; and David Chilton, *Paradise Restored* (Ft. Worth, TX: Dominion Press, 1985), chap. 7.

8. Kline states that "the Glory-Spirit provided a preview of the finished creation-structure, for this theophanic Spirit-formation was a divine paradigm as well as a divine power for the work of creation. Cosmos and man alike were to be formed after this archetypal temple pattern in the heavens." *Kingdom Prologue* 1:49.

9. R. Laird Harris, Gleason L. Archer, Jr., and Bruce K. Waltke, eds., *Theological Wordbook of the Old Testament*, 2 vols. (Chicago: Moody Press, 1980) 2:861, no. 2217.

10. In addition to the works of Meredith Kline, noted above, a valuable study of the glory-cloud is R. E. Hough, *The Ministry of the Glory Cloud* (New York: Philosophical Library, 1955). Also see David Chilton, *Paradise Restored*, chap. 7, and Chilton, *Days of Vengeance*.

11. Richard M. Davidson, *Typology in Scripture: A Study of Hermeneutical TYPOS Structures* (Berrien Springs, MI: Andrews University Press, 1981), pp. 115-190.

12. The best introduction to the study of typology is Davidson, referenced above. Davidson refines and perfects the perspective found in Patrick Fairbairn's nineteenth-century study, *The Typology of Scripture*, 2 vols. (New York: Funk and Wagnalls, 1876). Davidson is an Adventist, but the peculiarities of that position seldom interfere with the value of his five-hundred-page study. The student may wish to look at the following studies as well: G. W. H. Lampe and K. J. Woollcombe, *Essays in Typology.* Studies in Biblical Theology 22 (London: SCM Press, 1957); Francis Foulkes, *The Acts of God: A Study of the Basis of Typology in the Old Testament* (London: The Tyndale Press, 1958); R. T. France, *Jesus and the Old Testament* (Downers Grove, IL: Inter-Varsity Press, 1971); Moisés Silva, *Has the Church Misread the Bible* (Grand Rapids: Zondervan, 1987). An excellent popular introduction to the typological reading of the Bible is S. G. DeGraaf, *Promise and Deliverance*, 4 vols., trans. H. Evan Runner and Elizabeth W. Runner (St. Catherines, Ontario: Paideia Press, 1977).

13. Jean Daniélou, *From Shadows to Reality: Studies in the Biblical Typology of the Fathers*, trans. Wulstan Hibberd (Westminster, MD: Newman Press, 1960), p. 1.

14. Ibid., p. 57. "In an unpublished thesis, Fr. Delcuve has shown that [Philo's] *Allegorical Commentary on the Laws* was entirely a symbolical interpretation of the Aristotelian theory of knowledge," p. 58.

15. Ibid., p. 58.

16. Herbert Schlossberg, *Idols for Destruction* (Nashville: Thomas Nelson, 1983), p. 11.

17. Notice how the description of Jesus Christ in Revelation 1 matches the description of His bride, New Jerusalem, in Revelation 21-22. The bride has been remade in the image of her Husband.

Chapter 5 — Sun, Moon, and Stars

1. Judges 5:31; 1 Thessalonians 5:1-11; Genesis 15:12; 32:23-30; Exodus 12:29; 2 Samuel 23:4; Isaiah 60:1-3; Zechariah 1-6; Malachi 4:1-2; Luke 1:78; John 3:2. See James B. Jordan, "Christianity and the Calendar," Chapters 2 and 3. Available from Biblical Horizons, P.O. Box 132011, Tyler, TX 75713.

2. See James B. Jordan, *Judges: God's War Against Humanism* (Tyler, TX: Geneva Ministries, 1985), pp. 107, 144, 236.

3. There may be an intended association between the east-west motion of the rising sun and the east-west motion of God's glory as it enters His house. Notice the imagery of Deuteronomy 33:2; Judges 5:4; Ezekiel 43:1-5.

4. M. Barnouin, "Remarques sur les tableaux numériques du libre des Nombres," *Revue Biblique* 76 (1969):351-64; Barnouin, "Recherches numériques sur la généalogie de Gen. V," *Revue Biblique* 77 (1970):347-65; Barnouin, "Les Recensements du Livre des nombres et l'Astronomie Babylonienne," *Vetus Testamentum* 27 (1977):280-303; English translation, "The Censuses of the Book of Numbers and Babylonian Astronomy," available for $5.00 from Biblical Horizons, P.O. Box 132011, Tyler, TX 75713; cf. also Gordon Wenham, *Numbers: An Introduction and Commentary* (Downers Grove, IL: Inter-Varsity Press, 1981), pp. 64-66; and Wenham, *Genesis 1-15* (Waco, TX: Word Books, 1987), pp. 133-34.

5. There is a considerable literature on the synagogal zodiacs. See Bernard Goldman, *The Sacred Portal: A Primary Symbol in Ancient Judaic Art* (Lanham, MD: University Press of America, 1986); and Rachel Hachlili, "The Zodiac in Ancient Jewish Art: Representation and Significance," *Bulletin of the American Schools of Oriental Research* 228 (December, 1977):61-77. Most modern authors are slow to associate these zodiacs with the twelve tribes, but Josephus as an ancient source is probably more reliable, and he does do so. In his *Antiquities*, 3:7:7, he associates the twelve stones of the High Priest's breastpiece with the twelve months and the twelve signs. The names of the tribes were on these stones.

6. See Joseph A. Seiss, *The Gospel in the Stars; or, Primeval Astronomy* (Grand Rapids: Kregel, [1882] 1972); Ethelbert W. Bullinger, *The Witness of the Stars* (Grand Rapids: Kregel, [1893] 1967); and a more moderate presentation, Duane E. Spencer, *The Gospel in the Stars* (San Antonio, TX: The Word of Grace, 1972).

7. R. H. Allen, *Star Names: Their Lore and Meaning* (New York: Dover, 1963), pp. 57, 362.

8. For further study, see Ernest L. Martin, *The Birth of Christ Recalculated*, 2d ed. (Pasadena, CA: Foundation for Biblical Research, 1980), pp. 167-172; Austin Farrer, *A Rebirth of Images: The Making of St. John's Apocalypse* (Gloucester, MA: Peter Smith, [1949] 1970), chaps. 7, 8; Farrer, *The Revelation of St. John the Divine* (Oxford: Clarendon Press, 1964); David Chilton, *The Days of Vengeance: An Exposition of the Book of Revelation* (Fort Worth, TX: Dominion Press, 1987), pp. 300-303. Farrer's approach is not the same as Martin's. The student will find that the faces in Numbers 2 are transposed from their positions in the zodiac. The explanation for this is that Judah replaced Reuben as firstborn. See also Joan André Moore, *Astronomy in the Bible* (Nashville: Abingdon, 1981), pp. 85-91.

9. On Revelation 6 in detail, see Chilton, *Days of Vengeance*, pp. 196-199.

10. On the overall interpretation of Matthew 24, see J. Marcellus Kik, *An Eschatology of Victory* (Phillipsburg, NJ: Presbyterian and Reformed Pub. Co., 1971); Ralph Woodrow, *Great Prophecies of the Bible* (Box 124, Riverside, CA: Woodrow Evangelistic Association, 1971); David Chilton, *The Great Tribulation* (Fort Worth, TX: Dominion Press, 1987); William R. Kimball, *What the Bible Says About the Great Tribulation* (Grand Rapids: Baker, 1983); and James B. Jordan, "Lectures on Matthew 24," eleven-tape series (available from Biblical Horizons, P.O. Box 132011, Tyler, TX 75713). On verse 29, see Kimball and Jordan.

Chapter 6 — Rocks, Gold, and Gems

1. Some very interesting observations on the context of this verse (the headwaters of the Jordan flow from a huge rock, and other matters) are discussed in Stanley L. Jaki, *And On This Rock: The Witness of One Land and Two Covenants* (Notre Dame, IN: Ave Maria Press, 1978). Jaki is a conservative Roman Catholic, and argues for the office of the papacy in this book. Nonetheless, many of his observations are very useful.

2. There is a reference to bdellium in Revelation 2:17, "To him who overcomes, to him I will give some of the hidden manna, and I will give him a white stone, and a new name written on the stone which no one knows but he who receives it." Like everything in Revelation, this verse ties together many Old Testament passages; but with manna and white stone both mentioned together, a reference to the bdellium of Havilah cannot be excluded from the list.

3. On the identification of these stones, see Ruth V. Wright and Robert L. Chadbourne, *Gems and Minerals of the Bible* (New Canaan, CT: Keats Publishing, Inc., 1970); and Athalya Brenner, *Colour Terms in the Old Testament*. Journal for the Study of the Old Testament Supplement Series 21 (Sheffield, England: Department of Biblical Studies, University of Sheffield, 1982).

4. On the land as Israel and the sea as Gentiles, see Chapter 12.

Chapter 7 — Trees and Thorns

1. For more on Joseph as baker and cupbearer, and its wider meaning, see James B. Jordan, *Primeval Saints: Studies in the Patriarchs of Genesis*, chap. 10. Available from Biblical Horizons, P.O. Box 132011, Tyler, TX 75713.

2. For a fuller discussion of the history of Assyria, its conversion and apostasy, see James B. Jordan, "Nahum," three taped lectures (available from Biblical Horizons, P.O. Box 132011, Tyler, TX 75713).

3. The strong possibility that Christ was crucified on the Mount of Olives only corroborates this. See Ernest L. Martin, *The Place of Christ's Crucifixion: Its Discovery and Significance* (Pasadena, CA: Foundation for Biblical Research, 1984).

4. See Carol F. Meyers, *The Tabernacle Menorah: A Synthetic Study of a Symbol from the Biblical Cult*. American Schools of Oriental Research Dissertation Series 2 (Missoula, MT: Scholars Press, 1976).

5. This becomes more pregnant if Martin is right and the tree is an olive. See note 3 above.

6. On the identification of these and other Biblical trees and plants, see W. E. Shewell-Cooper, *Plants, Flowers, and Herbs of the Bible* (New Canaan, CT: Keats Publishing, Inc., 1977), and United Bible Societies, *Fauna and Flora of the Bible*, 2d ed. (New York: United Bible Societies, 1980).

7. On the degrees of glory, see James B. Jordan, "From Glory to Glory: Degrees of Value in the Sanctuary" (available from Biblical Horizons, P.O. Box 132011, Tyler, TX 75713).

8. See Francis X. Weiser, *Handbook of Christian Feasts and Customs* (New York: Harcourt, Brace, and Co., 1952), pp. 98-103.

Chapter 8 — Birds and Beasts

1. See my remarks on this in James B. Jordan, *The Law of the Covenant: An Exposition of Exodus 21-23* (Tyler, TX: Institute for Christian Economics, 1984), pp. 122-124.

2. Such passages as Leviticus 26:6, Ezekiel 34:25, and Isaiah 11:6-9 indicate that when men are faithful to God, the dangerous animals become peaceable. These passages are often taken symbolically, but there is no particular reason to exclude a literal meaning as foundational for the symbolic. If the wild animals were once peaceful before the Fall, there is no reason to believe that they cannot once again become peaceful when the world is converted to Christ. Our discussion of the angelic world, Chapter 9, will provide a scientific basis for such a change.

3. Much of the rest of this chapter is taken from my studies *Food and Faith: The Mosaic Dietary Laws in New Covenant Perspective* (available from Biblical Horizons, P.O. Box 132011, Tyler, TX 75713).

4. Elijah Judah Schochet, *Animal Life in Jewish Tradition: Attitudes and Relationships* (New York: Ktav Publishing House, 1984), pp. 35-36. This book is a gold mine of information. On animals in the Bible, see also Alice Parmelee, *All the Birds of*

the Bible (New Canaan, CT: Keats Publishing, Inc., 1959); Roy Pinney, *The Animals of the Bible* (New York: Chilton Books, 1964); United Bible Societies, *Fauna and Flora of the Bible*, 2d ed. (New York: United Bible Societies, 1980); George S. Cansdale, *All the Animals of the Bible Lands* (Grand Rapids: Zondervan, 1970).

5. Though men are indeed more like animals than plants, we note that plants also keep the sabbath (Leviticus 25), also experience the blessing and curse of the covenant in the form of rain and drought, and their firstfruits are also given to God. Also, cereal offerings were made along with the animal sacrifices (Leviticus 2). Both wood and animals were brought up on the altar, though the wood is not called a sacrifice. Thus, while the analogies between men and animals are closer and more pronounced, there are similar analogies between men and the vegetable kingdom.

6. Greek: *pantos*.

7. Carmichael basically advocates just this point. As regards Deuteronomy 22:10, he argues that it is not expressly forbidden to plow a field with yoked ox and ass, but only to plow with them together in general, language used for sexual relations and finding its background and fulfillment in human affairs. He also calls attention to the parallel in Leviticus 19:19, which prohibits breeding ox and ass together; Calum M. Carmichael, "Forbidden Mixtures," *Vetus Testamentum* 32 (1982):394-415. For my own views, see James B. Jordan, "The Law of Forbidden Mixtures" (available from Biblical Horizons, P.O. Box 132011, Tyler, TX 75713).

    As regards Deuteronomy 25:4, he argues that the text does not forbid muzzling the ox while he is treading grain, but only while he is treading in general, language again used for sexual relations and finding its background and fulfillment in human affairs; Carmichael, *Law and Narrative in the Bible: The Evidence of the Deuteronomic Laws and the Decalogue* (Ithaca, NY: Cornell University Press, 1985), pp. 292-295; and Carmichael, " 'Treading' in the Book of Ruth," *Zeitschrift für die Alttestamentliche Wissenshaft* 92 (1980):248-266. Carmichael's writings abound in useful connections between animal laws and human affairs, but are marred by his commitment to a critical view of the dating of Deuteronomy.

8. Schochet, p. 37.

9. Schochet comprehensively summarizes these in his excellent discussion, ibid., Chapter 3. For a very interesting modern attempt to extend these principles, see the lavishly illustrated volumes published by the Institute for Basic Youth Conflicts (Box One, Oak Brook, IL 60522) entitled *Character Sketches: From the Pages of Scripture, Illustrated in the World of Nature* (1976, 1978, 1982).

10. See Paul S. Taylor, *The Great Dinosaur Mystery and the Bible* (San Diego: Master Book Pub., 1987).

11. I have discussed the animal kingdoms in greater depth in *Food and Faith*.

12. See ibid.

13. Schochet, p. 39.

14. Ibid., p. 41. The serpent can be seen to symbolize God in Exodus 4:3 and 7:9-12, Numbers 21:8, and John 3:14.

15. See Jordan, *Food and Faith*.

Chapter 9—Angels

1. From *The Service Book of the Holy Orthodox-Catholic-Apostolic Church*, trans. by Isabel F. Hapgood, rev. ed (Englewood, NJ: Antiochian Orthodox Christian Archdiocese of North America, [1922] 1983), p. 94.

2. Herman Bavinck, *Our Reasonable Faith*, trans. Henry Zylstra (Grand Rapids: Baker Book House, [1956] 1977), p. 178.

3. Auguste Lecerf, *An Introduction to Reformed Dogmatics*, trans. André Schlemmer (Grand Rapids: Baker Book House, [1949] 1981), p. 147.

4. Vern S. Poythress, *Symphonic Theology: The Validity of Multiple Perspectives in Theology* (Grand Rapids: Zondervan, 1987), p. 106.

5. Louis Berkhof, *Systematic Theology*, 4th ed. (Grand Rapids: Eerdmans, 1949), pp. 171-172. Berkhof sets out three errors to be avoided in connection with the doctrine of concurrence: 1. That it consists merely in a general communication of power, without determining the specific action in any way. 2. That it is of such a nature that man does part of the work and God a part. 3. That the work of God and that of the creature in concurrence are co-ordinate; rather, the work of God always has priority. Berkhof discusses the mystery of the relationship between Divine concurrence and sin. See pp. 172-175.

6. This implies that they did indeed cease during the Flood, which means that the Flood year was an extended miraculous event, and casts some doubt on the ability of creation scientists to account for its every detail in terms of uniformity of causation.

7. John Calvin, *Commentaries on the First Twenty Chapters of the Book of the Prophet Ezekiel*, trans. Thomas Myers (Grand Rapids: Baker Book House, [1849] 1979), pp. 334-335. Italics added. Calvin's lectures on Ezekiel were his last work—he died before finishing the book—and reflect his maturest thought.

8. These twenty-four elders are sometimes identified as the twenty-four chief priests of the Temple service. In light of the progression of thought in Revelation 4 and 5, however, I believe we have to see the twenty-four elders as the angelic archetypes of the twenty-four chief priests on earth.

9. See Menahem Haran, *Temples and Temple-Service in Ancient Israel* (London: Oxford University Press, 1978), p. 247.

10. On the Levite guards, see James B. Jordan, "The Death Penalty in the Mosaic Law: Five Exploratory Essays" (available from Biblical Horizons, P.O. Box 132011, Tyler, TX 75713), chap. 3.

Chapter 10—Breaking Bread: The Rite of Transformation

1. Henry Van Til, *The Calvinistic Concept of Culture* (Grand Rapids: Baker, 1959), p. 27.

2. The material on the "six-fold rite" in the remainder of this chapter was originally published in a slightly different form as part of James B. Jordan, "Christian Piety: Deformed and Reformed," *The Geneva Papers* 2:1 (September 1985). It is also found, again with some changes in emphasis, in James B. Jordan, *Primeval Saints: Studies in the Patriarchs of Genesis*, chaps. 1 and 2. Both are available from Biblical Horizons, P.O. Box 132011, Tyler, TX 75713.

3. Biblical names are descriptive. Thus, Abraham means "Father of a Multitude," and Isaac basically means "Laughter." When Adam named the animals, he did not simply assign random sounds to each. Rather, he gave each an appropriate descriptive name. He had the wisdom to interpret the world rightly, and to recognize the character God had placed in each creature.

4. This is an act of primordial oblation, offering God's world to Him, apart from human works. It is, thus, an act of faith apart from works. It corresponds to the sabbath as the first day of man's week.

5. This is an act of eschatological oblation, offering God's world to Him as transformed by human works. It is, then, an act of faith that embraces human works. It corresponds to the sabbath as the last day of the week.

6. I am building on the discussion of the "four-fold" action found in Gregory Dix, *The Shape of the Liturgy* (Westminster, England: Dacre Press, 1945).

7. Covenant-making in the Bible always entails the act of dividing and restructuring. Thus, Eve was divided from Adam, and then rejoined to him in the one-flesh relationship. Similarly, when covenant was made with Abraham, the animals were divided in half (Genesis 15). See O. Palmer Robertson, *The Christ of the Covenants* (Grand Rapids: Baker, 1980), especially pp. 127ff.

8. See note 6 above.

9. See note 2 above.

10. For an example, see James B. Jordan, "Hexameron: Theological Reflections on Genesis One (A Syllabus)" (available from Biblical Horizons, P.O. Box 132011, Tyler, TX 75713), chap. 19.

11. See James B. Jordan, *Covenant Sequence in Leviticus and Deuteronomy* (Tyler, TX: Institute for Christian Economics, 1988). Significant literature on the subject includes George E. Mendenhall, *Law and Covenant in Israel and the Near East* (Pittsburgh: Biblical Colloquium, 1955). Mendenhall divides the covenant into seven basic parts. Klaus Baltzer, *The Covenant Formulary: In Old Testament, Jewish, and Early Christian Writings*, trans. David E. Green (Philadelphia: Fortress Press, [1964] 1971). Baltzer finds six basic parts. Meredith G. Kline, *The Structure of Biblical Authority*, rev. ed. (Grand Rapids: Eerdmans, 1972). Kline also sees six "standard sections," p. 121.

12. See John M. Frame, *Doctrine of the Knowledge of God* (Phillipsburg, NJ: Presbyterian and Reformed Pub. Co., 1987).

13. The most expansive treatment of the five-fold approach is found in Ray R. Sutton, *That You May Prosper: Dominion by Covenant* (Tyler, TX: Institute for Christian Economics, 1987); cf. Sutton, *Who Owns the Family?: God or the State?* (Fort Worth: Dominion Press, 1986); *Second Chance: Biblical Principles of Divorce and Remarriage* (Dominion, 1988). See also Sutton's newsletter, *Covenant Renewal*, published by the Institute for Christian Economics, P.O. Box 8000, Tyler, TX 75711.

   Gary North has worked with this model in several books, including *The Sinai Strategy: Economics and the Ten Commandments* (Tyler, TX: Institute for Christian Economics, 1986); *Liberating Planet Earth: An Introduction to Biblical Blueprints* (Fort Worth: Dominion Press, 1987); *Inherit the Earth: Biblical Principles for Economics* (Dominion, 1987); *Healer of the Nations: Biblical Principles for International Relations* (Dominion, 1987).

   Other significant literature employing one or another version of this model includes David Chilton, *The Days of Vengeance: An Exposition of the Book of Revelation* (Fort Worth: Dominion Press, 1987); Gary DeMar, *Ruler of the Nations: Biblical Principles for Government* (Dominion, 1987); George Grant, *The Changing of the Guard: Biblical Principles for Political Action* (Dominion, 1987).

Chapter 11 — Man: The Agent of Transformation

1. From *The Oxford Book of Carols* (London: Oxford University Press, [1928] 1964).

2. These are actually sayings of Agur (Proverbs 30:1), but they are regarded as part of Solomon's collection. Agur means "sojourner," and scholars have hypothesized that these proverbs came from Jacob, or possibly Moses. See Roland E. Murphy, *Wisdom Literature* (Grand Rapids: Eerdmans, 1981), p. 80.

3. The expression "deep sleep" refers to a state near death, or even death itself (Psalm 76:6; Proverbs 10:5; 19:15). During "deep sleep" God appears to men in

dreadful visions (Job 4:13; 33:15; Daniel 8:18; 10:9). During "deep sleep" God cut His covenant with Abram (Genesis 15:12). The church fathers regarded Adam's deep sleep and the birth of Eve from his side as a very important type of Christ's death and the birth of the church from His side. See the discussion in Jean Daniélou, *From Shadows to Reality: Studies in the Biblical Typology of the Fathers*, trans. Wulstan Hibberd (Westminster, MD: Newman Press, 1960), pp. 48-56.

4. On the priests' duty to guard the sanctuary boundary, see James B. Jordan, "The Death Penalty in the Mosaic Law: Five Exploratory Essays" (available from Biblical Horizons, P.O. Box 132011, Tyler, TX 75713), chap. 3.

5. "Create" in Hebrew does not carry with it only the idea of making out of nothing, but primarily carries the idea of a new and wondrous work.

6. Adam was encouraged to eat of the Tree of Life. God had singled it out (Genesis 2:9), and had told Adam to eat freely of every tree except the Tree of Knowledge. It is an unsupportable speculation to maintain, as some have, that Adam was not supposed to eat of the Tree of Life. See the discussion of this in Gary North, *The Dominion Covenant: Genesis*. Economic Commentary on the Bible I, 2d ed. (Tyler, TX: Institute for Christian Economics, 1987), pp. 102-106.

7. I have discussed this phenomenon of exclusion at length in my books, *The Sociology of the Church* (Tyler, TX: Geneva Ministries, 1986), chap. 3; and *Sabbath Breaking and the Death Penalty: A Theological Investigation* (Tyler, TX: Geneva Ministries, 1986), chap. 2.

8. The need for a robe of authority, to deal with Satan, is implied by Adam's nakedness. For a full discussion, see James B. Jordan, "Rebellion, Tyranny, and Dominion in the Book of Genesis," in Gary North, ed., *Tactics of Christian Resistance*. Christianity and Civilization 3 (Tyler, TX: Geneva Ministries, 1983); and also James B. Jordan, *Primeval Saints: Studies in the Patriarchs of Genesis* (available from Biblical Horizons, P.O. Box 132011, Tyler, TX 75713).

9. Abraham J. Heschel, *The Prophets*, 2 vols. (New York: Harper and Row, 1955) 1:21.

10. See Jordan, "Rebellion."

11. George Vandervelde, "The Gift of Prophecy and the Prophetic Church," *ICS Academic Papers* (August 1984), p. 10. Distributed by the Institute for Christian Studies, 229 College St., Toronto, Canada M5T 1R4. I owe Vandervelde a debt of thanks for many of the insights in this section. The allusion to Heschel is to his *Prophets* 1:22.

Chapter 12 — Eden: The World of Transformation

1. Solomon's Temple proper: 1 Kings 5-7 plus 2 Chronicles 2-5 equals 178 verses. Temple personnel (the man in the Garden): 1 Chronicles 22-28, for 168 verses. The Mosaic Tabernacle is described in Exodus 25-31, 35-40, for 459 verses. The animals of the new Garden (sacrifices) and the new Adam (priest) are described in Leviticus 1-9, for 255 verses. Restrictions on access to the Garden occupy 238 verses in Leviticus 11-16. The symbolic organization of the nation of Eden around the Garden takes up 188 verses in Numbers 1-4. Other passages from the Pentateuch could be added in as well.

2. On the Abyss, see David Chilton, *The Days of Vengeance: An Exposition of the Book of Revelation* (Fort Worth, TX: Dominion Press, 1987), p. 244.

3. For additional thoughts on water, see James B. Jordan, "Hexameron: Theological Reflections on Genesis One (A Syllabus)" (available from Biblical Horizons, P.O. Box 132011, Tyler, TX 75713), chaps. 15-16.

4. On the cross, see James B. Jordan, *The Sociology of the Church* (Tyler, TX: Geneva Ministries, 1986), pp. 212-218.

5. See C. S. Lewis, *The Discarded Image* (New York: Cambridge University Press, 1964), pp. 28, 61, 140ff.; and Daniel J. Boorstin, *The Discoverers* (New York: Random House, 1983), pp. 94, 98, et passim.

6. Some useful insights, and some questionable ones, into the location of Eden in the north are provided by D. F. Pocock, "North and South in the Book of Genesis," in J. H. M. Beattie and R. G. Lienhardt, *Studies in Social Anthropology: Essays in Memory of E. E. Evans-Pritchard by his former Oxford Colleagues* (Oxford: Clarendon Press, 1975), pp. 273-284.

7. Had God been coming from Jerusalem to Ezekiel, He would have come from the west. The "north" here must, thus, point back to Ararat and Eden.

8. Zechariah's prophecy concerns the evangelization of the Northern empires, Babylon and Persia, under Daniel and Esther. Egypt, to the south, would not be converted at this point in history.

9. Useful reflections on this complex subject will be found in Klaas Schilder, *Heaven: What Is It?*, trans. and condensed Marian M. Schoolland (Grand Rapids: Eerdmans, 1950); Schilder, *Christ and Culture*, trans. G. van Rongen and W. Helder (Winnipeg: Premier Pub., 1977); Henry R. Van Til, *The Calvinistic Concept of Culture* (Grand Rapids: Baker Book House, 1959); and Francis Nigel Lee, *The Central Significance of Culture* (Phillipsburg, NJ: Presbyterian and Reformed Pub. Co, 1977).

10. See George Ernest Wright and Floyd Vivian Filson, *The Westminster Historical Atlas to the Bible*, rev. ed. (Philadelphia: Westminster Press, 1956), p. 105. Also "Zion," in John McClintock and James Strong, *Cyclopedia of Biblical, Theological, and Ecclesiastical Literature* (Grand Rapids: Baker Book House, [1867-87] 1981) 10:1100-1102. Zion's elevation was 2550', while Moriah's was 2440'.

11. McClintock and Strong, "Olivet," 7:353-355. Olivet was 2665' above sea level. As we saw in Chapter 7, olive was the wood of the Most Holy Place. Jesus' descent from Olivet to Jerusalem at the triumphal entry may be seen as a descent from heaven (Matthew 21:1). Jesus walked out of Zion and cursed it and Moriah from Olivet (Matthew 24:1-3). It was on holy Olivet that He offered His high priestly prayer (Matthew 26:30). From Olivet He ascended into heaven (Acts 1:12). See further our remarks in Chapter 7.

12. See Boorstin, chap. 10.

13. Notice also the association of mountains and men in Revelation 17:9-10, "The seven heads [of the beast] are seven mountains on which the woman sits, and they are seven kings."

14. The Hebrew for "mountain of God" is *har'el*, while "hearth" is *'ari'eil*. The two words are obviously quite different, but in spite of this the following Bibles translate them both as "hearth": The New American Standard Version, the New International Version, the Jerusalem Bible, and the New King James Version. The old King James sidesteps the problem and just translates both words as "altar." The assumption that the *har'el* is to be changed to "hearth" is based solely on supposition and the LXX, and is utterly unsupportable, even though occasionally advocated by conservatives; e.g., Patrick Fairbairn, *An Exposition of Ezekiel* (n.p.: National Foundation for Christian Education, [reprint] 1969), p. 475.

This mistranslation in otherwise conservative translations of the Bible (which are not known for following the LXX!) is all the more peculiar because so many conservative commentaries on Ezekiel have strongly maintained that *har'el* is not to be tampered with, and that verse 15 clearly and unmistakably calls either the whole altar or the top section "the Mountain of God." See for instance, C. F. Keil, *Biblical Commentary on the Prophecies of Ezekiel*, 2 vols., trans. James Martin (Grand Rapids: Eerdmans, 1968) 2:287; E. W. Hengstenberg, *The Prophecies of the Prophet Ezekiel Elucidated*, trans. A. C. Murphy and J. G. Murphy (Edinburgh: T. & T. Clark, 1869), p. 425; and Charles Lee Feinberg, *The Prophecy of Ezekiel* (Chicago: Moody Press, 1969), p. 254.

   Albright suggests that the *heq ha'arets*, translated "base on the ground" in the NASV of Ezekiel 43:14, and "gutter on the ground" in the NIV, should be rendered more cosmically as "the foundation of the earth." Such a translation makes sense in light of the cosmic "mountain of God" imagery in verse 15. It has been disputed on technical grounds, however. "Gutter" also would have important symbolic associations, since it would point to the "gehenna" area at the base of the mountain. See W. F. Albright, *Archaeology and the Religion of Israel*, 5th ed. (Baltimore: Johns Hopkins, 1968), pp. 146-147; and summary of criticisms by David P. Wright, *The Disposal of Impurity: Elimination Rites in the Bible and in Hittite and Mesopotamian Literature*. Society of Biblical Literature Dissertation Series 101 (Atlanta: Scholars Press, 1987), p. 151.

15. See also Isaiah 51:13-16, which speaks of "planting" the heavens, in context a clear reference to the founding of Israel as God's "planting" (see Chapter 7). See also Jeremiah 4:23-31. A particularly useful sermon on the New Heavens and Earth by Puritan expositor John Owen is found in Owen, *Works*, 16 vols. (London: Banner of Truth Trust, 1965-68) 9:131ff. See also Chilton, *Days of Vengeance*, pp. 538-545.

16. See Chilton, pp. 197, 238-239.

Chapter 13 — The World of Noah

1. Translated from Welsh original by the author and Peter Williams.

2. On the Day of the Lord, the sabbath, and judgment, see James B. Jordan, *Sabbath Breaking and the Death Penalty: A Theological Investigation* (Tyler, TX: Geneva Ministries, 1986); and Jordan, "Christianity and the Calendar (A Syllabus)" (available from Biblical Horizons, P.O. Box 132011, Tyler, TX 75713).

3. On time as burden or opportunity, as cyclical or linear, see various works of Mircea Eliade, especially *Cosmos and History: The Myth of the Eternal Return*, trans. Willard R. Trask (New York: Harper Torchbooks, [1949] 1959); and Gary North, *The Dominion Covenant: Genesis*. An Economic Commentary on the Bible I, 2d ed. (Tyler, TX: Institute for Christian Economics, 1987), pp. 118-131, 440-441. C. S. Lewis also has some interesting remarks on this subject in his novel *The Great Divorce*.

4. See commentaries on Genesis. The alternatives are that the sons of God were angels who married with men, but this is based on Jewish fables and makes no sense in the light of Matthew 22:30. A modification sees the "sons of God" as demonized men, thus angelic in that sense. The other view sees the "sons of God" as powerful warrior kings who took whatever women they wanted, precursors of Nimrod. There is much to be said for this view, but I believe it is guilty of importing to the context considerations that are absent. In context we need an explanation for what happened to the godly line of Seth. The intermarriage interpretation alone provides it.

5. Meredith G. Kline, *Kingdom Prologue*, 3 vols. (by the author, 1983) 2:105.

6. Ibid.

7. For a detailed discussion of these animal lists, and what accounts for the differences among them, see James B. Jordan, *Food and Faith: The Mosaic Dietary Laws in New Covenant Perspective* (available from Biblical Horizons, P.O. Box 132011, Tyler, TX 75713).

8. Kline, 100-109; Jean Daniélou, *From Shadows to Reality: Studies in the Biblical Typology of the Fathers*, trans. Wulstan Hibberd (Westminster, MD: Newman Press, 1960), pp. 69-102.

9. See Kline, ibid.; and Jordan, "Christianity and the Calendar," chap. 23.

10. On the robe of invested authority, see James B. Jordan, *Primeval Saints: Studies in the Patriarchs of Genesis* (available from Biblical Horizons, P.O. Box 132011, Tyler, TX 75713); and Jordan, "Rebellion, Tyranny, and Dominion in the Book of Genesis," in Gary North, ed., *Tactics of Christian Resistance*. Christianity and Civilization 3 (Tyler, TX: Geneva Ministries, 1983), pp. 38-80.

11. Evidence suggests that the world before the Flood was warm from pole to pole, a situation often explained by the suggestion that the "waters above the firmament" had a literal as well as a symbolic existence in the world before the Flood, taking the form of a water vapor canopy over the earth, which created a "greenhouse" effect, and which collapsed at the Flood. Revelation 4 and other passages show that there is still a "heavenly sea" associated with the firmament, but this does not exclude the possibility of a literal canopy. See Joseph C. Dillow, *The Waters Above: Earth's Pre-Flood Vapor Canopy* (Chicago: Moody Press, 1981); and James B. Jordan, "Hexameron: Theological Reflections on Genesis One (A Syllabus)" (available from Biblical Horizons, P.O. Box 132011, Tyler, TX 75713), chaps. 14-16.

12. Noah's drunkenness might seem to be the new sin in the new garden, but the Bible focuses on Ham's sin and Noah's judgment of him. I have discussed this at length in Jordan, *Primeval Saints*, chaps. 3 and 4.

13. The Tree of the Knowledge of Good and Evil had to do with investiture with rule and authority. See Jordan, *Primeval Saints*, chap. 9, and Jordan, "Rebellion."

14. On the numerological structures in Genesis 10, see Umberto Cassuto, *A Commentary on the Book of Genesis, Part II: From Noah to Abraham*, trans. Israel Abrahams (Jerusalem: Magnes Press, [1949] 1964), pp. 175-180.

15. In Hebrew, there is one word meaning "earth" in the sense of an ordered cosmos, and another word meaning "soil" or "ground," from which man was made. The tower was made of bricks (Genesis 11:3). Abram's blessing would extend to all the families who were made of soil (Genesis 2:7; 12:3). Thus, the curse on the soil, and by extension on humanity, would be removed through the Seed of Abram (Genesis 3:17, 19).

Chapter 14 — The World of the Patriarchs

1. Olivers wrote this paraphrase in 1770. Shortened versions are found in many hymnals. The text used in the present book is complete, and taken from John Julian, ed., *A Dictionary of Hymnology* (New York: Dover Pub., [1907] 1957), p. 1150.

2. I do not believe that this rule applied to the Gentiles outside the land and nation of Israel. The uncircumcised Gentile priest, Jethro, led Israel in worship in Exodus 18, and then returned to his own land. Did he cease worshipping at altars thereafter? There is no reason to think so. God-fearing Gentiles continued under the Noahic covenant until the New Covenant. The only change for them

during the Old Testament was that after the Abrahamic covenant, they were obligated to recognize the special priestly status of Israel.

3. The author's study of "The Life of Abraham" provides an in-depth examination of the history of Abraham and its meaning in the context of Genesis. This is a set of twelve tapes with a forty-six-page syllabus, and is available from Biblical Horizons, P.O. Box 132011, Tyler, TX 75713.

4. David Daube, *The Exodus Pattern in the Bible* (London: Faber and Faber, 1963). This is the standard work on the subject, but is marred by critical (liberal) assumptions. My own comments entail significant expansions of Daube's initial study.

5. The Mountain the angels offered Lot was the mountain where Abraham was. Lot refused it. He wound up in another mountain, living in a cave, a symbol of being returned to dust in death. Lot's exodus was a warning to Israel. Note the unleavened bread (Genesis 19:3), the angels guarding the doorway, and the midnight passover exodus. When Israel refused to conquer Canaan, they repeated Lot's mistake, and received the same judgment. They did not learn from typology.

6. Christian ethicists have generally not regarded the deception of tyrants as evil. A familiar example is the way Dutch Christians hid Jews from the Nazis, and boldly lied about it. In his sermons on Genesis, Luther exonerated Abraham and Isaac for deceiving Pharaoh and Abimelech. See my comments on this in Jordan, *Primeval Saints: Studies in the Patriarchs of Genesis*. Available from Biblical Horizons, P.O. Box 132011, Tyler, TX 75713.

7. The details of the Jacob-Laban episode correlate to the laws of slavery in Exodus 21. See my remarks on this in Jordan, *The Law of the Covenant: An Exposition of Exodus 21-23* (Tyler, TX: Institute for Christian Economics, 1984), pp. 33-34.

8. Deposit "under the oak near Shechem" implies that these gods were humbled under the trampling feet of God, whose ladder to heaven was the tree.

9. An extensive discussion of this pattern and its wider ramifications can be found in Meredith G. Kline, *The Structure of Biblical Authority*, rev. ed. (Grand Rapids: Eerdmans, 1975), pp. 76-93.

10. Lot's exodus (Genesis 19) and Abraham's (Genesis 20-21) are a study in parallels and contrasts.

11. See my extended remarks in James B. Jordan, *Judges: God's War Against Humanism* (Tyler, TX: Geneva Ministries, 1985), pp. 279-290.

12. Eber had two sons, Peleg and Joktan (Genesis 10:25). Abraham was a descendant of Peleg (Genesis 11:16-27). In the "Table of Nations" of Genesis 10, Eber and Peleg each count as distinct "nations" in the list of seventy. The Pelegites had apostatized and worshipped strange gods in Ur (Joshua 24:14). The converted Abraham and his clan considered themselves not as Pelegites but as the true Eberites (Hebrews).

13. Joseph's sheaves are to be associated with the earth, in light of Genesis 1:9-13. Thus, the picture of Israel as both dust (sheaves) and stars is found in Joseph's dreams (Genesis 37:6-10).

14. This verse does not refer to purchased slaves but to converts. See the remarks of Umberto Cassuto, *A Commentary on the Book of Genesis, Part II: From Noah to Abraham*, trans. Israel Abrahams (Jerusalem: Magnes Press, [1949] 1964), p. 320.

15. Tree and altar, Genesis 12:7; 13:18; 35:7-8; tree, well, and worship (altar implied), 21:30-34; altar and well, 26:23-25, 32-33.

16. On the cloud and the Spirit, see Meredith G. Kline, *Images of the Spirit* (Grand Rapids: Baker, 1980), passim. On oil, pp. 45-46.

17. See Jordan, *Primeval Saints*, chap. 10.

18. In light of the conversion of Egypt, there is no reason to think that Potipherah was a heathen priest. The Joseph who was too pure to become involved with Potiphar's wife would hardly have joined himself to a heathen woman.

Chapter 15 — The World of the Tabernacle

1. Notice that God's people are said to continue and be established after God has changed the heavens and earth. This could apply to the Resurrection and the new physical universe, but more likely applies to an in-history covenant change.

2. As mentioned in the previous chapter, there were so many servants that the Hebrews were given the entire land of Goshen in which to dwell. Most of these "servants" were adopted freemen, which is what the expression "born of the house" means (Genesis 14:14). On this see James B. Jordan, *The Law of the Covenant: An Exposition of Exodus 21-23* (Tyler, TX: Institute for Christian Economics, 1984), pp. 76-84. The retinue of the patriarchal sheikdom are referred to in Genesis 24:2; 26:19, 25, 32; 32:16.

3. It can be argued that the entire Tabernacle and sacrificial system flowed from Passover. At Passover, God claimed the firstborn sons of Israel as His priests. They fell into sin at the Golden Calf, and the Levites were substituted for them. Also at Passover, God put blood on the houses of the Israelites and spared them His plague. These protected houses can be correlated to the Tabernacle, itself a symbol of the nation of protected houses. Thus, the nation-under-blood, and the Tabernacle as its symbol, were created as Passover. All the new sacrifices added to the original burnt offering had to do with Tabernacle-access. All the laws of cleanness had to do with Tabernacle-access. Thus, all of this stemmed from Passover.

4. See James B. Jordan, *Sabbath Breaking and the Death Penalty: A Theological Investigation* (Tyler, TX: Geneva Ministries, 1986); and Jordan, "Christianity and the Calendar (A Syllabus)" (available from Biblical Horizons, P.O. Box 132011, Tyler, TX 75713).

5. This is the tendency, if not the actual position, of the "theonomic" writings of R. J. Rushdoony and Greg Bahnsen. See Rushdoony, *Institutes of Biblical Law* (Nutley, NJ: Craig Press, 1973); Bahnsen, *Theonomy and Christian Ethics* (Nutley, NJ: Craig Press, 1977). For a critique, see Vern S. Poythress, *Understanding the Law of Moses* (forthcoming). It should be noted that the "theonomic" positions of Rushdoony and Bahnsen are much more theologically sophisticated and moderate than the radical "Mosaic theocracy" views spouted by certain militant Anabaptists at the time of the Reformation and by certain extreme wings of the Puritan movement a century later. Modern "theonomists" do not believe in social reform via political revolution.

6. I have explored some of the ramifications of this in James B. Jordan, "The Death Penalty in the Mosaic Law: Five Exploratory Essays" (available from Biblical Horizons, P.O. Box 132011, Tyler, TX 75713).

7. Some have argued that "cutting off" is the same as execution, but this is impossible. Leviticus 18:29 states that all the abominations of Leviticus 18 are punished by "cutting off," but in Leviticus 20, these same crimes are discussed, with a variety of punishments. Only a few are capital offenses. Clearly, then, "cutting off" does not mean execution. It probably implies that God will deal with the sinner—God will cut him off—but since the officers of the Church know that God has set His face against the person, excommunication must be the

church's response. Thus, "cutting off" always implies ecclesiastical censure. See ibid., chap. 5.

8. See James B. Jordan, *Judges: God's War Against Humanism* (Tyler, TX: Geneva Ministries, 1985).

9. See James B. Jordan, "The Israelite Militia in the Old Testament," in Morgan Norval, *The Militia in 20th Century America: A Symposium* (Falls Church, VA: Gun Owners Foundation, 1985).

10. There are clear sabbatical patterns in Genesis, though, such as the seven years of plenty and the seven years of famine, or Genesis 8:6-12. Whether the sabbath day was a day of worship is unclear. For a very careful and detailed summary of the evidence on this question, see Francis Nigel Lee, *The Covenantal Sabbath: The Weekly Sabbath Scripturally and Historically Considered* (London: The Lord's Day Observance Society, 1966).

11. See Jordan, *Law of the Covenant*, pp. 64, 75.

12. Meredith G. Kline, *The Structure of Biblical Authority*, rev. ed. (Grand Rapids: Eerdmans, 1975), p. 80.

13. Ibid.

14. The discussion that follows is "short on argument, long on assertion." I have given my reasons for this in the Introduction. Also, much of the "argument" is woven into the warp and woof of this book, in that it entails a Biblical worldview perspective.

Although some writers, such as Fairbairn, have minimized the symbolic character of the Tabernacle in its cosmic and human dimensions, they must virtually swallow camels to do so. E.g., Patrick Fairbairn, *The Typology of Scripture*, 2 vols. (Grand Rapids: Zondervan, [1876] n.d.) 2:201-223. In a real sense, the failure of such writers as Fairbairn is their lack of a worldview approach, and thus they fail to see worldview models in the Bible when they appear. All the same, the worldview interpretation of the Tabernacle and Temple is ancient, and has an honorable history in mainstream Christian thought, as Davidson (see below) has demonstrated.

Sound expositions of the multilayered symbolism of the Tabernacle can be found in Meredith G. Kline, *Images of the Spirit* (Grand Rapids: Eerdmans, 1980); and Vern S. Poythress, *Understanding the Law of Moses* (forthcoming). See also Erich Sauer, *The Dawn of World Redemption*, trans. G. H. Lang (Grand Rapids: Eerdmans, 1952), pp. 137-140; Richard M. Davidson, *Typology in Scripture* (Berrien Springs, MI: Andrews University Press, 1981), pp. 336ff.; Angel Manuel Rodríguez, "Sanctuary Theology in the Book of Exodus," *Andrews University Seminary Studies* 24 (1986):127-145; James B. Jordan, "From Glory to Glory: Degrees of Value in the Sanctuary" (available from Biblical Horizons, P.O. Box 132011, Tyler, TX 75713).

15. See Menahem Haran, *Temples and Temple-Service in Ancient Israel* (Oxford: Clarendon Press, 1978), chap. 13. 1 Samuel 4:4; 2 Samuel 6:2; 2 Kings 19:15; Isaiah 37:16; Psalm 80:2; 99:1.

16. See Kline, *Images*, chap. 2.

17. For a full exposition, see Jordan, "Death Penalty in the Mosaic Law," chap. 4.

18. See various commentaries on Revelation, at Revelation 1:16, 20.

19. See Bernard Goldman, *The Sacred Portal: A Primary Symbol in Ancient Judaic Art* (Lanham, MD: University Press of America, 1986), esp. pp. 20, 21, 60, 63. Goldman does not realize the connection of this sequence with the Tabernacle, unfortunately. See also Jacob Neusner, "Studying Judaism through the Art of the Synagogue," in Doug Adams and Diane Apostolos-Cappadona, *Art as Religious Studies* (New York: Crossroad, 1987).

20. A fuller exposition of this theme is found in Rodríguez, "Sanctuary Theology."
21. On the changes in priesthood, and for a detailed study of the boundaries and their guards, see Jordan, "Death Penalty in the Mosaic Law," chap. 3.
22. For a complete study of the veils and their symbolism, see Jordan, "From Glory to Glory."
23. I have argued for these correlations in ibid.
24. A very useful study of Jesus' association of the Temple with His body is Lucius Nereparampil, *Destroy This Temple: An Exegetico-Theological Study on the Meaning of Jesus' Temple-Logion in Jn 2:19* (Bangladore, India: Dharmaram [College] Publications, 1978).
25. Kline, *Images*, chap. 1.
26. On the heart and mind, and other aspects of the human person in the Bible, see Hans Walter Wolff, *Anthropology of the Old Testament*, trans. Margaret Kohl (Philadelphia: Fortress Press, 1974).

Chapter 16 — The World of the Temple

1. A comparison of this genealogy with others, and with the chronology of the period, shows that there were doubtless more than ten generations involved. David was born 406 years after the entrance into Canaan (1 Kings 6:1; 2 Samuel 5:4). Perez was born about two hundred years before the Exodus, assuming that the Hebrews lived in Goshen 215 years, dating the 430 years of Egyptian captivity from the time Abraham moved out of Canaan into (Egyptian) Philistia, after the destruction of Sodom (Genesis 19–20). Judah was about forty-two when the Hebrews moved to Goshen, and Perez was his grandson. Thus, the story of Judah in Genesis 38 has been recorded out of chronological order, for theological reasons, and actually took place after the Hebrews had relocated their homes to Goshen. At any rate, this puts about six hundred years between Perez and David, which is a rather long time for ten generations. Also, Nahshon was Aaron's age (Exodus 6:23), and Salmon was Rahab's husband (Matthew 1:5). Their marriage took place about four hundred years before David's birth. We know that Jesse was David's true father, and since David was his eighth son, we can put Jesse's age at about fifty, and thus Jesse's birth about 356 years after the Conquest. The genealogy is Salmon—Boaz—Obed—Jesse. We know that Boaz was the true father of Obed (Ruth 4). Thus, there is a considerable gap either between Salmon and Boaz, or between Obed and Jesse, or both. I have argued elsewhere that for Biblical theological reasons the birth of Obed might well be correlated with the births of Samson and Samuel. If this guess be correct, then Obed was Jesse's true father. This means that the gap would be between Salmon and Boaz. On the birth of Obed, see James B. Jordan, *Judges: God's War Against Humanism* (Tyler, TX: Geneva Ministries, 1985), pp. 239-240.
2. The expression "there was no king in Israel" refers to the Lord's kingship, not to a lack of human kingship. This is clear from the entire context of Judges, which sets the Lord's kingship against human kingship at this stage of history. For extended comments on this theme in Judges, see Jordan, *Judges*, passim.
3. 1 Samuel 13:2; 14:52; 23:13; 24:2; 25:13; 2 Samuel 15:18; 20:7. See James B. Jordan, "The Israelite Militia in the Old Testament," in Morgan Norval, ed., *The Militia in 20th Century America: A Symposium* (Falls Church, VA: Gun Owners Foundation, 1985), pp. 34-36.

4. Judges 13; 1 Samuel 1. On the decline and on the simultaneity of Samuel's and Samson's births, see Jordan, *Judges*, esp. pp. 229-230, 238-238.

5. Samson was not the fool he is often mistaken for. An analysis of his shrewd revival methods is found in Jordan, *Judges*, chaps. 12-14.

6. Lucius Nereparampil, *Destroy This Temple: An Exegetico-Theological Study on the Meaning of Jesus' Temple-Logion in Jn 2:19* (Bangladore, India: Dharmaram [College] Publications, 1978), pp. 67-73.

7. I have treated the theology of the Saul narratives (1 Samuel 9-15) at length in two essays: James B. Jordan, "Saul: A New Adam for Israel," and "Saul: A Study in Original Sin," *The Geneva Papers* 2:9 (July, 1987), 11 (July, 1988).

8. It would be interesting to make a full study of the typological parallels, and differences due to the maturation of history, between the Mosaic wilderness wanderings and David's wilderness experience. Notice for instance that David begins by getting showbread from the Tabernacle (1 Samuel 21:1-6), which we should associate with manna in the wilderness. Saul becomes a new Pharaoh pursuing David. Like Moses, David must fight Amalekites (1 Samuel 30).

9. "And therefore I have sworn to the house of Eli that the iniquity of Eli's house shall not be atoned for by sacrifice or offering forever." I believe this refers specifically to the High Priest's sacrifice on the Day of Atonement (Leviticus 16:11-14), not to other sacrifices. In other words, the house of Eli was demoted to the status of ordinary Aaronic priests.

10. On the textual problems with this verse, where Ahimelech and Abiathar seem to have been transposed, see commentaries on 1 Chronicles.

11. This seems to be implied by 1 Chronicles 16:37-40, where only Zadok is mentioned as ministering at Gibeon. First Chronicles 24:5 says that both Ithamarites and Eleazarites served as both officers of the sanctuary (Tabernacle) and officers of God (the Ark?). Thus, if there was a distinction of duties in David's time, it may not have been very rigid.

12. See Jordan, "Saul: A Study in Original Sin."

13. On the tribal republics, see E. C. Wines, *The Hebrew Republic* (originally published as *Commentary on the Laws of the Ancient Hebrews*, vol. 2; reprint, Rt. 1, Box 65-2, Wrightstown, NJ 08562: American Presbyterian Press, n.d.).

14. See James B. Jordan, *Sabbath Breaking and the Death Penalty: A Theological Investigation* (Tyler, TX: Geneva Ministries, 1986), pp. 47-49.

15. Gehenna or the Valley of Hinnom was "a deep narrow glen to the south of Jerusalem, where, after the introduction of the worship of the fire-gods by Ahaz, the idolatrous Jews offered their children to Moloch (2 Chronicles 28:3; 33:6; Jeremiah 7:31; 19:2-6). In consequence of these abominations, the valley was polluted by Josiah (2 Kings 23:10); subsequently to which it became the common lay-stall of the city, where the dead bodies of criminals, and the carcasses of animals, and every other kind of filth was cast, and, according to late and somewhat questionable authorities, the combustible portion consumed with fire. From the depth and narrowness of the gorge, and, perhaps, its ever-burning fires, as well as from its being the receptacle of all sorts of putrefying matter, and all that defiled the holy city, it became in later times the image of the place of everlasting punishment. . . . In this sense the word is used by our Lord, Matthew 5:29-30; 10:28; 23:15, 33. . . ." "Gehenna," in John McClintock and James Strong, *Cyclopedia of Biblical, Theological, and Ecclesiastical Literature* (Grand Rapids: Baker Book House, [1867-87] 1981) 3:764.

16. See Chapter 12, note 14 (on p. 302 above), on the gutter at the base of the altar as perhaps the symbolic equivalent of Gehenna.

17. For instance, the word "socket" or "pedestal" in Song of Solomon 5:17 occurs in Job 38:6 referring to the foundation of the earth, and the only other use of this word is for the sockets that held up the pillars of the Tabernacle, in connection with which it is used fifty-two times in Exodus 26, 27, 35–40, Numbers 3, 4. The comparison of Solomon to a pillar correlates with the bronze Boaz pillar of the Temple, which represented the King.

18. Psalm 45 is generally taken as the key to Song of Solomon. I highly recommend G. Lloyd Carr, *The Song of Solomon: An Introduction and Commentary* (Downers Grove, IL: Inter-Varsity Press, 1984), though I put more stock in the traditional typological aspects than he does. Compare for instance the call of the bride in Song of Solomon 8:14 with the call of the Bride in Revelation 22:17-21.

19. The Most Holy of the Tabernacle was a cube ten cubits on a side, or one thousand cubic cubits. In the Temple it was twenty cubits on a side, or eight thousand cubic cubits. The Holy Place in the Tabernacle was twenty by ten by ten, or two thousand cubic cubits. In the Temple the Holy Place was forty cubits long, twenty cubits wide, and thirty cubits high, for twenty-four thousand cubic cubits.

20. On the names of Jachin and Boaz, see 1 Chronicles 24:17; 2 Kings 11:14; 23:3. For a full study of this, see James B. Jordan, "Thoughts on Jachin and Boaz" (available from Biblical Horizons, P.O. Box 132011, Tyler, TX 75713).

21. The number 666 is hardly included by accident here. See my discussion in James B. Jordan, "Revelation Made Practical," a six-tape series with a thirty-seven-page study syllabus, available from Biblical Horizons, P.O. Box 132011, Tyler, TX 75713.

22. *The Open Bible* (Nashville: Thomas Nelson, 1985), p. 28.

23. For more on this, see Jordan, "Jachin and Boaz."

Chapter 17 — The Worlds of Exile and Restoration

1. Generally speaking, the post-exilic period is overlooked in books on the history of the covenants. It is often viewed as a time of weakness rather than of strength, which is the opposite of my contention here. Additionally, the visionary Temple of Ezekiel is usually referred to the New Covenant, instead of first and foremost to the Restoration. But see the works referred to in note 5 below.

2. This is an inference from such passages as 1 Kings 18:4; 20:35; 2 Kings 2:7; 4:1; 6:1. "Sons" of the prophets means "disciples," and implies apprenticeship. Obviously, *somebody* was conducting routine pastoral ministry in Israel. Who else could it have been?

3. The approach of older Christian commentators, such as John Calvin, to the subject of prophecy is a valuable corrective to the modern evangelical approach, which generally leaps over the post-exilic period. In his remarks on Jeremiah 23:7-8, Calvin writes that "Christians have been too rigid in this respect; for passing by the whole intermediate time between the return of the people and the coming of Christ, they have too violently turned the prophecies to spiritual redemption." Calvin on *Jeremiah*, trans. John Owen (Grand Rapids: Baker Book House, reprint 1979) 3:149.

4. When Ezekiel's wife died, he was forbidden to mourn, a condition levied only on the High Priest (Ezekiel 24:16-18; Leviticus 21:10-12). He entered his ministry, like any other priest, in his thirtieth year (Ezekiel 1:1).

5. Sadly, many have completely overlooked the first fulfillment of this prophecy in the inter-testamental era. Commentators who are aware of the immediate Restoration fulfillments of Ezekiel 38-39, and who see Ezekiel's Temple as relating to the Restoration first of all, include Matthew Henry, Matthew Poole, Adam Clarke, and E. W. Hengstenberg. See *Matthew Henry's Commentary* (numerous editions); Matthew Poole, *A Commentary on the Holy Bible* (London: Banner of Truth Trust, [1685] 1962); Adam Clarke's *Commentary* (numerous editions); E. W. Hengstenberg, *The Prophecies of Ezekiel Elucidated*, trans. A. C. Murphy and J. G. Murphy (Minneapolis, MN: James Publications, reprint: 1976). See also Ralph Woodrow, *His Truth is Marching On: Advanced Studies on Prophecy in the Light of History* (Riverside, CA: Ralph Woodrow Evangelistic Association, 1977), pp. 32-46.

6. See the works in note 5 above, and also Katheryn Pfisterer Darr, "The Wall Around Paradise: Ezekielian Ideas about the Future," *Vetus Testamentum* 37 (1987):271-279.

7. Note how our interpretation eliminates all the problems that plague so many approaches to these chapters. The sacrifices were indeed set back up in Zechariah's time. These chapters in Ezekiel do not point to restored sacrifices in a millennium, nor do these chapters have to be "totally spiritualized" to refer only to the New Testament situation. Like Leviticus, they refer to actual sacrifices, and like Leviticus, they have typological relevance to the New Testament church.

8. On the problem of nations and empires in Biblical perspective, see Gary North, *Healer of the Nations: Biblical Principles for International Relations* (Fort Worth, TX: Dominion Press, 1987), and James B. Jordan, "The Bible and the Nations (A Syllabus)" (available from Biblical Horizons, P.O. Box 132011, Tyler, TX 75713).

9. On the detailed predictions in Daniel 11 and 12 I have found Adam Clarke's *Commentary* to be of greatest help, though I do not agree with every detail of his analysis.

10. The establishment of "chief priests" was one of the changes David made in the original Mosaic system.

11. I have made a very detailed study of these visions in a series of thirteen lectures available on cassette from Biblical Horizons, P.O. Box 132011, Tyler, TX 75713. An expanded version of this survey of Zechariah 1-6, focusing on the bronze mountains, is James B. Jordan, "Thoughts on Jachin and Boaz" (available from Biblical Horizons, P.O. Box 132011, Tyler, TX 75713).

12. For this important insight, I am indebted to David L. Petersen, *Haggai and Zechariah 1-8: A Commentary* (Philadelphia: Westminster Press, 1984), pp. 194-202. "Zechariah's concerns here involve meta-ritual. How can the whole temple ritual system be set in motion again if everyone is unclean? The high priest cannot bear anyone's guilt since he, or at least his clothing, is soiled. What happens in this vision of Zechariah makes the restoration of the ritual system possible, and this by means of an ad hoc cleansing ritual in the divine council. The normal purification rituals are impossible and therefore not invoked," p. 201.

13. The idea of the "ten lost tribes" is wholly mythical. For conclusive proof we need only call attention to Luke 2:36. The northern tribes were carried off by Assyria, and joined up with the southern exiles later on.

Chapter 18 — The New World

1. Theologians sometimes use "Old Covenant" to refer to the Mosaic covenant. There is truth to this in that the Mosaic covenant published most fully the distinctive character of the Adamic covenant under curse. Yet, ultimately, the Old Covenant is the covenant of the original garden of Eden. Ultimately there are two covenants, Old and New. There are two Adams, Adam and Jesus. There are two heavens and earth, the first in Adam and the second in Christ. See my discussion of this in Jordan, *The Law of the Covenant: An Exposition of Exodus 21–23* (Tyler, TX: Institute for Christian Economics, 1984), pp. 196-198.

2. On this see Vern S. Poythress, *Understanding the Law of Moses* (forthcoming), Appendix: "Does the Greek Word *Pleroo* sometimes mean 'Confirm'?".

3. In my book *The Law of the Covenant* (Tyler, TX: Institute for Christian Economics, 1984), I took a different view of these verses, arguing that the passing of the heavens and earth is the end of the physical world, and that Christians are still supposed to keep the "fundamental principles" of the jots and tittles. I find that this interpretation, though it has weighty advocates, simply will not stand up in the light of the work presented in the present book as a whole. Thus, I must differ with so fine a work as John Murray, *Principles of Conduct* (Grand Rapids: Eerdmans, 1957), pp. 149ff. Murray simply does not take sufficient account of the redemptive historical setting of this passage, though his ethical exhortations are surely invaluable all the same. Let me direct the reader to an older work, equally Reformed and profound, that sets out what I now take to be the correct view of the passage: John Brown, *Discourses and Sayings of Our Lord Jesus Christ*, 3 vols. (London: Banner of Truth Trust, [1852] 1967) 1:171-174.

4. In non-Christian thought, including that of some liberal and "neo-orthodox" theologians, a paradox is a real contradiction that expresses a contradiction in "ultimate reality." This is not the Christian view. There is no contradiction in God, but God sometimes presents us with contradictions in order to goad us to wisdom.

5. Matthew 16:19 says "whatever you shall bind on earth shall have been bound in heaven, and whatever you shall loose on earth shall have been loosed in heaven." These future passives have the force of commands: Be sure you don't loose anything on earth unless you know it has already been loosed in heaven. And how shall we know? By the Scriptures.

6. The book of Revelation portrays the world-shaking power of church prayer and discipline. See James B. Jordan, *Revelation Made Practical*, a set of six tapes with a thirty-seven-page syllabus, available from Biblical Horizons, P.O. Box 132011, Tyler, TX 75713.

7. Romans 12:1. Baptism washes us and makes us clean sacrifices. Then, week by week as "we eat the body and drink the blood" of Christ, we are transformed into the image of His sacrificial life and resurrected power. Also, week by week the sword of His Word sacrifices and resurrects us (Hebrews 4:12-13).

8. Arthur W. Pink, *Exposition of the Gospel of John*, 3 vols. (Grand Rapids: Zondervan, 1945) 3:273.

9. According to John 20:7, the head cloth in which Jesus had been wrapped was separate from the linen wrappings of the body. This shows that Jesus had simply passed through them without undoing them. It is also possible, however, to correlate this with the fact that the Tabernacle was really two tents. The veil between the Holy Place (body) and the Most Holy (head, heart) acted to form two tents.

10. Satan had access to heaven in the Old Covenant, as Job 1-2 show. On the timing of Satan's removal from heaven, and all the many prooftexts for it, see Greg L. Bahnsen, "The Person, Work, and Present Status of Satan," in Gary North, ed., *The Journal of Christian Reconstruction* I:2, Symposium on Satanism (Winter 1984):11-43, esp. 33-37.

11. The Gentiles are consistently pictured as the Sea in Revelation, and the Jews as the Land. See James B. Jordan, *Revelation Made Practical*.

12. Thus, while the lampstand in the Tabernacle and Temple had one central shaft with seven branches, in the New Covenant each church is its own lampstand (Revelation 1:12, 20). The kingdom is decentralized on earth, and centralized in heaven.

13. For a full discussion of these degrees of access, see James B. Jordan, *The Sociology of the Church* (Tyler, TX: Geneva Ministries, 1986), pp. 83-124.

14. The New Jerusalem "is the Church of our Lord Jesus Christ, the Church that daily descends from heaven in our dispensation after the Pentecost festival. Prof. S. Greydanus writes: 'Two things are true of this Jerusalem: it already descends from heaven to earth, and it will not descend from heaven until the time of the end. This Jerusalem, after all, is the Church of the Lord.'" M. B. Van't Veer, *My God is Yahweh*, trans. Theodore Plantinga (Ontario: Paideia Press, [?] 1980), p. 26. The statement from Greydanus is from his *De Openbaring des Heren aan Johannes* (Amsterdam: H. A. van Bottenburg, n.d.), p. 422.

15. On the "last days," see David Chilton, *Paradise Restored: An Eschatology of Dominion* (Fort Worth: Dominion Press, 1985), pp. 115-124.

16. This emerges from a careful study of the chronology of Exodus. See my discussion in Jordan, *The Law of the Covenant: An Exposition of Exodus 21-23* (Tyler, TX: Institute for Christian Economics, 1984), pp. 55-58; and also Umberto Cassuto, *A Commentary on the Book of Exodus*, trans. Israel Abrahams (Jerusalem: Magnes Press, [1951] 1967), p. 229.

17. On the gift of tongues (xenolalia) as a sign of judgment upon Israel, and the modern practice of glossolalia (which is something different, but not necessarily wrong or unspiritual), see James B. Jordan, *The Sociology of the Church* (Tyler, TX: Geneva Ministries, 1986), pp. 169-174; and also Richard B. Gaffin, Jr., *Perspectives on Pentecost: New Testament Teaching on the Gifts of the Holy Spirit* (Phillipsburg, NJ: Presbyterian and Reformed Pub. Co., 1979), esp. Chapter 5.

18. Because the "Sardis" period of the Old Covenant history has less to do with the specific worldview concerns of this particular book, I have not discussed it in depth. The Sardis period is generally considered simply the later phase of the monarchy, and we have considered it that way in this book. On the other hand, Elijah is a clear Moses figure, challenging the Pharaonic kings of Northern Israel, and finally being taken to heaven in the very place Moses died (2 Kings 2:1-11, 16-18). After this, Elisha, a new Joshua, crosses the Jordan and reconquers Jericho (2 Kings 2:13-22). A series of miracle stories follow this, in which Elisha sets up the kingdom in a new form: the Remnant Church (2 Kings 4–6). Note the Exodus themes of borrowing, and of deliverance from slavery, in 2 Kings 4:1-7, the restoration of a firstborn son in 2 Kings 4:8-37, healing of food in 2 Kings 4:38-41, manna in 2 Kings 4:42-44, and especially the building of the new house for God's new people in 2 Kings 6:1-7. This new period of history, following Elijah and Elisha, is the period of the Writing Prophets (Isaiah, Jeremiah, Hosea, Amos, Joel, etc.). Thus, it is entirely possible to see the Sardis or Remnant period as a "new covenant" with new conditions, conditions related to being a faithful Remnant Church in an apostate land.

19. This matter is briefly discussed in Chilton, *Days of Vengeance*, pp. 86-89; and see also Eugenio Corsini, *The Apocalypse: The Perennial Revelation of Jesus Christ*, trans. and ed. Francis J. Moloney (Wilmington: Michael Glazier, Inc., 1983), pp. 104-111. It is interesting that Corsini, Chilton, and I each came up with this scheme separately at different times, and our schemes are virtually identical.

Chapter 19 — The Course of History

1. This is the third and fullest version of the hymn, designed for processional use. The first version, seven stanzas, dates from 1866. A five-stanza version dates from 1868, and it is on this one that most hymnals draw. Text and information from John Julian, ed., *A Dictionary of Hymnology*, 2 vols. (New York: Dover Pub., [1907] 1957) 2:1146-1147.

2. On the pervasiveness of "postmillennialism" in previous centuries, and the rise of "amillennialism" and "premillennialism" in recent years, see J. A. De Jong, *As the Waters Cover the Seas: Millennial Expectations in the Rise of Anglo-American Missions, 1640-1810* (Kampen, The Netherlands: J. H. Kok, 1970); Iain Murray, *The Puritan Hope: A Study in Revival and the Interpretation of Prophecy* (London: The Banner of Truth Trust, 1971); Gary North, ed., *The Journal of Christian Reconstruction* III:2, "Symposium on the Millennium" (Winter 1976-77), especially the essays by Greg L. Bahnsen, "The *Prima Facie* Acceptability of Postmillennialism," and James B. Jordan, "A Survey of Southern Presbyterian Millennial Views before 1930"; and Gary DeMar and Peter Leithart, *The Reduction of Christianity: An Answer to Dave Hunt* (Fort Worth, TX: Dominion Press, 1988), esp. pp. 206-299.

3. Leaven is not a symbol of evil in the Bible, but a symbol of growth. We want to avoid the old growth-principle of Egyptian and Pharisaical leaven, but we definitely do want the new growth-principle of Kingdom leaven. Thus, at Passover the old leaven was cut off, but new leaven, found in the Holy Land, was started. For proof, see Leviticus 23:17; 2:11-12; 7:13.

4. The author's opinion on the millennium can be found in James B. Jordan, *Revelation Made Practical*, six tapes with thirty-seven-page syllabus (Tyler, TX: Geneva Ministries, 1986). See also David Chilton, *Days of Vengeance: An Exposition of the Book of Revelation* (Fort Worth: Dominion Press, 1987), pp. 493-529. Compare Revelation 20:1-2 with Matthew 16:18-19.

5. On the rise and growth of Christianity, see Loraine Boettner, *The Millennium* (Phillipsburg, NJ: Presbyterian and Reformed Pub. Co., 1957), pp. 3-108; Kenneth Scott Latourette, *A History of Christianity* (New York: Harper and Row, 1975); and Latourette, *A History of the Expansion of Christianity*, 7 vols. (Grand Rapids: Zondervan, 1970).

6. A very interesting study of this, that goes into the change of symbolism in each era, is Eugen Rosenstock-Huessy, *Out of Revolution: Autobiography of Western Man* (Norvich, VT: Argo Books, [1938] 1966). See also Harold J. Berman, *Law and Revolution: The Formation of the Western Legal Tradition* (Cambridge: Harvard University Press, 1983).

7. And as I write this, the news media is filled with stories of how our "conservative, Christian" president's wife consults astrologers.

BIBLIOGRAPHY

This bibliography is by no means complete. Many other works were used in the present book, and they are found in the notes. Here I have simply listed those works I believe would be of greatest help for those wishing to follow up some of the themes in this book. My own previous studies naturally figure prominently in this list, since they form much of the background to the present work. All of my studies are available from Biblical Horizons, P.O. Box 132011, Tyler, TX 75713.

Some of the works referred to here are written from an orthodox Christian perspective, while others, though containing useful information, are not. I have used the term "liberal" to denote works that assume that the Bible is not the infallible Word of God, but the product of human authors. I have used the term "evangelical" to denote works that hold to the Christian view of the inerrancy of Scripture.

Albright, W. F. *Archaeology and the Religion of Israel*. Baltimore: Johns Hopkins, 1946.

Allen, R. H. *Star Names: Their Lore and Meaning*. New York: Dover Pub., 1963.

Bavinck, Herman. *Our Reasonable Faith*. Translated by Henry Zylstra. Grand Rapids: Baker Book House, (1956) 1977.

_____. *The Doctrine of God*. Translated by William Hendriksen. Edinburgh: The Banner of Truth Trust, (1918) 1977.

Beattie, J. H. M., and Lienhardt, R. G. *Studies in Social Anthropology: Essays in Memory of E. E. Evans-Pritchard by his Former Oxford Colleagues*. London: Oxford University Press, 1975.

Berkhof, Louis. *Systematic Theology*. Fourth Edition. Grand Rapids: Eerdmans, 1949.

315

typological patterns in Scripture. The author, an Adventist, later rejected the approach in this book and became a liberal.

Campbell, Roderick, *Israel and the New Covenant*. Tyler, TX: Geneva Ministries, (1954) 1983. Excellent study of prophetic symbolism; evangelical.

Carr, G. Lloyd. *The Song of Solomon: An Introduction and Commentary*. Tyndale Old Testament Commentaries. Downers Grove, IL: Inter-Varsity Press, 1984. A judicious conservative commentary on a highly symbolic book.

Cassuto, Umberto. *A Commentary on the Book of Exodus*. Translated by Israel Abrahams. Jerusalem: Magnes Press, 1967. Jewish; rather conservative perspective.

Chilton, David. *Days of Vengeance: An Exposition of the Book of Revelation*. Fort Worth, TX: Dominion Press, 1987. Evangelical.

_____. *Paradise Restored: An Eschatology of Dominion*. Fort Worth, TX: Dominion Press, 1985. Good introduction to prophetic symbolism; evangelical.

Clowney, Edmund P. *Preaching and Biblical Theology*. Phillipsburg, NJ: Presbyterian and Reformed Pub. Co., 1975. An excellent introduction to redemptive historical theology; evangelical.

Cornwall, Judson. *Let Us Draw Near*. Plainfield, NJ: Logos International, 1977. A fictionalized narrative about the building of the Tabernacle. A very readable presentation, with judicious interpretations based largely on Pink's *Exodus*.

Daniélou, Jean. *From Shadows to Reality: Studies in the Biblical Typology of the Fathers*. Translated by Wulstan Hibberd. Westminster, MD: Newman Press, 1960. Valuable study showing that the Fathers knew the difference between Biblical typology and philosophical allegory.

Davidson, Richard M. *Typology in Scripture: A Study of Hermeneutical TYPOS Structures*. Andrews University Seminary Doctoral Dissertation Series 2. Berrien Springs, MI: Andrews University Press, 1981. Thorough history of typology; invaluable study; conservative Adventist perspective.

De Graaf, S. G. *Promise and Deliverance*. 4 volumes. Translated by H. Evan Runner and Elizabeth W. Runner. St. Catharines, Ontario: Paideia Press, 1977. Popularly written theological Bible history, "typological" in method.

Dix, Dom Gregory. *The Shape of the Liturgy*. Westminster: Dacre Press, 1945. Seminal study of the structure of worship.

Edersheim, Alfred. *The Temple: Its Ministry and Services, As They Were at the Time of Christ.* Grand Rapids: Eerdmans, 1972. Evangelical.

Fairbairn, Patrick. *The Typology of Scripture.* New York: Funk and Wagnalls, 1876. Classic evangelical study of typology; see Davidson.

Farrer, Austin. *A Rebirth of Images: The Making of St. John's Apocalypse.* Gloucester, MA: Peter Smith, (1949) 1970. Fascinating study of Biblical symbolism. Quasi-evangelical.

_____. *The Revelation of St. John the Divine.* Oxford: Clarendon Press, 1964. A follow-up study to *Rebirth of Images.*

Frame, John M. *The Doctrine of the Knowledge of God.* Phillipsburg, NJ: Presbyterian and Reformed Publishing Co., 1987. The most important work in evangelical epistemology in several decades.

Haran, Menahem. *Temples and Temple-Service in Ancient Israel.* Oxford: Clarendon Press, 1978. Liberal perspective.

Hough, R. E. *The Ministry of the Glory Cloud.* New York: Philosophical Library, 1955. A valuable redemptive-historical study. Evangelical.

Institute for Basic Youth Conflicts. *Character Sketches: From the Pages of Scripture, Illustrated in the World of Nature.* Three volumes. Oak Brook, IL: Institute for Basic Youth Conflicts, 1976, 1978, 1982. Evangelical.

Jaki, Stanley. *The Road of Science and the Ways to God.* University of Chicago Press, 1978. A Christian critique of Kuhn's subjectivism.

Jordan, James B. "The Bible and the Nations (A Syllabus)." Biblical Horizons, P.O. Box 132011, Tyler, TX 75713.

_____. "Christianity and the Calendar (A Syllabus)." Biblical Horizons, P.O. Box 132011, Tyler, TX 75713.

_____. *Covenant Sequence in Leviticus and Deuteronomy.* Tyler, TX: Institute for Christian Economics, 1988.

_____. "The Death Penalty in the Mosaic Law: Five Exploratory Essays." Biblical Horizons, P.O. Box 132011, Tyler, TX 75713.

_____. "Dragons and Dinosaurs in Biblical Perspective." Biblical Horizons, P.O. Box 132011, Tyler, TX 75713.

_____. "From Glory to Glory: Degrees of Value in the Sanctuary." Biblical Horizons, P.O. Box 132011, Tyler, TX 75713.

_____. "Hexameron: Theological Reflections on Genesis One (A Syllabus)." Biblical Horizons, P.O. Box 132011, Tyler, TX 75713.

_____. *Judges: God's War Against Humanism*. Tyler, TX: Geneva Ministries, 1985.

_____. *The Law of the Covenant: An Exposition of Exodus 21–23*. Tyler, TX: Institute for Christian Economics, 1984. Out of print. Photocopies available from Biblical Horizons, P.O. Box 132011, Tyler, TX 75713.

_____. *Primeval Saints: Studies in the Patriarchs of Genesis*. Biblical Horizons, P.O. Box 132011, Tyler, TX 75713.

_____, editor. *The Reconstruction of the Church*. Christianity and Civilization 4. Tyler, TX: Geneva Ministries, 1985.

_____. *Sabbath Breaking and the Death Penalty: A Theological Investigation*. Tyler, TX: Geneva Ministries, 1986.

_____. *The Sociology of the Church*. Tyler, TX: Geneva Ministries, 1986.

_____. "Thoughts on Jachin and Boaz." Biblical Horizons, P.O. Box 132011, Tyler, TX 75713.

_____. *Food and Faith: The Mosaic Dietary Laws in New Covenant Perspective*. Biblical Horizons, P.O. Box 132011, Tyler, TX 75713.

Keel, Othmar. *The Symbolism of the Biblical World: Ancient Near Eastern Iconography and the Book of Psalms*. Translated by Timothy J. Hallett. New York: Seabury Press, 1978. Liberal perspective, but valuable, highly illustrated study.

Kik, J. Marcellus. *An Eschatology of Victory*. Phillipsburg, NJ: Presbyterian and Reformed Pub. Co., 1971. Evangelical study in prophetic symbolism.

Kline, Meredith G. *Images of the Spirit*. Grand Rapids: Baker, 1980. Evangelical study in Biblical symbolism.

_____. *Kingdom Prologue*. 3 volumes. By the author (Gordon-Conwell Theological Seminary, South Hamilton, MA), 1981, 1983, 1986. Evangelical study in Genesis, focussing on literary structures and symbolism at many places.

_____. *The Structure of Biblical Authority*. Revised Edition. Grand Rapids: Eerdmans, 1972. Evangelical study of literary structures in the Bible.

Kuhn, Thomas S. *The Structure of Scientific Revolutions*. Second Edition. University of Chicago Press, 1970.

Lecerf, Auguste. *An Introduction to Reformed Dogmatics*. Translated by André Schlemmer. Grand Rapids: Baker Book House, (1949) 1981. Evangelical.

Lee, Francis Nigel. *The Central Significance of Culture*. Phillipsburg, NJ: Presbyterian and Reformed Pub. Co., 1977. Evangelical.

Lewis, C. S. *The Discarded Image: An Introduction to Medieval and Renaissance Literature*. Cambridge University Press, 1964. Valuable presentation of a worldview different from the modern one.

——————. *An Experiment in Criticism*. Cambridge University Press, 1961. Outstanding introduction to the art of literary reading.

Lovejoy, Arthur O. *The Great Chain of Being*. Cambridge: Harvard University Press, 1936.

North, Gary. *The Dominion Covenant: Genesis*. An Economic Commentary on the Bible I. Revised edition. Tyler, TX: Institute for Christian Economics, 1987. Evangelical.

——————, editor. *Tactics of Christian Resistance*. Christianity and Civilization 3. Tyler, TX: Geneva Ministries, 1983. Contains James B. Jordan, "Rebellion, Tyranny, and Dominion in the Book of Genesis."

Pink, Arthur W. *Gleanings in Exodus*. Chicago: Moody Press, 1971. Evangelical.

Poythress, Vern S. *Symphonic Theology: The Validity of Multiple Perspectives in Theology*. Grand Rapids: Zondervan, 1987. Evangelical.

Robertson, O. Palmer. *The Christ of the Covenants*. Grand Rapids: Baker, 1980. A careful presentation of the sequence of covenants in the Bible.

Rosenstock-Huessy, Eugen. *Out of Revolution: Autobiography of Western Man*. Norwich, VT: Argo Books, (1938) 1969. Survey of the revolutionary transformations in culture in Western history.

Rushdoony, Rousas J. *The Mythology of Science*. Nutley, NJ: Craig Press, 1967.

——————. *The One and the Many*. Tyler, TX: Thoburn Press, [1971] 1978.

Schilder, Klaas. *Christ and Culture*. Translated by G. van Rongen and W. Helder. Winnipeg: Premier Publishers, 1977. Very important evangelical discussion of Christian worldview.

——————. *Heaven: What Is It?* Translated and condensed by Marian M. Schoolland. Grand Rapids: Eerdmans, 1950. Very important evangelical discussion of Christian worldview.

Schlossberg, Herbert. *Idols for Destruction: Christian Faith and its Confrontation with American Society*. Nashville: Thomas Nelson, 1983. Important evangelical discussion of Christian worldview.

Schmemann, Alexander. *For the Life of the World*. Crestwood, NY: St. Vladimir's Seminary Press, 1973. Seminal "renewed Russian Orthodoxy" discussion of Christian worldview.

Silva, Moisés. *Has the Church Misread The Bible? The History of Interpretation in the Light of Current Issues*. Foundations of Contemporary Interpretation 1. Grand Rapids: Zondervan, 1987. Important evangelical introduction to the art of Biblical interpretation.

Sutton, Ray R. *That You May Prosper: Dominion by Covenant*. Tyler, TX: Institute for Christian Economics, 1987. Extended somewhat popular introduction to the pattern of Biblical covenants. Evangelical.

Terry, Milton S. *Biblical Apocalyptics*. New York: Eaton and Mains, 1898. Moderately evangelical discussion of Biblical symbolism.

_____. *Biblical Hermeneutics*. New York: Phillips and Hunt, 1883. Moderately evangelical, includes much useful material on Biblical symbolism.

Van Til, Henry. *The Calvinistic Concept of Culture*. Grand Rapids: Baker Book House, 1959. Very important evangelical discussion of Christian worldview.

Wenham, Gordon J. *The Book of Leviticus*. The New International Commentary on the Old Testament. Grand Rapids: Eerdmans, 1979. Evangelical.

_____. *Numbers: An Introduction and Commentary*. Tyndale Old Testament Commentaries. Downers Grove, IL: Inter-Varsity Press, 1981. Evangelical.

Whitcomb, John C. *The Early Earth*. Grand Rapids: Baker Book House, 1972. Evangelical discussion of six-day creationism.

Wolff, Hans Walter. *Anthropology of the Old Testament*. Translated by Margaret Kohl. Philadelphia: Fortress Press, 1974. Liberal but useful.

Woodrow, Ralph. *Great Prophecies of the Bible*. P.O. Box 124, Riverside, CA: Woodrow Evangelistic Association, 1971. Evangelical and sensible.

Woolley, Paul, ed. *The Infallible Word: A Symposium*. Third Edition. Phillipsburg, NJ: Presbyterian and Reformed Pub. Co., 1967. Contains Cornelius Van Til's seminal essay, "Nature and Scripture."

SCRIPTURE INDEX

OLD TESTAMENT

Genesis		Genesis	
1	9ff., 41ff., 145f., 250	2:19	32
1:1	41, 42, 45, 105, 106	2:23	135
1:2	24, 43, 106	2:24	135f., 198
1:2-3	43	3	121, 207
1:2-2:4	118ff.	3:6	170
1:3	43,	3:14	100
1:4-5	130	3:15	96, 100, 102
1:5	11	3:17	100, 101, 303
1:5ff.	32	3:18	81
1:6	43	3:19	303
1:6-8	130	3:24	113, 137, 174
1:7	45, 161	4	169
1:8	41	4-6	102
1:9	144f.	4:16-24	175
1:9-10	130	4:17	122, 125
1:9-13	304	5	58
1:10	146	5:14	58
1:11	81	5:23-24	170
1:14	1f., 12, 58, 60	5:23	58
1:14-18	45, 53ff.	5:31	58
1:17	41	5:32	188
1:20	41, 45	6:2	170, 184
1:21	137	6:3	125
1:24	12	6:4	175
1:26	23, 31, 95, 133, 214	6:5	125
1:27	25, 31	6:6	24
1:28	95	6:7	125, 172
1:28-30	120	6:20	172
1:29	81	7:8	172
2	81, 121, 133ff., 150f.	7:10	205
2:7	90, 269, 303	7:11	172
2:8	152	7:12	205
2:9	81, 90, 276	7:14	172
2:10-12	73	7:21	172
2:10-14	207	7:23	172
2:15	113, 133f.	8:2	172
2:18	95	8:4	150
2:18-20	96	8:6-12	306

NEW TESTAMENT

AUTHOR INDEX

SUBJECT INDEX

astral bodies/imagery, 1, 3, 12, 20, 45, 46, 53ff., 189, 270
astrology, 67
astronomy, 53
Assyria, 83, 178
Aaron's rod, 217
Abel, 81
Abiathar, 225
abomination, 244
Abram, Abraham, 20, 58f., 61, 82, 88, 90, 139, 154, 178, 182ff.
abyss, 145f., 228
acacia, 91f.
Adam, 15, 122, passim
  Israel's king as, 228
adoption, 305
Ahimelech, 225
Agur, 299
Alexandrian exegesis, 17
allegory, 50f.
almond, 86
altar, 88, 147f., 158f., 161, 190, 234, 252, 285
  Elijah's, 236
  Ezekiel's, 158f., 235f., 301f.
analogy, 24, 32
angels, 2, 31, 46, 55, 105ff., 173, 302, 304
animals, 1, 3, 12f., 95ff., 134, 137, 269
anticipation, 198
Antiochus Epiphanes, 245
appearance, 12, 46
Ararat, 174
Ark of Covenant, 14, 90, 183, 217, 223f., 226, 253, 269
Ark of Noah, 150, 170ff.
Armenia, 150
army, 204f., 222, 235
art, 134

Babylon, 62f., 65, 178
Bach, J. S., 13, 21
baptism, 72, 136, 267, 311
bastards, 221
bdellium, 73f., 295
beasts, 13, 96
  Beast of Revelation, 15f.
Beersheba, 223f.
Beethoven, 21
Being, 22, 29, 291
bells, 216f.
benedicamus, 128f.
Bethel, 191
Bible, heavenly blueprint, 47
birds, 100, 102
  see dove, eagle
blame, 185f.
blood, 174
blue, 45, 46
blueprints, 41ff.
body, human, 216f.
body politic, 24f., 213ff.
boundary, 46, 136, 213, 300
bread, 82, 84
bride, assaulted, 184
burning bush, 74, 84f.

Cain, 81, 125, 128, 169
Carmel, 235f.
catechisms, 30
cedar, 82, 91f., 227
chariot, Divine, 231, 244, 252
  see cloud-chariot
cherubim, 46, 49, 61, 75, 99, 101, 105, 111, 112, 113, 148, 206, 207, 231, 244, 252, 264
chiasm, 55
Christmas tree, 93
chronology of Bible, 291
church, 264

COLOPHON

The typeface for the text of this book is *Baskerville*. Its creator, John Baskerville (1706-1775), broke with tradition to reflect in his type the rounder, yet more sharply cut lettering of eighteenth-century stone inscriptions and copy books. The type foreshadows modern design in such novel characteristics as the increase in contrast between thick and thin strokes and the shifting of stress from the diagonal to the vertical strokes. Realizing that this new style of letter would be most effective if cleanly printed on smooth paper with genuinely black ink, he built his own presses, developed a method of hot-pressing the printed sheet to a smooth, glossy finish, and experimented with special inks. However, Baskerville did not enter into general commercial use in England until 1923.

Substantive editing by Michael S. Hyatt
Copy editing by Barbara Sorensen
Cover design by Kent Puckett Associates, Atlanta, Georgia
Typography by Thoburn Press, Box 2459, Reston, Virginia 22090
Printed and bound by Maple-Vail Book Manufacturing Group
Manchester, Pennsylvania
Cover Printing by Weber Graphics, Chicago, Illinois